Hope you enjoy,

Gary Walter

A General History of the Civil War

the Civil War

THE SOUTHERN POINT OF VIEW

By

Gary C Walker

i

Proof Reader
David A. Saville
3713 Bohon St.
Roanoke, Va. 24012

ISBN 0-9617898-6-7
C-2004
A & W Enterprise
3747 New Spring Branch Rd. S. E.
Roanoke, Va. 24014

GOD'S WAYS ARE SO DIFFERENT THAN MAN'S WAYS THAT PERHAPS OFFERING A CUP OF COOL WATER TO A THIRSTY MAN IS MORE IMPORTANT IN GOD'S EYES THAN THE BRAVEST DEED DONE ON THE FIELD OF BATTLE.

This book is proudly dedicated to, two people who have dedicated their lives to His service:

Ray and Ina Forbes.

A very special thanks to those people who shared their time and information so generously: Rev. Roy S. Whitescarver, Wayne D. Carson, Jo Ann Breaux, Robert Howlett, Joe Grissom, Patricia Buck, Walter H. Ring, III, Rev. Pete Isenberg, Karen Dinkins, Robert E. Wimmer ,Donald and Carol Whitacer, Peggy Aldhizer, Jay H. Combs, Effie J. Erhardt, James D. Poindexter, Jr., Fred Averill, Rev. Rondel Rumburg, Walter L. Meeks, Becky Wimmer Sloan, Don W. Link, George Russell "Slick" Inge, Raymond Douglas Camper, III and Patrick Schroder.

Thank you beautiful wife for the love, support and the hours you spent preparing this manuscript.

iii

President Jefferson Davis

iv

CHAPTERS

Page

INTRODUCTION

This book is written so both younger and adult readers will be able to understand the true history of America's greatest war. It also uses many of the words that were used during that time. Although each battle, skirmish and event is important, this is a general history and cannot cover everything. Guidelines for the Standards of Learning were consulted. A list of material will be given so that the reader can get more in-depth information.

The war was fought from 1861 to 1865 and it has a lot of names. Here are the ones most commonly used: Civil War, War Between the States, North against the South, War of the Rebellion, War of Northern Aggression, War for Southern Independence, Second American Revolution, and the War for Constitutional Government. Its real name is The War between the United States of America and the Confederate States of America. In this book we will simply call it the "War."

The soldiers who fought for the Confederacy were known by many names. They were called: Confederates, Southerners, Rebels (Rebs), Johnnys, Secessionists (Secesh, Sesh), Dixie Boys and Gray Backs.

The soldiers who fought for the United States were called U. S. Soldiers, Federals, Union, Yankees (Yanks), Damn Yankees, Northerners, Billys, Blue Bellys, and Blue Coats.

People living in this country who came from Africa have been called many things during history. They were referred to as "Negroes" during the war, so they will be called the same in this book.

This book reflects the Southern point of view. However, the objective reader will see that it is less biased than textbooks that are now in schools.

The United States today is a big country. It goes from the Atlantic to the Pacific Ocean and out to Hawaii and Alaska but in 1861 it was much smaller. The country was divided because of money (economics) and politics long before the shooting started. The line that roughly divided the country was called the "Mason-Dixon Line." The line was named for the two surveyors (men who are trained to find where the line runs that separates one person's property from another) who made the line that separates the states of Maryland and Pennsylvania. That line was drawn across the country and it separated the Northern states from the Southern States. Most, but not all, the people living south of the line were for the Confederate States. Most, but not all, the people living north of the line were for the United States.

There were 22 million people living north of the line. South of the line, there were about 4 ½ million white people, 4 million slaves, and ½ million free Negroes. There were more people living in the North and they had more votes in Congress. They passed laws that helped their part of the country. When war came the North put 1 ½ million men into uniforms compared with the South's 600,000 to 900,000. All these numbers are close but no one really knows the exact count.

There were many causes for the War. Most writers start with false beliefs; sometimes they write them down, other times they don't. The wrong beliefs are that the South did not have the right to leave the Union and that the war started because of slavery; and that slavery was a racist and cruel system. These false beliefs made the people living in the South evil and the ones who started the war. This is not true. The United States Government had neither a moral nor a legal basis to attack the people in the south just because they no longer wished to be part of the United States.

After America's first Revolutionary War, the defeated English signed 13 peace treaties with 13 new countries. There was the country of Georgia, of New York, of Virginia, etc. Instead of calling them countries, they were called "States," which meant the same thing. These 13 new countries formed a union called the United States of America. It would be stupid to think any state would join a union they couldn't leave, even if that union turned against what the people of the state (country) wanted.

The people of the South did not fight to take over the Union or make any demand on the people of the North; they just wished to leave the Union and live in peace. It was the government of the United States that did not want the Southern States to leave and was willing to fight to force them to stay in the union of states.

✗ The War did not start because of slavery. The person who commanded all Union forces was their president, Abraham Lincoln. Lincoln said many times, "My paramount [biggest] object in this struggle [war] is to save the Union, and is not either to save or to destroy slavery. If I could save the Union without freeing any slaves, I would do it, and if I could save it by freeing all the slaves, I would do it: and if I could save it by freeing some and leaving others also, I would also do that. What I do about slavery, and the colored race, I do because I believe it helps save the Union.....✗

The slaves were the workers for their masters. They cost a lot of money. It is stupid to believe that the master would beat his slaves so that they would be worth less money. It is stupid to believe that the master beat his workers so that the workers would be unhappy and would not want to work. There are always mean people in every age. There were some masters who were mean to their slaves but they were few and far between.

Most slavery was white masters and black slaves. The North had as many slaves as did the South during Colonial times. The Yankees were starting to get rid of their slaves because they couldn't make money with them. The people up North always owned more white slaves (Indentured Servants) than the South. Some Indians were slaves. Indians owned black slaves, white slaves and other Indian slaves.

In the South, few slaves had last names. When slavery ended in 1865, they got to choose any last name they wanted. Most chose their old master's name because they truly loved, not hated him. (For more information on this important subject, see my book *The Truth about Slavery*.)

Napoleon was a French general who fought wars in Europe a few years before our war. He was the most winning general of his time. Military schools around the world taught his ways of war. He taught that men should stand shoulder-to-shoulder and start firing when their lines were about two hundred yards away from each other. Napoleon's troops used a musket. A soldier was lucky to hit a man at that distance. The rifle was invented before our war. With a rifle at two hundred yards, a soldier was unlucky not to hit a man. The leaders on both sides studied and used Napoleon's tactics. That is the reason so many men were killed during the war.

There were many, many things that caused the war but the two that were the most important and which couldn't be worked-out were money and politics; these go together. The people of the South made their living farming. Slaves were used. The people in the North were starting to make a lot of their money using factories. Both the people in the South and in the North wanted to make as much money as they could, so, both sides wanted laws (politics) passed to help them. There were more people living in the North and they had more votes. They passed laws so that the people in the South had to pay almost 100% of the taxes. They also passed high tariff laws. These laws put such a high tax on the goods from Europe that they forced the people in the South to buy goods made in Northern factories. The people of the South didn't like paying most of the taxes and thought Northern made goods cost too much and weren't as good as the ones they could get from Europe.

During this period of time, Harriet Beecher Stowe wrote a novel (a story she made up) about slavery. Stowe was never in the South and knew little about slavery but people in the North believed that *Uncle Tom's Cabin* was true. The book made people in the North hate people in the South.

Religion and politics often come together. Many people up North wanted to call slavery "bad and evil" but the Bible says that slavery is good, not bad. In order to call slavery "evil" and slave owners "sinners," the Yankees had to leave the word of God behind. The people in the South said the Bible, as written, must be followed. Many people up North disagreed. This is what led to the split between the Northern and Southern Baptists, Methodists and others. Because the people of the South believed that Northerners had left the word of God behind, they called them "Damned Yankees."

Something happened as the national elections of 1860 got close. In 1859, John Brown and a small group of his followers took over the Federal Arsenal (a place that made guns and gun powder) at Harpers Ferry, Virginia. It later was made part of West Virginia. These men were "abolitionists." That is to say that they were against people who owned slaves. This did not mean that they believed Negroes were equal to white people. John Brown thought that all he had to do was start a slave revolt and that slaves everywhere would murder their masters and their masters' families. Brown knew that he was breaking the law when his band of outlaws took over the arsenal. Among the first to get killed by the Brown Gang was a former slave who was spreading the alarm that Brown was taking the arsenal. There was no slave revolt as Brown thought would happen. Colonel Robert E. Lee came and took the arsenal back from Brown. JEB Stuart was one of the men who helped him. Brown was given a fair trail and was hanged for treason and murder.

There weren't that many abolitionists but they owned some Northern newspapers and made a lot of noise. They were very unhappy that there was no slave revolt and that masters and slaves were still living and working together. They said many bad things about the South.

The people in the South were angry that people up North wanted their slaves to revolt and kill them. The people of the whole country were angry and divided as they moved toward the 1860 election.

The country was divided. Instead of two big parties and two men running to be president, there were four parties and four men running. No one person, who wanted to be president, won over half of the votes but the president is not really elected by "people" votes. The president is elected by "electoral" votes. Each state gets two votes for being a state and then it gets more votes based on how many people live in that state. The more people the more votes. In most cases, Lincoln barely won over half of the popular votes in most of the big northeastern states, except in Vermont where he carried 75% of the vote. In many Southern states, there weren't even enough Republican voters to get Lincoln on the ballot. All states allow write-in votes. However, in Alabama, Arkansas, Florida, Georgia, Louisiana, Mississippi, North Carolina, South Carolina, Tennessee, and Texas, Lincoln received no votes at all! In non-deep-South states, he didn't do well either. For example, Kentucky had 146,216 votes cast, Lincoln got 1,364; Maryland 92,505, Lincoln 2,294; Missouri 165,563, Lincoln 17,028; Virginia 166,891, Lincoln 1,887. Because this country is founded on the principal of the "consent of the governed;" Lincoln could not claim a "mandate" (a right to be president) in very many states.

The people of the South did not like or vote for Lincoln. Lincoln said that if he were elected president, he would not let any more states whose people owned slaves come into the Union. The people of the South already knew that the people of the North out-voted them. If no more slaveholding states could come into the Union, then each new state that came into the Union would vote with the North and against the South. It was possible that someday the Northern people would wish to stop slavery altogether. The people of the South did not want to lose their rights, money or property.

On November 6, 1860 Lincoln was elected president and people all across the South started talking about leaving the Union. James Buchanan was still the president until Lincoln would take office. Buchanan did not want the Union to break apart. On December 4th, he made a speech and said, "...the long-continued and intemperate interference of the Northern people with the question of slavery in the Southern States has at length produced its natural effects." In other words, he said the people in the North were hate filled and should not have said bad things about the people of the South because Southerners owned slaves. It was the people in the North who forced the people in the South to start talking about leaving the Union (Secession). In the same speech, President Buchanan said that he did not believe the people of the South had the right to leave the Union.

He called it "revolution." The speech didn't help because people on both sides now got mad at Buchanan.

In South Carolina, there was already strong talk about leaving the Union but no one wanted war. So on December 19, 1860 politicians from South Carolina met with President Buchanan and said there would be no attack on Fort Sumter, a fort in Charleston harbor, as long as the U. S. Government did not send "reinforcements" (more troops). The troops already there could stay but no more could come.

On December 20, the State of South Carolina, by free vote, voted itself out of the Union, thus becoming the "Nation of South Carolina" once again. The newspapers read, "THE UNION IS DISSOLVED!!!" In two days, the new nation sent three men (commissioners) to Washington to tell the foreign government of the United States that it must remove its forces from their nation but that South Carolina wanted no war and would pay for the property.

On December 31, President Buchanan told the commissioners that he wasn't going to get into a dispute with South Carolina but would let Congress work with the problem. He also said he would not remove troops from South Carolina.

As the year was ending, several other Southern states were taking votes and talking about secession. Because South Carolina had left the Union first, it was the center of attention. If the United States could get South Carolina back into the Union by talk or by force, it was believed that no more states would leave: Thus ended the year 1860.

BACKGROUND: the Southern people knew that there were more Yankees. It was probable the South would have to fight to stay free nations but there were several things that the Southern people believed would happen that would allow them to stay out of the Union. It was okay to leave a union where the government wasn't liked; the colonists did that in the first Revolution. This would just be the second Revolution. The Yankees didn't like the people of the South, so why would they fight to force them to stay in the same union? If the South just showed those Yankees they would fight to not be part of their union, then the Yankees would just let them go. If these things did not happen, there is one thing that would surely happen that would let the South be free. England, at this time, was the world "Super Power." England had the best navy and army in the world. If England wanted to do something, no other country could stop her. The factories in England used a lot of Southern cotton. If the North would not let Southern cotton reach England then the English navy and army would come and help the South. With English support, the South would remain free. Southern people referred to how important cotton was by calling it, "King Cotton." It would be a very short, glorious war, they thought. Many of the soldiers who signed up to fight this war signed up for 90 days because everyone knew it would be over by then.

General Robert E. Lee

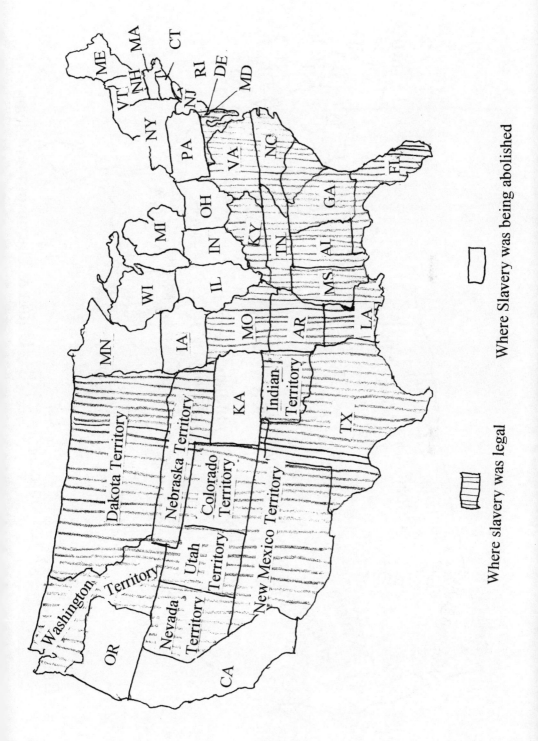

Where slavery was legal

Where Slavery was being abolished

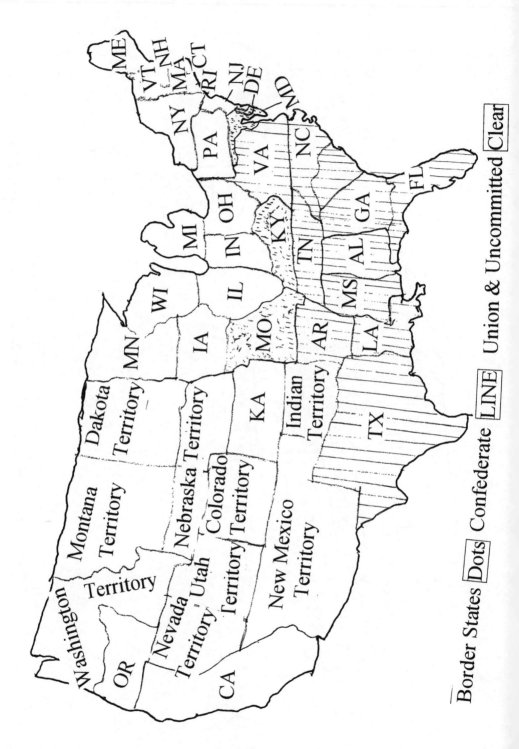

Border States Dots Confederate LINE Union & Uncommitted Clear

- 14 -

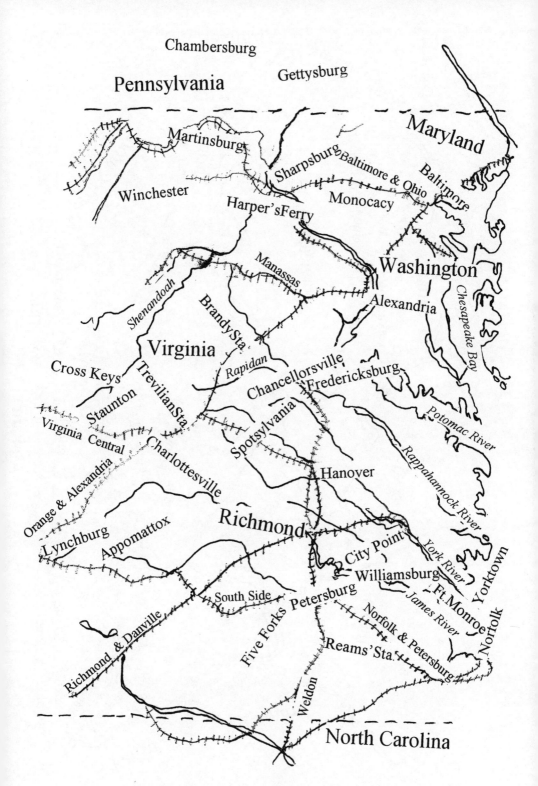

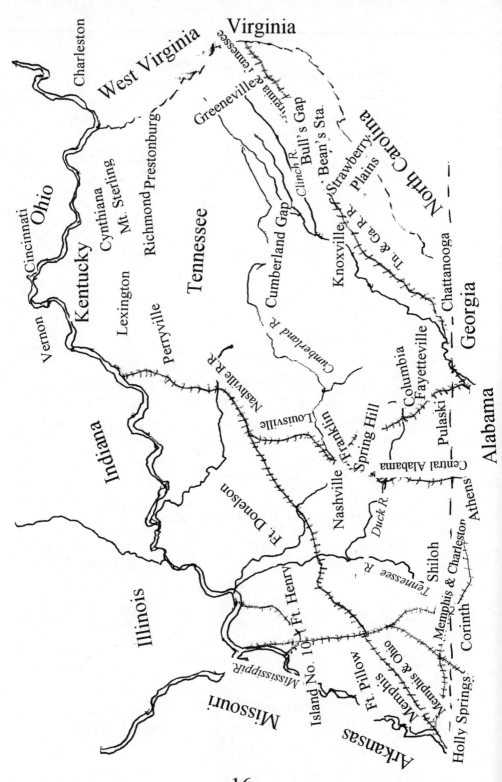

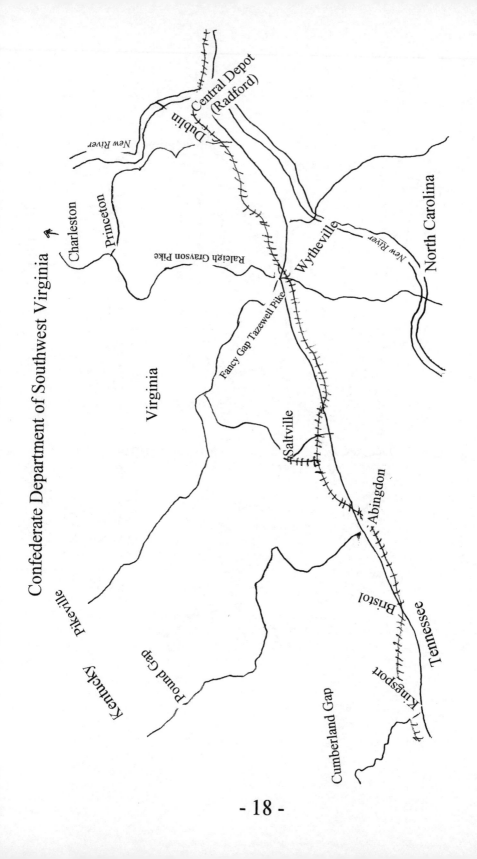

Confederate Department of Southwest Virginia

Charleston

Princeton

New River

Central Depot (Radford)

Dublin

Raleigh Grayson Pike

Wytheville

North Carolina

New River

Virginia

Fancy Gap Tazewell Pike

Saltville

Abingdon

Pikeville

Kentucky

Pound Gap

Cumberland Gap

Bristol

Kingsport

Tennessee

- 18 -

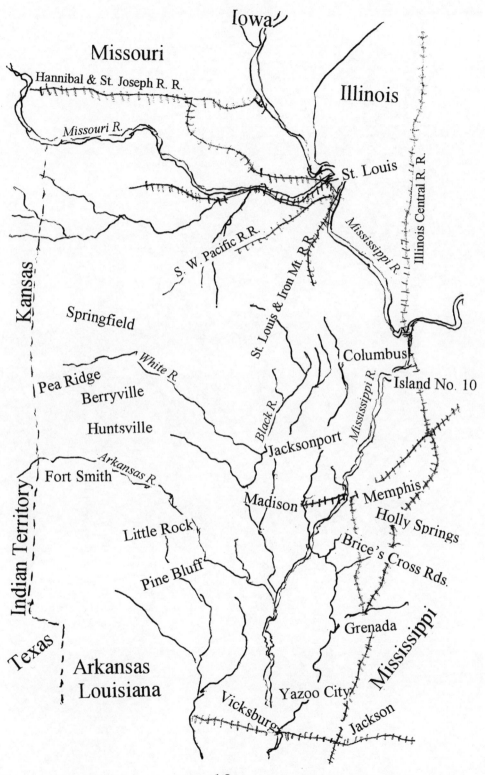

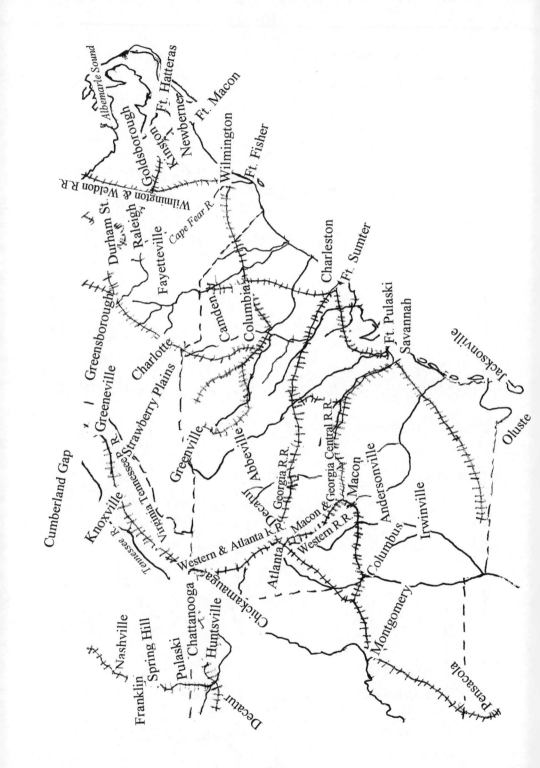

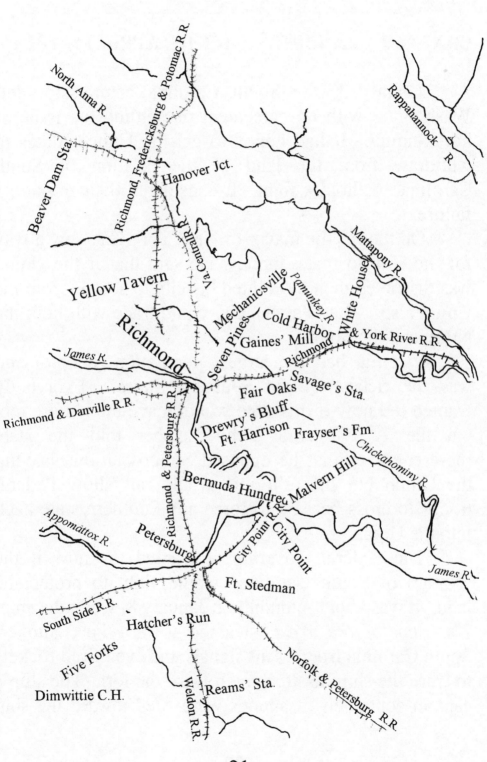

CHAPTER 1 JANUARY 1, 1861--- APRIL 14, 1861

January 3, the South Carolina commission left Washington with no agreement on settling the issue of Fort Sumter. It had hoped to get the United States to withdraw from the land of the "Nation of South Carolina" without a fight. It considered their mission a failure.

On the 6[th,] the mayor of New York City saw a way for the City to make money. He said that if the Union was dissolved then he wanted his city to secede from the Union also. That way his city could trade with both the North and the South.

Virginia had the largest population (people) and was the richest of the Southern States. Everybody wanted to know if this state would leave the Union, too. On the 7[th,] Governor John Letcher told the state representatives that he opposed South Carolina leaving the Union but that Virginia would not allow Federal troops to cross her soil to force any Southern state back into the Union.

The Federal Government wanted to know if the "Nation of South Carolina" would fight to protect its land. It was about midnight on January 8, when the ship, *The Star of the West*, steamed toward Fort Sumter. South Carolina troops sent signals and even fired rockets to warn the ship not to come toward the fort. The ship's captain continued. Cannons were fired toward the ship before it turned around. South Carolina showed that it would fight to stay out of the Union!

That same day, Mississippi, by free vote, left the Union. For the first time, the first "unofficial" Confederate flag was flown. The "Bonnie Blue Flag" was raised over the Capital Building in Jackson. . This flag had one white star on a field of blue. It was never an official flag but it was used throughout the war.

On the 10th, Florida left the Union. On the 11th, Alabama left the Union. On the 19th, Georgia also left; Louisiana left on the 26th. On the 29th, Kansas joined the Union. On February 1st, Texas left.

The 4th of February could be called Southern Independence Day. On this day at Montgomery, Alabama, the Confederate States of America was born.

President Buchanan announced that the "unofficial" truce with South Carolina was off and that he would not even consider giving up Fort Sumter. The President had already broken the truce by sending a ship toward the Fort.

Today the Indians aren't very important. During the war they controlled a lot of land, mostly in the western part of the country. The Indians had seen the United States break many treaties; so that on the 7th, the Choctaw Nation gave its support to the Confederacy.

On 10 February 1861, Jefferson Davis was made President of the Confederacy. He received the news at his plantation near Vicksburg, Mississippi.

Both Davis and Lincoln were born in Kentucky. On the 11^{th,} both Presidents headed toward their capitals to take the Oath of Office (become President). Davis left from Mississippi and Lincoln from Illinois. Both men said they needed God's help.

On the 16^{th,} Jefferson Davis rode in to Montgomery and a big crowd welcomed him. He made a speech. He said, "The time for compromise has now passed, and the South is determined to maintain her position (The Southern States will not be talked into re-joining the Union) and make all who oppose her smell Southern powder and feel Southern steel if coercion is persisted in (If the U. S. tried to use the military to force the states back into the Union, the South will fight), …We ask nothing, we want nothing (The South just wanted to be left in peace)." One man said of Davis, "The Man and the hour have met." The next day, the band played "Dixie" as he took the oath. He had a very big job to do because the South had no army or navy and very little government. The new president had to build a new country.

At 6 A. M. on the 23^{rd,} Abraham Lincoln sneaked in to Washington. He was afraid to travel through Baltimore, Maryland because the people were rioting against him.

On the 27^{th,} President Davis appointed three Commissioners from the Confederate Government to go to Washington to try and get the Federals out of Fort Sumter without a fight.

March 1st, Davis sent a message and a man to South Carolina Governor Francis Pickens. The message was that the Confederate States of America was taking over the troops in Charleston and the man to take command was Brigadier General Pierre Gustave Toutant Beauregard.

On 4 March 1861 Lincoln became President of the United States. In his speech he said that he had no intention of interfering with the institution of slavery where it existed. Lincoln said the Union was "perpetual" (could not be broken). Those states that had left the Union were, "insurrectionary and revolutionary…the laws of the Union must be faithfully executed in all the States." He went on to say that the Army of the United States would not be the first one to attack.

From the 4th until the 28th, the South tried to talk or bully the Yankees to get out of Fort Sumter. No shots were fired. Lincoln had to make it look like the South was the one that wanted war, so on the 29th, he announced "I desire that an expedition, to move by sea, be ready to sail as early as the 6th of April next…" Lincoln said that the ships would bring supplies to the Fort and maybe more troops. He put the South on notice that the United States was going to keep its forces on foreign soil and would not leave without a fight!

Lincoln could not officially say that the government of the Confederate States existed. If he did then he would admit that he was making war on another country. He could not officially admit that any state was out of the Union. If he did then he admitted that he was not their president and could not force his government on them. That is the reason that on the 6th he sent a message to the Governor of South Carolina and not the President of the Confederate States. Lincoln told the governor that he was sending supplies but if there was fighting he also had troops.

April 9th the steamer *Baltic* left New York City for Charleston. Lincoln was making good on his threat.

On the 10th Lincoln met a group of men calling them selves the Chiriqui Improvement Company. The company was formed to "colonize." That is to say they all, including Lincoln, wanted to send the Negroes back to Africa.

On the 11th the Confederacy demanded Maj. Robert Anderson and his troops leave Fort Sumter or they would be fired upon.

At 11 P. M. Beauregard sent another message asking Anderson to surrender. Anderson sent a message back that he would not; he was waiting on the supply ships. In the early morning hours of the 12th Beauregard sent word that he would start firing at 4 A. M. but it wasn't until 4:30 A. M. a when a signal shot was fired. Many believe that Edmund Ruffin fired the first shot toward Fort Sumter. Ruffin was a very old Virginian who had worked most of his adult life to help bring the Confederacy into being. For this reason he was given the honor of firing the first shot of the war. Others say the story is untrue. For the next 36 hours Charleston

Harbor roared as cannons fired. "The time for compromise has now passed, and the South is determined to maintain her position, and make all who oppose her smell Southern powder and feel Southern steel if coercion is persisted in…" The Yankee ships came to Charleston during the bombardment but could not take part in the fight.

Over 4,000 shots were fired. The fort was much damaged but by some miracle, no one was killed. On the 13th, Major Anderson sent word that he would surrender.

On the 14th, Fort Sumter formally surrendered. In Washington, Lincoln was following the events closely by telegraph. He had forced the South into firing the first shots. He had the war he wanted. He now had an excuse to call for 75,000 troops to put the "Rebellion" down.

Robert Anderson

P. G. T. Beauregard

General Albert S. Johnston

General Thomas "Stonewall" Jackson

CHAPTER 2 APRIL 15- JULY 23, 1861

On the 15th several northern states wired the President that they would send troops. Kentucky and North Carolina said they wouldn't send troops. On the 16th Governor John Letcher of Virginia informed Lincoln that the state would oppose any Federal attempt at "subjugation" of a southern state! On the 17th both Missouri and Tennessee told Lincoln he would receive no troops.

A secession flag was raised on Federal Hill in Baltimore. Maj. Anderson and his men arrived to a hero's welcome and Kansas troops were "camped" in the East Room of the White House; all on the 18th.

From the 19th almost to the end of the month there were pro-secession riots in Baltimore. Washington was cut off from the rest of the United States. The people wanted Maryland to leave the Union. Lincoln sent troops to fight the citizens; both soldiers and citizens died. Maryland called for a Secession Convention. Lincoln who took an oath "to protect and defend the Constitution of the United States;" he went back on his word. He suspended the right of habeas corpus. Now the government arrested official Maryland representatives and put them in jail without a crime being charged and no trial being given. The people of Maryland didn't get a fair vote on secession.

The Lincoln government had asked Col. Robert E. Lee to command the Federal Army. On the 20th Lee resigned the army; he could not fight his nation, Virginia. Later Lee would command all Confederate field armies. It is a very unusual thing in history for the same man to be asked to command the armies of countries at war with each other.

On the 22nd, Arkansas refused Lincoln's request for troops; a Yankee Army was stationed at Cairo, Illinois, where the Mississippi and Ohio Rivers meet; and Lee took command of Virginia state troops.

Col. Thomas Jackson took command of Virginia troops at Harper's Ferry but still let Northern trains pass through because he still hoped Maryland would vote to leave the Union. On the 29th, with many of the pro-Southern representatives still in jail, Maryland voted not to leave the Union.

On the 30th, the "Five Civilized Indian Tribes" (Cherokees, Chickasaws, Choctaws, Creeks, and Seminoles) decided to be on the Southern side.

The South did not have very many factories. On May 1st, Col. Jackson began to ship gun making equipment from Harper's Ferry to Richmond. This machinery produced many guns for the South during the war.

England "received" Confederate commissioners in London. This did not mean that England officially thought the Confederacy was a true country but it moved her along that road. The South was sure England would come to her aid. Lincoln was very upset by the English.

May 6th Arkansas and Tennessee also left the Union. In Knoxville, riots broke out between pro- and anti- Confederates. On the 10th, riots also broke out in St. Louis, Missouri. These kept going for many days, many people were killed. Also on the 10th, Lee got command of all Confederate troops in Virginia. Maryland asked Lincoln to stop the war.

On the 13th, the South got a setback from England; for the time being England would remain "neutral."

On the 14th, Jackson stopped the trains at Harper's Ferry. He did something many thought impossible. He shipped trains overland (not by rail) to Winchester.

The United States Constitution says it gets its power from "We the People." The Confederate Constitution got its power from God. On this date, President Davis declared the first National Day of Fasting and Prayer for the South!

Everybody was expecting a big fight in the Harper's Ferry area so on the 15th, Gen. Joseph E. Johnston came and took over command from Col. Jackson.

On the 16th, Kentucky said it wanted to be "neutral."

On the 20th, North Carolina left the Union. Both Kentucky and Missouri were claimed by the South before the end of the war. Thus, there are eleven stars on the Confederate Battle Flag.

On the 24th, Yankee troops entered Alexandria, Virginia without a fight. Col. Elmer Ellsworth with the

New York Zouave Company (Zouaves dressed in fancy red uniforms) saw a Secessionist Flag flying over the Marshall House Hotel. He and two others climbed the steps and pulled it down. As they were coming down the stairs, the inn keeper, James Jackson took his shotgun and blew Ellsworth into eternity. Jackson was also shot to death. Both sides called the dead men heroes (martyrs) for their side. Ellsworth "laid in state" (kept) in the White House until the burial. Jackson's deed inspired others to write poems, songs, and make paintings.

Lincoln always claimed that no state had left the Union but on the 26th, the Post Master for the United States said there would be no more deliveries in those states out of the Union.

On the 27th, the Chief Justice of the Supreme Court ruled that Lincoln did not have the right to suspend the right of habeas corpus. Lincoln's arrests were illegal and the people must be let out of jail. Lincoln was a lawyer before he became President but said he didn't care what the Chief Justice said. Lincoln kept arresting and jailing people without a trial throughout the war.

Everybody was expecting a fight in the Northern part of Virginia and on the 28th, Brig. General Irvin McDowell took command of the Union forces in the area. On the 31st, Beauregard was sent to counter McDowell.

June 2 Beauregard took command of the troops in Northern Virginia. The Confederacy was a new nation and things changed quickly. Beauregard's army was known by several names. One of them was the "Army of the Potomac." Later the Federals would call their army by the same name.

Irvin McDowell

On the 3rd, Lincoln lost both a friend and opponent. Stephen Douglas had run against Lincoln for the Senate and opposed Lincoln in the Presidential election of '60. Lincoln was sad that Douglas was dead.

The first land battle of the war occurred at Phillippi, (W) Virginia on the 3rd. Forces under Gen. George McClellan defeated the Confederates.

Past Governor of Virginia and now Confederate Brigadier General, Henry Wise got command of the troops in the Kanawha Valley (Today near Charleston, W. Va.) on the 6th.

On the 8th, Lee became an adviser to the President.

The Engagement of Big (Great) Bethel Church took place on the 10th. Out-numbered Confederates sent the Yankees running.

On the 11th, a meeting took place at Wheeling, (W) Virginia. Very few people knew or cared about the meeting but this meeting started the formation of the State of West Virginia. Francis Pierpoint became the first "Governor." Most of the delegates wanted their area to secede from Virginia. It appears that many people in the area just wanted to stay out of any war.

Governor Claiborne Jackson of Missouri called for troops to keep the Yankees from overthrowing the government on the 12th but on the 15th he had to leave the capital at Jefferson City anyway. The government of the United States wanted Missouri, Kentucky and Maryland to be on their side. They would use any method, legal or illegal, to keep them in the Union.

Things were starting to heat up in the Shenandoah Valley. Johnston fell back from Harper's Ferry to Bunker Hill, near Winchester. Union General Patterson moved slowly after Johnston.

Back in Missouri: after running the elected government out of the capital, Unionist, Nathaniel Lyon, attacked the Governor and won at Boonville, on the 17th. On the $19^{th,}$ pro-Southern forces won a victory at "Cole Camp." Alarmed, the next-door Governor of Kansas called for troops to stop any attempt by pro-Confederate forces from taking his state, on the 20th.

History was made on the 23rd when Professor Thaddeus Lowe took his balloon up at Falls Church, Va. to watch the Rebs. This was the first use of a balloon to observe the enemy.

The North had started to blockade Southern ports. On the $30^{th,}$ Raphael Semmes took command of the blockade runner, C. S. S. Sumter (C. for Confederate; S. for States; S. for Service).

July 2^{nd,} instead of following the Supreme Court's ruling, President Lincoln took the right of habeas corpus away from anyone from New York City southward.

By the 2^{nd,} McDowell had decided to attack the Rebs at Manassas Junction but only a few people knew his plans. To keep Gen. Joseph E. Johnston from sending troops to help Beauregard, McDowell ordered Gen. Robert Patterson to cross the Potomac and attack Johnston. Patterson attacked Col. Thomas Jackson near Falling Waters. Jackson's smaller command fell back to join Johnston near Winchester. On the 3^{rd,} Patterson entered Martinsburg and sent reports of his "great victory" to McDowell.

In a July 4^{th,} speech to Congress, Lincoln said that "maybe" some of the things he had done were beyond his powers as President but that he believed Congress would go along with them.

On the 5th in Missouri, Gov. Jackson's troops attacked Franz Sigel's, mostly German speaking, Northern troops at Carthage, Mississippi. and defeated them.

McClellan had defeated the Rebs at the Battle of Phillippi in June. On the 11^{th,} McClellan defeated the Confederates at Rich Mountain. On the 13^{th,} the first general to die was Confederate Gen. Robert Garnett; killed near Cheat Mountain. The North called

McClellan the first "hero general." His army took Beverly, WV..

July 16th McDowell's Army of 35,000 began to march south from Washington; its object was the railroad junction at Manassas. Washington City was thrilled that at last the forces of the "Righteous Union" were going to destroy the Rebel Army, take Richmond and force all those states that had dared to leave back into the Union. Both armies were untrained and the Union Army only moved 6 miles the whole day. When the Yanks entered Virginia some looting occurred. This was just the beginning of the Yankees' evil deeds. By the time the first Federals left the city, Beauregard knew how many Yankees were coming and where they were going because of a Confederate spy,

When the last of the Union Army left town, they were followed by Congressmen and their families and the common folk. Everybody was sure it was the end of the Rebel Nation. It was a holiday spirit with drink and food.

Beauregard had to wire Richmond to get his superior officer, Johnston, to move to Manassas. Johnston wired back to Richmond that he couldn't move because Patterson was about to attack him. Patterson didn't attack because he was sure that Johnston had as many troops as he did. Beauregard did not know that Johnston wasn't on his way. Beauregard made plans. Bull Run Creek is a small stream with high banks. There were only a few places where a large army could cross and Beauregard began to place troops and cannons at these fords; his line stretched for eight miles. Beauregard wanted to attack and not defend. He was making plans to use Johnston's men once they arrived.

As Beauregard thought, the Yankees were looking for a place to cross Bull Run. On the 18^{th,} the 1st Massachusetts ran into the Rebels, under Gen. James Longstreet, at Blackburn's Ford. Gen. Daniel Tyler sent the 2nd Michigan and 12th New York plus artillery to knock a hole through the Rebel's line. Longstreet brought his own cannons on line and attacked

Robert Garnett

with two regiments. The New Yorkers were completely routed and the rest of the Yankees fell back. There were 19 Yankees killed, 38 wounded and 26 missing. Southern loses were 15 killed and 53 wounded. When McDowell got the news of the defeat, he knew it wasn't going to be easy to take Manassas Junction; he would have to change his whole battle plan. Also on the 18^{th,} Johnston got the orders from Richmond to move toward Beauregard. Johnston started moving some of his men by road and others would be moved by rail. When the armies came together there would be 35,000 Southern troops.

On the 19th and 20^{th,} McDowell didn't move. He was making new plans to attack Manassas. He also didn't know that Johnston's Army was moving toward Manassas. At 4 P. M. on the 19^{th,} Beauregard and his staff were at the home of Wilbur McLean when they were very surprised to see Col. Jackson's men arrive. Later his men were called "Foot Cavalry" because they could march so fast. On the 20^{th,} Johnston arrived and took command. Both sides made plans to attack the next day. The South would attack the North on their left flank (side). The North would attack the South on their left flank. This would almost have the armies move in a circle.

At 2:30 A. M. on the 21^{st,} 37,000 green (untested) troops and their green generals started toward battle. McDowell's plans called for Gen. David Hunter and Col. Samuel Heintzelman to march their divisions (about 13,000 men) away around the Southern line and attack from the rear. McDowell's plan began to fall apart at once because of McDowell. McDowell had placed Tyler's division on the road ahead of the others. Tyler was heading to the creek to pretend to attack the Rebs, just to hold their attention. Tyler moved very slowly and everything fell behind schedule. It was 9 o'clock before Col. Ambrose Burnside, under Hunter, crossed the Sudley Ford. Confederate scouts told Gen. N.G. "Shanks" Evans, who was about a mile from the crossing. Evans saw the danger and without orders rushed his small unit of 1,100 men to fight the enemy.

He sent word to Johnston. (The Southern plan wasn't going anywhere. There was a mix-up and no orders to attack were ever given!) Although outnumbered, the Rebels attacked with great fury; much of the fighting was hand-to-hand. At first Burnside's men fell back but because there were so many of them they began to push the Rebels back. Evans called for help but Confederate troops were far away at the railroad. Against great odds, Evans held the line until 11 A. M. when Gen. Barnard Bee's two Georgia regiments arrived. By now, the heat of the day was working against both sides.

Burnsides, too, called for help. Two batteries of cannons arrived and Tyler attacked at Stone Bridge. "Seemly a thousand rifles were flashing and the air was alive with whistling bullets" along a quarter mile line. The Southern forces broke and fell back towards the Warrenton Pike and Henry House Hill. "Victory! Victory!" screamed the Yankees as they chased the Rebs but Evans heroes turned and stood. They held the line for two hours. During this time, Beauregard had found out that his planned attack was going no where and that the real battle was going on. Beauregard rode on the scene in time to see Hampton's Legion of 600 men move toward Evans but before they got there the Yankees struck again. The Southern line fell back in confusion toward Henry House Hill.

McDowell looked from his side of the line and decided that the battle was won. He did not press the attack.

Col. Jackson did not have orders but marched his five regiments to the top of Henry House Hill. As Bee fell back, he told Jackson that the enemy was pushing his men hard. Jackson said that he was there to fight! Bee of Georgia then tried to stop his men from retreating further. Of all the words Bee had spoken in his life time, those near his end are the only ones that history remembers. "Look! There stands Jackson like a stone wall! Rally behind the Virginians!" Moments later Bee fell to rise no more. His words had taken away the first two names of a nutty professor from Virginia Military Institute and now history knows him as "Stonewall" Jackson.

McDowell decided that the battle wasn't over and ordered his men forward at 2 P. M. With his numbers, he was sure to win. McDowell sent 2 batteries (5 guns) to within 300 yards of the Confederate lines. Before the cannons could fire at the South, the South was firing at them. Southern cannon found their mark and so did Jackson's men from the top of the hill. Yankee gunners fell at their

Barnard Bee

guns. The New York Zouaves in their fancy uniforms started to run. Col. James Ewell Brown "JEB" Stuart saw the red uniforms in flight and chased them.

The Confederates saw that the guns might be taken so the 33rd Virginia Regiment under Col. Authur Cummings moved toward the guns. Yankee artillery saw the Rebs but did not fire because these Rebels were wearing blue uniforms. If they were blue uniforms; they must be Yanks, it was believed. The Confederacy was a new nation and its army was a new army. Many units came in the uniforms they had worn when part of the local militia, before the war. The 33rd wore those blue uniforms. No one shot at them but at 70 yards they fired on the gunners that were left. The 33rd took the guns (cannons). The 14th Brooklyn (New York City) tried to take them back but "Stonewall's" men fired on them and then charged. The 14th Zouaves and the Marines began to run in terror.

Other Northern units attacked the exposed Confederates. Col. William Franklin sent the 1st Michigan and the 2nd Massachusetts against the Rebs but they were driven back.

For the next hour, charge and counter charge took place outside the window of the house on Henry Hill. Troops from Maine and Vermont were force marched in the afternoon sun and sent straight into battle. At 3:30 the last Union attack against Henry Hill began; it was beaten back. As the Federals fell back more Southern reinforcements were moving on the hill.

At about 4 P. M. Brig. Gen. Edmund Kirby Smith's boys rushed on the field to Jackson's left. As Smith began the attack, he was wounded but Col. Arnold Elzey led the attack.   Smith's boys hit the Maine and Vermonters, who had already taken a beating.   The Yanks began to run.   When Gen. Beauregard saw the enemy's right flank falling apart, he ordered all his troops to attack at once.   Southern troops charged off the hill; this is where the "Rebel Yell" may have been born!

At Bull Run, Federals ran for their lives.   A Confederate cannon shell hit a wagon on the Cub Run Bridge, the main retreat road.   Men couldn't fall back. Panic set in and the whole army just dissolved.   The Congressmen and other sightseers got more than they bargained for.   Instead of watching a military operation, they were now part of it as they too ran away.

At first, the Southerners chased the Yankees but Beauregard got a false report that said the enemy was getting ready to attack his right flank.   He stopped the chase until he found out the report was wrong.   By then it was 7 P. M. and too late to attack.

Both armies were tired and disorganized.   Both armies had suffered in battle.   The North lost 470 dead, 1,071 wounded, and 1,793 missing.   The South dead were 387; 1,582 wounded and 13 missing.

President Davis arrived as the victory was won. Through the years questions have been raised, "why the South did not attack Washington because it appeared, to all, that the city could easily be taken?"   Davis had made it clear that the South had no desire to attack the North. Washington was the United States capital; it would not be attacked. In years to come, many would regret that it wasn't attack.

As the South received the news there was laughter, joy and celebration. Children born across the country were being named for the new Southern heroes, Johnston, Beauregard, Davis, and "Stonewall." The South was a real country and had a major victory to prove it. The Southern soldier had met and beaten his Yankee counterpart. Surely the South would now live in peaceful independence!

As the news was received in the North, there was astonishment, heartache and depression. Those states that had left the Union were just puffed up windbags and pretenders; they weren't a real nation. Their new nation with a brand new army had whipped the Union's best. No new born children were named for McDowell or Patterson; they were both fired in disgrace. They were the first of many to have their reputation and careers ruined in Virginia.

On the 22^{nd,} the Confederate Congress declared a day of National Thanksgiving to God.

In Washington, "Hero General" George B. McClellan (Mac) was named to replace McDowell and Gen. N. P. Banks was named to replace Patterson.

CHAPTER 3 JULY 23- DECEMBER 31, 1861

On the 24[th,] Gen. Henry Wise retreated towards Gauley Bridge (Ferry); Union General, Jacob Cox pursued from Charleston.

On the 25[th,] the Senate also passed the "Crittenden Resolution." The President Lincoln and both Houses were now on record that the war was "not to interfere with established institutions such as slavery." That same day, Maj. Gen. John Fremont took command of the Western Department.

In New Mexico Territory, Confederates under John Bayor, moving up the Rio Grande and were attacked by Maj. Isaac Lynde at Mesilla. The following day the Yankees retreated. The next day the whole Union command surrendered to a much smaller Southern force.

Horace Greeley was a powerful man and ran the *New York Tribune*. On the 29[th,] he wrote Lincoln saying he should talk to the South about peace and staying out of the Union.

On the 30[th,] Gen. Benjamin Butler wrote the War Department and asked what to do with 900 Negroes that had come into his camp. Were they property? Should they be returned as run-away-slaves? Should they be stolen from their masters?

On the 31[st,] a pro-Union government was put in Missouri.

On August 1st, Robert E. Lee was sent by the President to help out in Western Virginia.

After his great victory, Baylor made New Mexico and Arizona part of the Confederacy.

The first income tax law was passed by the U. S. Congress on the 2nd.

A balloon rose into the air off a Union boat in Hampton Roads and became the world's first "aircraft carrier" on the 3rd.

On the 7th, Hampton, Virginia was burned by Confederate General John Magruder. He wanted to stop the Negroes from running to Butler.

Brig. Gen. U. S. Grant took command of the District of Ironton, Missouri.

The Secretary of War wrote to Butler that he must keep the slaves that ran to his camp. If the state were out of the Union the slaves must be stolen from their masters. If the state was still in the Union the slaves would be returned to their masters.

On the 10th, the biggest battle fought in Missouri took place. At the Battle of Wilson's Creek, Federal General, Nathaniel Lyon attacked with more men and much better equipment. At first he pushed the Southern Army, under Gen. Benjamin McCulloch, back. Sterling Price and Missouri State Troopers were there to fight the Yanks. An attack by Gen. Franz Sigel and his mostly German Union fighters "failed miserably." The Confederates counter attacked. The Yanks started to fall back. Lyon tried to stop the Rebels but was shot dead.

After that, the Union Army ran from the field. This was the second big battle of the war and the South won this one also. The North lost about 1,300 men and the South about 1,200 but the South won the battle!

On the 11th, Gen. John Floyd took command in the Kanawha Valley. Floyd had been the Governor of Virginia and he did not like Henry Wise, who also had been a Governor of Virginia.

President Davis had done so good with his day of Thanksgiving to the Lord that Lincoln decided to get God on his side, so he said that the last Thursday of September would be a "day of humiliation, prayer and fasting...."

Most Indian tribes supported the South but Chief Nicholas of the Mescalero Apaches did not. From ambush his braves killed 15 Confederate soldiers.

On the 14th, President Davis issued a proclamation saying if people living in the Confederate States could not support the Confederacy they should go or be sent north.

The U. S. Government had already been putting people in jail without any law being broken now they started to attack a "free press." Most people got their news from newspapers. The government did not want the people to hear anything good about the South so they charged many papers with "disloyalty" and stopped them from printing their newspapers. Lincoln took away the freedom of the press. On the 16th, the *Journal of Commerce, Daily News, Day Book Freeman's Journal,* and Brooklyn *Eagle* (all New York City papers) were put out of business. Later papers at West Chester and Easton, Pennsylvania were closed. Not only was the Haverhill, Massachusetts paper closed; its editor was "tarred and feathered." Later, all the papers in New York State, that were thought to be pro-Southern, were "suppressed." No one knows how many papers were closed but there were many; including those in Paducah, Kentucky and Philadelphia. In more modern times the United States Government called the communist "evil" because they arrested people without charges and would not let their people hear the truth.

This author found only one pro-Union newspaper that was stopped by the South. It was the *Whig* in Knoxville, Tennessee.

On the 17th, the Union officially created the Army of the Potomac for the northern part of Virginia. On this date Lincoln made Henry Halleck a general; he also asked Simon Buckner to be a Yankee general but Buckner quit the Union Army and became a general for the South.

Rose Greenhow and Mrs. Philip Phillips were arrested in Washington on the 24th, on charges of "corresponding with the Confederates." The Yankees never found out how important these spies were to the South. On the 26th, King Kamehmeha said his Hawaiian Islands would stay neutral during the war. That must have made Lincoln more relaxed.

Fort Hatteras fell to the enemy on the 28th. This gave the Federals a base in North Carolina and helped stop blockade runners.

As if Lincoln wasn't having enough trouble with the Rebels, one of his own generals started a fire storm on the 30th. Maj. Gen. John Fremont thought of himself as more than a general. He lived a very rich life style in St. Louis, Missouri. He declared "martial law." That is he took all the people's rights away. He arrested and

Henry Halleck

took property from anyone he wished. Any pro-Southern man found with a gun would "be shot." Because of the "disorganized condition, helplessness of the civil authority (the U. S. Government)" he declared the very first "Emancipation Proclamation." Slaves of pro-Southerners were "free." Those of pro-Union men were still slaves. "The cry against the order was immediate and largely unanimous...." President Lincoln and Congress had said that this war was not about slavery; now Fremont was trying to change that. The people of the United States were against Fremont and so was the President. Lincoln called Fremont a dictator. Northern newspapers wrote bad things about Fremont;

only a few abolitionist newspapers liked what he had done.

The Federals had just taken control of the Kentucky government and ran their flag up the capital pole. Kentucky had many slaves and Lincoln worried that the Emancipation would "alarm our Southern Union friends," who owned slaves. Fremont had gone too far and started setting policy for Lincoln.

On September 3, Confederate troops entered Kentucky. Gen. Leonidas Polk wanted Kentucky to side with the South. Because the South had been the first to invade the state, many people in Kentucky got mad at the South because the state was still officially "neutral."

On the 6th, Grant invaded to Paducah as both sides fought for Kentucky.

Lincoln sent Gen. David Hunter on the 9th, to advise Fremont to back off of the Emancipation.

On the 10th, Gen William Rosencrans' Federals attacked John Floyd at Carnifix Ferry. Floyd wanted Wise to help him but Wise did not. Even Robert E. Lee couldn't make the two Confederate generals work together. Because of this campaign the South lost effective control of Western Virginia. Western Virginia was the biggest wool producing section east of the

Leonidas Polk

Mississippi River. Few knew this fact and even fewer cared in '61. It was to be a "short war." After '63 everyone knew that there wasn't enough wool to make Southern uniforms.

Rosencrans' boss, Jacob Cox, would later burn the Boone County Courthouse. By destroying courthouses, it would cause the Rebel counties problems for generations to come.

Gen. Albert Sidney Johnston took command of Southern troops in Tennessee, Missouri, Arkansas, and Kentucky.

Late that night in Washington, Mrs. Fremont met with the President. She told Lincoln that he should support her husband in the Emancipation. Lincoln was polite but not friendly to Mrs. Fremont. The next day Lincoln wrote Fremont and told him to withdraw that hated Emancipation. Fremont ignored the President and continued to take slaves from pro-Southerners.

Lincoln had more pro-Southern, Maryland delegates locked up. The legislature decided not to even try to meet with so many of their delegates in jail.

In Western Virginia things had not gone well for the South. Because of rough mountains, bad weather and two generals that would not work together, "Lee's plan had failed miserably...." A lot of newspapers wrote bad stories about Lee.

On the 19th, Gen. Zollicoffer took his troops into east Tennessee and stopped the bridge burners. The people of east Tennessee weren't so much for the Union;

they were just against west Tennessee folk. It is very similar to northern Mississippi and southern Mississippi. People in the mountains didn't think that they had much of a say so in their government so they hated the people in the flat land more than they did the Yankees.

Col. James Mulligan had been expecting reinforcements from Fremont but Fremont was too busy stealing slaves to send any men. In a last attack on Lexington, Missouri the Confederates under Gen. Sterling Price used big bales of cotton as shields which they rolled toward the Union line. On the 20th Mulligan surrendered to Price. When a newspaper in St. Louis said that Fremont should have sent troops to help Mulligan, Fremont closed the newspaper and arrested the editor.

On the 25th, Gen. Henry Wise was fired from command because he did not work with Floyd.

On October 2nd, the Confederacy signed a peace treaty with the Great Osage Indians and later that month with the Shawnee, Seneca and Cherokees.

The English were divided over our war. The *Post* wanted to back the South; the *London Times* backed the North.

On the 8th, Brig. Gen. William Sherman took command of the Union Department of the Cumberland while Lincoln continued to worry about Fremont.

The Union blockade got a little tighter on the 9th when Federals took Fort Pickens guarding Pensacola Bay, Florida.

The Confederates were usually friends with the Indians but on the 11th, it was Confederates that attacked the Indians near Fort Inge, Texas.

On the 12th, John Slidell and James Mason commissioners to France and England sailed away from the Confederacy.

Yankees captured Lexington, Missouri on the 16th.

On the 19th, the C. S. S. Florida and U. S. S. Massachusetts fired at each other off Ship Island, Mississippi. Both sides knew how important the Mississippi River was.

On the 21st, there was a battle, best known as Ball's Bluff. It was also known as Leesburg, Harrison's Island, or Conrad's Ferry. It was another Union disaster. About 1,700 Yankees crossed the Potomac to attack about the same number of Rebels. In the morning, the Federals pushed the Confederates but the Confederates came roaring back. They fought very well and pushed the Yankees back to the river. The Union commander Col. Edward Baker was shot dead near the river and the Yankees panicked. The Federals ran to their boats but many over turned and men drowned. Other Yanks were shot and many surrendered. The North lost 921 men to the South's 155. The North was shocked that the South had beaten them so badly again!

Brig. Gen. Charles Stone was in over all Union command. The newspapers and high officials said Stone was really pro-Southern and just pretending to love the North. They said he was guilty of "treason." That was all it took. The Lincoln government threw Stone in jail, without charges, like it had done so many others. Later he was released but he was through in the army.

On the 24th, the first Transcontinental Telegraph was completed and Western Union became a part of America until this day.

Federal cavalry charged a small Southern force, under Price, at Springfield, Mo. The cavalrymen shouted, "Fremont and the Union." Some people believed that Fremont wanted to start his own nation.

After the battle, Fremont and Price signed an agreement on exchanging prisoners and also release of some of the political prisoners which, without charges, Fremont had taken. Although Fremont won the battle, his days as Department Commander were numbered.

Benjamin Franklin Kelley took Romney, (W) Virginia on the 26th. This put the Yanks within striking distance of Winchester.

On the 31st, the Missouri legislature voted the state out of the Union. The thirteenth star was added to the Confederate flag!

General-in-Chief of the Union Army and hero of the War with Mexico, Winfield Scott left the army. He was just too old. McClellan took his place.

Off Cape Hatteras, North Carolina on the 1st of November stood the biggest invasion fleet in the history of the United States. Seventy-seven vessels and 12,000 men were moving to attack Port Royal, near Savannah.

There was also a very big storm and many men and ships went down.

Fremont knew that he had acted against Congress and the President. He knew there may be an attempt to get rid of him, so he told his "Royal Guard" not to let anyone through to see him unless, he said it was okay. The "Royal Guard" was a company of Kentucky soldiers all of whom were over 6 feet tall and completely loyal to Fremont. No one had gotten through until the 2nd when a courier with orders from the President slipped through the guards. Fremont was fired and Gen. David Hunter replaced him. Lincoln did not know as much about Hunter as he thought he did. Lincoln broke the agreement with Price. When Lincoln sent someone to jail, even without charges, he was going to stay there! Lincoln is known in history as the "Great Emancipator," because of his supposed love for the slaves and overwhelming desire to make them free. However, it was Lincoln who destroyed Fremont's Emancipation Proclamation and said there would be not one slave freed!

On the 4th, "Stonewall" became commander of the Shenandoah Valley Military District. On the 5th Lee took command of South Carolina, Georgia, and East Florida. On this same day, Union General William Nelson moved troops into Prestonsburg, Ky.

Confederate elections on the 6th made Jefferson Davis President for 6 years. The country would end before his term expired.

Although the wind had damaged the fleet, the Yankees took Port Royal and later Hilton Head Island. This gave the ships a port to re-supply and get coal; it was a big help to the North.

Grant moved by boat and attacked near Columbia, Kentucky. Later Confederates under Polk forced Grant to retreat. Losses were about the same in both armies, somewhere over 600 but the South still held.

By the 8th, the Confederate Commissioners to France and England had left their Southern vessel in Cuba and taken an English ship, the *Trent*, toward London. Off Cuba, the *U. S. S. San Jacinto* caught the *Trent* and took the Commissioners prisoner. This made the North happy, the English mad and the Southerners excited! It became known as the "Trent Affair." The Yankees thought they had stopped the South from getting aid from England. However, Federals had made the English Government angry because they had boarded an English ship and arrested people who had committed no crime. Lincoln had been doing it on land for a long time, so why not on the sea? The South was excited because they were sure England would now come to the aid of the Confederacy.

Lincoln had trouble with Fremont and now McClellan had quit sending Lincoln answers to his letters. So Lincoln and an aid rode to McClellan's house and waited for him to come in that night. The President humbly waited to speak to one of his employees (Lincoln was the boss and McClellan served under him).

When he did arrive, McClellan went straight to bed without one word to the President. Lincoln was angry because he thought someone should pay attention to him.

On the 14th, the Young Men's Christian Association (YMCA or Y) was formed to help with the religious needs of the Union soldier.

Near Round Mountain in Indian Territory, pro-Confederates and pro-Union Indians fought an engagement.

Judah Benjamin, who was Jewish, was named Secretary of State for the Confederacy on the 21st. On the 22nd, the Confederate Department of Indian Territories was created and Brig. Gen. Albert Pike made its head.

On the 24th, Bedford Forrest started the first of many raids on the Federals.

On December 3rd, in a speech to Congress, Lincoln called for "...colonization of free Negroes..." In other words, he wanted to ship all Negroes out of the country!

Maj. Gen. William Hardee took command of the Confederate Central Army of Kentucky on the 5th.

On the 8th, the American Bible Society said it would give 7,000 copies of the Bible to Union troops, only. It wasn't just because the Yankees were the biggest sinners; it was that the Society backed the North.

The English were angry about the Trent Affair and sent a message to Washington on the 19th and troops toward Canada on the 20th. As the troops left England, the band played *Dixie*.

On the 22nd, Maj. Gen. H. W. Halleck announced that any Southerner in Missouri found burning a bridge would be shot.

The show of force by England was too strong for Lincoln. On the 26th, he admitted that the arrest of the Southern Commissioners was "illegal" and that they would be sent to Europe without delay. Lincoln was too smart to risk a war with England and the Confederacy at the same time. He only hoped the English would not come to the aid of the South.

As the year closed, the two warring countries, which shared the same history, also shared the same view on race. Neither side said the war was about slavery. Fremont tried to change things but he was gone and Lincoln still said it was not about slavery. It was still a "white man's" war. The North didn't recruit Negro soldiers. In the South where there were large free Negro population centers (like New Orleans, Atlanta, Savannah, and Richmond), Negroes had volunteered to serve the Confederacy. President Davis thanked the volunteers kindly but the role of a Negro was that of a slave. They were not considered, by North or South, to be the equal of a white person. One Southern general summed it up well: "If Negroes make good soldiers our whole concept of slavery is subject to question."

As the year closed, there were gay parties across the South. At the first of '61 there was no Southern nation; now there was. The new nation had whipped the Yankee invaders badly in the east and more than held their own in the west. The Damn Yankees hadn't crushed Southern Independence as they had bragged. On the other hand, England had not supported Southern Independence as all Southerners believed that she would. "King Cotton" was still on His throne and a Confederacy, living in peace, was sure to come in '62.

Joseph E. Johnston

CHAPTER 4 JANUARY 1 - APRIL 7, 1862

On New Years Day, Lincoln sent the Confederate Commissioners on their way. McClellan remained ill with probably typhoid fever.

On the 3rd, "Stonewall" left Winchester on his Romney Campaign to break-up the Baltimore & Ohio Railroad. On the 5th, he was at Hancock, Md.

Pvt. Archibald Carnaghan of the 7th Kansas Cavalry didn't want his parents to worry about him so he wrote them a letter on the 6th. "We kill and strip as we go...We live on the top of the heap. We have splendid horses to ride and jacket-full of money, although I have not been paid any. We have and take money, watches, jewelry, horses, mules, sheep, hogs, cattle and bed-clothes, burn their houses and kill all who have ever taken up arms against the government. We take no prisoners...My love to all."

On the 7th, there were skirmishes in eastern Kentucky at Paintsville and Jennie's Creek. On the 10th at Prestonsburg, Union Brig. Gen. James Garfield struck the Confederate line of Gen. Humphrey Marshall. The Yanks retreated but Garfield still claimed victory. Garfield was a politician at heart and would later be President. Also on this date, "Stonewall" marched into Romney, Virginia. Back in Washington where Lincoln claimed that no states were really out of the Union, Missouri Senators, Waldo Johnson and Trusten Polk, were thrown out of office because they believed in the Southern Cause.

A fleet of about 100 vessels under Commodore Louis Goldsborough sailed south from Hampton Roads, Virginia carrying 15,000 troops under Burnside.

"Politics makes strange bedfellows." On the 13[th,] Lincoln appointed Edwin Stanton Secretary of War. Stanton hated the South and didn't like Lincoln either. He had called Lincoln a "Buffoon" (clown). He was considered "…crafty, dishonest, arbitrary (impulsive), and unfit for his position." This wasn't a good move for "Honest Abe."

This date, McClellan basically told the President of the United States to "Drop Dead" when he refused to tell Lincoln any of his battle plans.

In Kentucky on the banks of the Cumberland River on the 19[th,] the battle with many names was fought. It was called Mill Springs, Logan Cross Roads, Fishing Creek, Somerset and Beech Grove. Confederate General, George Crittenden, sent General Zollicoffer to attack. At first the Confederates were pushing the Yankees back. Zollicoffer was shot and killed. A Virginia-Yankee, Gen George Thomas, brought more troops and the Southern line broke. There were about 4,000 men on each side. The Federals lost 39 killed, 207 wounded and 15 captured. The South withdrew across the Cumberland having lost 125 killed, 309 wounded, and 99 missing.

On the 20th, the Northern navy sunk several old ships in the harbor at Charleston, hoping to block the channel. It didn't work but they tried the same thing at other Southern ports.

McClellan wouldn't talk to the President so Lincoln talked to McClellan and the rest of his generals on the 27th. He told them all to advance on the 22nd of February. They all ignored General War Order No. 1 and no one moved by the 22nd.

On the 3rd of February, Lincoln wrote a thank-you but no thank-you note to the King of Siam. It was nice of the king to offer to send a herd of war elephants anyway.

This month, the *Atlantic Monthly Magazine* printed Julia Ward Howe's poem, *"The Battle Hymn of the Republic."* It became one of the most popular Yankee songs of the war. Many people believe it to be a "religious song" but it is not Biblically based. The song calls the Union Army the Lord's "Swift sword" and says the South was evil, "where the grapes of wrath are stored." Later in the war when the North began to attack civilians and their property, the Yankee troops sang this song with glee as they burned Southern towns and defiled Southern women! It is best described as a "Hymn of Hate."

On the 4th, Federal troops landed north of Fort Henry in Tennessee just south of Kentucky.

Indiana Senator, Jesse Bright, was the next to be thrown out of the U. S. Senate.

By the 6[th,] most of the Confederates had left Fort Henry for Fort Donelson. Without a fight Brig. Gen. Lloyd Tilghman surrendered to Grant. It was another serious loss to the South. After this Federal gunboats moved down the Tennessee River so they could go up the Cumberland to attack Donelson. Southerners moved all the troops in the area toward Donelson.

Elsewhere, Burnside and the Yankee fleet took Roanoke Island in North Carolina and the Federals re-entered Romey as "Stonewall" fell back on Winchester.

Yankee General, Charles Stone, (of Ball's Bluff) hadn't been out of jail long when he was again thrown back into jail. Again, there were no charges. He would be released again on Aug. 16th.

Lincoln kept up with the war news but he was very worried about William "Willie" Lincoln, his son who was very sick with typhoid.

On the 13[th,] delegates in Wheeling, (W) Va. were adopting a constitution for a possible new state. There was an "unwelcome" sign hung out for the Negroes "...no slavery or free person of color should come into the state...." This same day fighting started at Fort Donelson. The next day four ironclad and two wooden gunboats arrived and started shelling the fort but the Dixie Boys were ready. By day's end, the two wooden boats were badly damaged and two of the four ironclads drifted helplessly down stream. Despite a Dixie-Victory that day, the Confederate generals decided that Donelson couldn't be held. On the morrow, they would fight their way out to safety.

At 5 A. M. on the 15th, the attack was launched. The Federal line was broken; a safe way to Nashville was open but nobody moved. There were too many generals, who couldn't decide anything, so with escape open, senior commander Floyd (who had done so badly in Western Virginia) called the men back into the fort. That night the generals decided to surrender the fort but Generals Floyd and 2nd in command, Gideon Pillow, decided to run. Col. Forrest said he didn't want to spend the war in a Union prison camp so he and his command ran also.

On the 16th, Confederate General Simon Buckner asked Grant for terms. Grant sent these words back, "No terms except unconditional and immediate surrender...." Grant got a nickname, "Unconditional Surrender Grant" and the South suffered a great loss. Grant got promoted to Major General and the South lost control on the upper Mississippi. When the news reached Richmond, President Davis was very angry at his generals, especially Floyd.

Despite the good war news on the 20th, there was much crying in the White House. "Willie" died. Mrs. Mary Todd Lincoln would not stop crying. Later she tried to contact Willie through use of mediums (almost like witches). Many believed that she was crazy and his death just added to her problems.

The South got a little good news on the 21st. After a sharp engagement at Valverde, in New Mexico Territory, Southern forces pushed toward Santa Fe. The Yankees lost 68 killed, 160 wounded, and 35 missing. Southern loses were 31 dead, 154 wounded and 1 missing.

On the 23rd, Lincoln made Andrew Johnson, a Tennessean, Military Governor of that state. Johnson had been elected by the people to represent their state in the Senate. A tailor by trade, he turned Senator. Tennessee left the Union but Johnson didn't. His voters said he had turned "traitor." On the 25th, Union forces took over the capital, Nashville.

The South knew that Lincoln was jailing anyone he pleased with no charges. The Confederate Congress gave their president the same power on the 27th but Davis used it very little during the entire war.

On the last day of February, there was a "day of fasting and prayer." After the losses in Kentucky and Tennessee, the South needed

Andrew Johnson

all the help She could get. In Washington, Lincoln asked McClellan why there had been no movement on the 22nd but McClellan had an excuse and Lincoln let the matter drop.

On March 1st, President Davis used the power Congress had given him. He declared martial law in Richmond and arrested some pro-Northerners.

In New Mexico Territory, Gen. H. H. Sibley was still pushing the Union back. This time the Yanks left Santa Fe on the 4th.

On the 5th, Union General Nathaniel Banks moved from Harper's Ferry toward Winchester and "Stonewall" fell back. In Tennessee, Beauregard took command of the Army of Mississippi.

In a message to Congress on the 6th, Lincoln called for a law to give money to states that would adopt gradual abolition (slowly stop slavery). The money would help pay the masters for their slaves. This law was aimed mostly at Delaware, Maryland, Kentucky, and Missouri. The other Northern states were already starting to get rid of their slaves. It was not morality that was causing the Yankees to get rid of slavery; it was because they couldn't make money with their slaves. Those four states were in a southern climate and were making money from their slaves. They refused Lincoln's bribe money. In the same message, Lincoln again called for shipping free Negroes to Africa or South America.

It was a cold morning in Elkhorn Tavern, Arkansas where the Battle of Pea Ridge was fought on the 7th. Four divisions of Federals under Samuel Curtis lay in wait for Earl Van Dorn's small Confederate army, which included Indians. The Yankees thought he would attack their front line but Van Dorn sneaked around to their back. At first the Federals were surprised but they did a good job of turning about to receive the attack. This started a day of attacks and counter-attacks. The Yankees accused the Indians of scalping their wounded and dead. Two Confederate generals were killed, Benjamin McCulloch and James McIntosh. Despite their deaths, the Yankees still couldn't break the line. The battle continued on the 8th as Union troops fought well and drove Van Dorn's boys off the field and toward Van Buren, Arkansas. This was another big loss for the South. No longer was Arkansas part of the Confederacy and the South no longer controlled the entire Mississippi.

On this same date in Hampton Roads near Norfolk, Virginia, the Confederacy changed naval warfare for ever. The *Merrimack* was a wooden ship, it was covered with iron plate and renamed the *C. S. S. Virginia*. The iron plates made her very heavy and her steam engines could move her only very slowly but she did move against the wooden ships of the North. The *Congress* and the *Cumberland* went down and the *Minnesota* was badly damaged. While the *Virginia* was sinking Union ships, the Union's ironclad ship, the *Monitor* was moving toward Hampton Roads.

The next day, the *Virginia* came out to finish the *Minnesota* off but the *Monitor* was waiting. The *Monitor* had only two guns to the *Virginia's* many but the *Monitor's* guns were in a turret. To aim her guns the *Virginia* had to move the whole ship; to aim her guns the *Monitor* only turned the turret. The *Monitor* moved faster and set lower in the water than did the *Virginia*. Even though the *Monitor* had the advantages, she broke off and steamed away from the fight. The iron plates protected both vessels and neither was badly damaged. The *Virginia* returned to Norfolk but never left port again. The English Navy ruled the world with wooden ships. They took notice of this sea battle.

March the 11th showed both the political power and weakness of Lincoln. In a show of power, he gave McClellan a slap when he fired him from the General-in-Chief's job. McClellan was still the head of the Army of the Potomac. In a show of weakness, Lincoln named Fremont to head the Mountain Department.

On the 12^{th,} the Federals took Winchester. This town would change hands 72 times during the war. On the 13^{th,} Burnsides took New Berne and McClellan made plans to send his army by water to attack Richmond.

Rebels started fortifying Island No. 10 to try to stop the Yankees from moving farther down the Mississippi River. On the 15^{th,} Fremont's former second in command, David Hunter, was given command of the Department of the South (at this time it was only a few islands off the South Carolina coast).

On the 19^{th,} Gen. James Shields was chasing "Stonewall" out of Strasburg. Shields had 9,000 men to Jackson's 3,500 but "Stonewall" decided to only fight a part of Shields' army. On the 23^{rd,} Jackson struck Shields hard at Kernstown near Winchester. Aided by his brilliant cavalry commander, Gen. Turner Ashby,

Jackson won a big victory. This was the first battle in Jackson's famous Shenandoah Valley Campaign. This campaign is studied in military schools to this day! Though fought near Winchester, it affected Washington. Lincoln was afraid that Washington would be attacked. He stopped the troops that McClellan wanted to attack Richmond with and sent some of them to the Shenandoah to fight "Stonewall." When McClellan found out that Lincoln had recalled his troops, he was very angry.

On the 24th, in Cincinnati, Ohio abolitionist, Wendell Phillips, tried to tell the crowd why the slaves should be freed. They didn't want to hear his propaganda. He was bloodied, hissed at, and eggs and rocks were thrown at him. His big talk ended in big fist fight and Phillips felt lucky to have escaped with his life.

In New Mexico Territory on the 28th, Jo Sibley was still pushing the Yankees back. Southern forces moved over the Santa Fe Trail and took the Federals on again at Pigeon's Ranch. Union commander, Col. John Slough, was taking a licking when about 400 Yankee reinforcements came from a different direction and struck the rear of the Confederates. They destroyed Southern supply wagons. This forced the Confederates to leave the area to the enemy.

By now, the Confederacy had learned that McClellan was coming by sea not by land. Gen. John Magruder only had a small force on the peninsula along the James River. President Davis ordered General Johnston to sent reinforcements.

On the last day of March, Lincoln further angered McClellan when he ordered some of McClellan's troops be returned to Washington. McClellan now believed that he did not have enough troops to attack. However his army far out numbered Magruder's small force.

April Fools Day was a day of jokes and sport both in the North and the South but the 2nd Baptist Church of Richmond did not decide to donate their bell to be made into cannon because it was April Fools Day. They donated it because they wanted their church to go to war and have an artillery unit named the "2nd Baptist Church Battery." Other churches also gave their bells. "Stonewall" was a very religious person and four of his guns were named, "Matthew, Mark, Luke and John." Together they were called, "The Gospels."

On the 2[nd,] it was the Yankees who were the "fools." They simply deported Rose Greenhow, Southern spy, to Virginia. If they would have known all that she had done for the South, they would have probably hung her.

On the 3[rd,] it was Lincoln who found-out that he had been fooled. McClellan had taken some of the troops Lincoln had ordered to stay and defend Washington. Lincoln was hot! He stopped other troops that were supposed to go to McClellan and ordered McClellan to "move against the enemy at once."

The U. S. Senate on this date, in a split vote, outlawed slavery in Washington.

McClellan was slowly moving on the 4th but not because of Lincoln's order. McClellan's army was huge, almost 100,000, and he was following Magruder's 15,000. The armies were at Yorktown and both sides knew the meaning of this town. Some of the men at Yorktown in 1862 had grand-fathers that fought there in America's First Revolutionary War. It was here that the climatic battle of that war took place. Oppressed Americans had thrown-off a big central government that had mistreated the Colonists and won their independence. The people of the South wanted to do the same thing.

Magruder put on a "play" for McClellan. McClellan thought that there were far more Confederates in front of him than there were. So Magruder had his men march all day, showing themselves at different points along the lines; this made McClellan believe he was seeing many troops. Magruder also had trees cut, shaped and painted to look like cannon barrels. These "cannon" could not shoot but McClellan did not know it. There were many people at this time that followed the Quaker religion. The Quakers did not believe in war. These cannons couldn't kill anyone so the soldiers started calling them "Quaker Cannon." Meanwhile Johnston was moving troops to oppose McClellan.

Out on the Mississippi, other Confederate cannons became useless. Island No. 10 had many cannons on it to stop the Yankees move down the river but Grant's men just dug a cannel below No.10 and moved their gunboats south of the island. Southern forces began to leave another important point.

On the 5th, Military Governor of Tennessee, Andrew Johnson, removed the mayor, aldermen and councilmen from their elected offices in Nashville. These brave men would not pledge allegiance to the Union.

The big Battle of Shiloh Church was fought on the 6th and 7th. Yankee forces under Grant had been steadily moving south with the aim of using the Mississippi River to cut into the heart of Dixie and maybe even to cut the Confederacy in two. There were more Yankees who were better equipped, better trained, better supplied and backed by gunboats. The South had little of those things but she did have the most brilliant Confederate general of the early war period, Albert Sidney Johnston.

The South had lost Forts Henry and Donelson, then Island No. 10 and the important manufacturing city of Nashville. Grant was pushing farther up the Tennessee River to threaten Corinth, Mississippi. It was believed that he may move along the railroad to Memphis. William Sherman was the first to arrive at Pittsburg Landing about 35 miles from Corinth. Grant later joined him and their forces numbered about 40,000. Grant had been "relieved of command" (fired) for a short time. The reason Grant was back was that his replacement, Gen. C. F. Smith, had hurt his leg in a fall. The leg got an infection and Smith died in five weeks. Grant was fired because he was a drunk. He had been thrown-out of the army in '54 for drinking and now the bottle caused him problems again. Many considered Sherman a "madman" and he too had been fired for a short time because he was nuts. The drunk and the crazy man brought their armies to Pittsburg Landing expecting to move south soon. They were ordered to stay there until Gen. Don Buell brought his 50,000 from Nashville. Buell was slow moving. Grant and Sherman were planning on attacking not being attacked so that they didn't make good defensive lines.

Gen. Johnston was watching and knew he must attack before Buell arrived. Johnston moved his men to a small Methodist Church called "Shiloh" (meaning Peace) about three miles from Pittsburg Landing on the 4th and skirmishing began between the two armies. Beauregard tried to get Johnston not to attack because he believed that Grant was just waiting for a Southern attack. Besides, Beauregard said Confederate troops were without supplies and very tried from the march. Johnston said "No" to Beauregard; the attack would be on the 6th. Grant later admitted, "I (had) scarcely the faintest idea of an attack being made upon us." Grant wasn't the sharpest tack in the box.

The Yankees went looking for the Rebs at Shiloh Church at 3:30 A. M. and found them. Skirmishing began between Hardee and five Federal companies. At 6:30, Johnston gave the order for the big attack.

Johnston was so sure he was going to win, he told another officer, "Tonight we will water our horses in the Tennessee River."

Hardee, Polk and Patrick Cleburne hit the Union right flank under Sherman. Sherman rode through "...a hail of bullets" to try and stop the Rebels. Col. Ralph Buckland's boys did slow the South down but then Bragg's Division hit. Sherman's line collapsed and Yankees ran for their lives. Then Col. Madison Miller's Union Brigade was attacked both from the front and side. To Miller's right Everett Peabody's Brigade was almost wiped-out. Peabody was killed while on his horse. By 8:45, the advanced brigades were running. Benjamin Prentiss's Brigade was behind and to the rear of Peabody's and Miller's. The Confederate attack slowed by the time it hit Prentiss's men. Union commander, John McClernand sent Prentiss reinforcements. This line held until 10 when Polk's Division attacked. This line of Yankees also broke and ran.

Federal Brig. Gen. William Wallace moved his brigade in to a sunken road bed and brought cannon forward. Prentiss's men joined Wallace. Grant rode toward Wallace's line and saw all the troops falling back. He knew his army was taking a beating. Grant's only hope was to hold out until Buel arrived.

By late morning, the attacking Rebels were almost as scattered and disorganized as the Yankees. Johnston and Beauregard didn't really know where the enemy was and didn't attack with a clear plan.

About 5,000 Yankees and six batteries of cannon fell in along the sunken road. The Confederates began attacking the road at 11 A. M.; they were still attacking at 2:00 P. M. with nothing but many dead to show for it. There was so much firing from the Union line, that the Southerners called it the "Hornet's Nest." Gen. Johnston wanted to break that line. He personally led a charge and Gen. John Breckinridge's boys followed. They smashed through on the Federals' left. Johnston got shot in an artery in his leg. Before he could be taken from his horse, the South's most brilliant general bled to dead. His last attack caused the Hornet's Nest to be surrounded; by 5 P. M. Rebels backed by 62 cannon were ready to destroy the Yankee line. Yankee Wallace joined Johnston in death and the Billys surrendered. While the fighting went on at the road, Southerners were also pushing the Billys on the left flank. The Confederates now felt that they would water their horses in the Tennessee. Although the Federals had lost their line at the road, it had given Grant time to set up a new line to receive the Confederate attack.

Bragg ordered an attack by Breckinridge. What Bragg didn't know was that one of the two brigades was almost out of bullets. What he also didn't know was that Grant had sent 60 cannon, some of them very big siege guns, to that area. Now that the Rebels were getting close to the Tennessee, Union gunboats could also fire on the Rebels. When all that artillery broke lose, the Confederates fell back. It was 6:30, and the day's work was done.

The South did not continue to attack for a number of reasons. They had been fighting for 12 hours, they were tired and hungry. The South had little extra food before the attack and now many Johnnys began to get food from the downed Yankees. Beauregard was at the rear when he got word that Johnston was dead and he was now the commander. So as the sun set, the Southern attack stopped.

What the South didn't know was that the first of Buell's army was crossing the river to Grant's aid.

Braxton Bragg

Through the night, it rained on the living, the dead and wounded. Through the night, Yankees poured across the river. The new commander, Beauregard, looked at the facts that night. The Yankees were beaten but his army was in no condition to attack. Many of his units had little or no ammo; little or no food; were very tired; were disorganized; they simply were not ready to fight. Beauregard decided to hold his position because he believed that Grant could not attack but would retreat across the Tennessee on the 'morrow.

Beauregard didn't know that more Union troops were arriving. Both Grant and Buell decided to attack on the 'morrow.

By dawn, there were 45,000 Yankees troops, many of them fresh and eager for battle. The South had less that 20,000 not ready for battle but Rebels outfought their Union counterparts at almost every engagement. At 7 A. M. the South was shocked when the Federals attacked. 15,000 fresh troops attacked on the South's right flank. Gen. Hardee called for reinforcements and by 10 A. M. it was the Federals falling back through the peach orchard. That area was covered by the wounded and dead from the day before. The Rebs advanced until the cannon of William Terrill's Battery spoke.

The Union attack on the center was stopped by a much weaker force of Confederates but the Confederates left gave way under a Union attack of 13,000 men commanded by Wallace. Brave Confederates fell trying to stop or slow the Yankees advance but by 11 A. M. the Federals were only a ½ mile from Shiloh Church.

Bragg thought he might split Wallace's attack with an attack of his own. Bragg ordered Cleburne to advance with only 800 men who were low on ammo. Cleburne told Bragg it was stupid to try the attack but Bragg ordered Cleburne forward. At first it appeared that Bragg was right because the little group of Confederates were pushing larger Yankees units before them. Then Lovell Rousseau's Brigade swung in on

Cleburne and it was all over. Cleburne's boys melted in the crossfire.

By now, Beauregard knew he was fighting Grant's and Buell's Armies. He was greatly outnumbered; the Yankees were approaching Shiloh Church; his line was near breaking. Beauregard shouted, "Retreat!" Beauregard, himself, took what few organized troops he had left and set up a defensive line to let the rest of the army retreat through. Southerners burned captured Union supplies and equipment as they retreated.

Grant and Buell knew the South was in full retreat. They had more troops and the daylight hours to smash the Confederate Army but they just let the Southern Army limp back toward Corinth.

The great Southern victory of the 6th was now the great defeat of the 7th. The Southern Army and Southern people were very sad and disheartened.

The U. S. Army numbered 65,000. They lost 1,754 killed, 8,408 wounded and 2,885 missing. The C. S. A. Army numbered 40,000. They lost 1,723 killed, 8,012 wounded and 959 missing.

There was more bad news for the South on this day. The Island No. 10 was taken.

CHAPTER 5 APRIL 8- JULY 1, 1862

On the 11^{th,} Fort Pulaski on the banks of the Savannah River, near the city with the same name, surrendered. Federal General, Quincy Gillmore used "rifled" artillery and "penetrating" shells for the first time in history. Col. Charles Olmstead surrendered to the Yankees and their blockade increased. On this date, Brig. Gen. Ormsby Mitchel occupied Huntsville, Alabama and broke the Memphis and Charleston Railroad. On the *C. S. S. Virginia's* last run, she captured 3 merchant vessels and offered fight to the *Monitor* but the *Monitor* would not leave the safety of port.

"The Great Locomotive Chase" began at breakfast time at Big Shanty, Georgia on the 12th. The train crew and most of the passengers had left the train to eat. Twenty-two men did not leave. They were Yankees, dressed as civilians, and under the command of James Andrews. The train crew was very surprised to see their locomotive, nicknamed *"The General,"* and three freight cars leave the station without them. The deceiving Yankees had left the passenger part of the train because it would slow them down. The left-behind-crew soon was chasing the stolen train using the locomotive *"The Texas."* Near Ringgold, *The General* ran out of steam and all the Yankees were captured. Andrews and 7 others were executed as spies and saboteurs. Six were paroled and 8 escaped. Nothing important happened because of the raid but it made good newspaper copy.

While the chase was on, Confederates were retreating from Albuquerque, New Mexico Territory. They wouldn't stop running until they got to El Paso, Texas.

Soon Lincoln would be scratching his head and wondering who was really running the country. David Hunter had served under Fremont, when Fremont made his "Emancipation Proclamation." Now Hunter did the same thing for the Department of the South but went much further. Hunter started to arm the run-away-slaves and started the first Negro unit in the Federal Army, the 1st South Carolina Volunteers. Soon the "Great Emancipator" would say this proclamation was no good either, this war is not about slavery! Lincoln disbanded the first Negro outfit; there was no room in the Union Army for Negro soldiers.

On the 16th, President Davis signed a conscription act to force Southerners to join the army.

On the 18th, The Battle for New Orleans began. The South knew the Yankee fleet was coming. Ships had been sunk in the channel, chains pulled across the water way, a small fleet of vessels assembled and forts Jackson and St. Philip below the city strengthened. The Union fleet under Flag Officer David Farragut was assembling at Ship Island, Mississippi. There was a mortar fleet under David Porter and invasion troops under Benjamin Butler. On this date, Porter started to shell the forts. This went on for six days and there was little damage done to the forts.

On the 23rd, navy action blocked the Chesapeake and Albemarle Canal in North Carolina. This was a major inland transportation link.

Farragut got tired of waiting on Porter's mortars to do something. At 2 A. M. on the 24th, he started for New Orleans. He hoped to sneak by under the cover of darkness. All was going well until the moon came out at 3 A. M. The night came alive with cannon fire and Confederate "fire rafts" (small boats set on fire and drifted toward the enemy in the hopes of setting their ships on fire or at least showing the enemy's position). By dawn, all but three Federal vessels were north of the forts; only the small Confederate fleet lying between it and the city.

The Southern ram (a ship made to sink another ship by running into it), the *Manassas* and her sister vessels tried their best but the Yankee ships were too many and much better. Only two Southern vessels escaped. Farragut tied his fleet up at the New Orleans docks on the 25th.

It was the South's biggest city and the people were very afraid. Someone set the dock area on fire but that didn't stop Farragut from coming on shore. Farragut demanded that someone of importance surrender the city to him. Confederate commander, Gen. Mansfield Lovell, told Farragut he would not surrender but would retreat his few men from the city. Next Farragut caught the mayor and demanded that John Monroe officially surrender the city to him. Monroe also refused. "This is no way to treat a conqueror," thought Farragut but he did not know the people of New Orleans and the depth of their hatred for the Yankees. One woman said, "We are conquered but not subdued."

Forts Jackson and St. Philip were cut off from supplies and surrounded. On the 28th, they too surrendered.

While the Battle for New Orleans went on the Battle for Fort Macon near Beafort, North Carolina came to an end. The Federals took the fort on the 28th and the blockade got tighter.

By the 29th, Grant had been down-moted to number two in his army. Gen. Henry Halleck now commanded over 100,000 men and he started from Pittsburg Landing toward Corinth.

On May 1st, began a reign of terror and suppression that finds few equals in the history of America. The corrupt administration of Benjamin Butler began in New Orleans. He earned two nicknames that would follow him the rest of his life. He was called "Spoons" and the "Beast of New Orleans." He, and those close to him, stole at will from the people of the city. It was said that he would even "steal the family silverware." Thus he became "spoons." Because of his suppression and insulting of the people, he was called "The Beast." While commander of the city, Butler had William Mumford hung because he tore down the U. S. flag at the mint building. All the newspapers were taken over by the Yankees. The people of the city did not show the respect Butler thought they should. No Southern lady would even speak to a Yankee soldier. Preachers didn't want to bury their dead. No one wanted them in their home or place of business. Sometimes women would throw the contents of their chamber pots (bodily waste) on to the proud conquerors walking the streets below high buildings. Butler issued his infamous order No. 28. Any woman "…by word, gesture or movement insult or show contempt for any (Damn Yankee)…" will be considered a whore and jailed. The citizens did not show the "proper respect" and many went to jail. Butler's order was designed to make Southern women ashamed but those so taken considered it a badge of honor. The hatred of this conqueror has not disappeared to this day! The picture of Ben Butler can still be found painted in the bottom of chamber pots.

For almost a month, Magruder's small force kept McClellan's big army from moving. Magruder was reinforced and the command changed to Johnston. On the 3rd, the Confederate Army left Yorktown and McClellan entered on the 4th. After being played for a sucker for a month, McClellan bragged "The success is brilliant." The following day, the head of McClellan's Army, Joseph Hooker and Phil Kearny tangled with James Longstreet and D. H. Hill at the Battle of Williamsburg. The old capital of Virginia saw blood as the Billys attacked. It took the Federals all day and more troops under Winfield Hancock to push the Rebels out but by sundown, Williamsburg was within the Union lines. About 500 Yankees had died, 1400 were wounded and 373 missing. The South suffered 133 missing and 1570 killed and wounded. On the 7th, there was another engagement at West Point as the Federals moved toward Richmond.

On the 8th, "Stonewall" attacked at McDowell (Battle of) or as some call it the Bull Pasture Mountain. The battle was on the mountains heading north from the Shenandoah. Jackson struck Robert Schenck's command, part of Fremont's army. It was a sharp fight but had less killed and wounded than did Williamsburg. After the victory "Stonewall" withdrew across the mountains and back to the Shenandoah.

Because of the Union advance up the Peninsula, Norfolk could not be defended. The navy base would fall into Union hands. There was no other deep water base so the *Virginia* was taken out for the last time and sunk by her crew, not the *Monitor*. Lincoln arrived in time to see his troops take the city.

On May 10th, a small group of Confederate vessels calling itself the "Confederate River Defense Fleet" attacked superior armored gunboats at Plum River Bend or Plum Point near Fort Pillow, Tennessee on the Mississippi. Capt. James Montgomery boldly attacked even though he knew there was little chance of winning. When the smoke cleared the Union owned the river but the Federal ironclads, *Cincinnati* and *Mound City* were at the bottom of it.

In Charleston, a very unusual thing happened on the 13th when Negroes disloyal to the South took over the steamer the *Planter* and turned it over to Yankee blockaders. Martial law was then declared in the city.

Back on the Peninsula, the Federals tried to attack Richmond by way of the James River

Benjamin Butler

on the 15th. The Monitor and four more vessels got to Drewry's Bluff eight miles below Richmond before Confederate cannon stopped them. Johnston fell back to a defensive line as close as three miles from the city. Richmond was in near panic.

This day, Lincoln created the Department of Agriculture.

On the 18^{th,} Farragut's fleet from New Orleans arrived at Vicksburg, Mississippi and demanded the city surrender. The Southerners replied, "No," and the Yankees sailed away but said they would be back.

Yankee cavalry struck the Virginia Central Railroad at Jackson River Depot (today Salma, near Covington) on the 20th.

"Stonewall" had been marching and counter marching since the Battle of McDowell, this kept the enemy confused. On the 23[rd,] his little army struck the Yankees at Front Royal and defeated them. Again he marched and counter marched until he was at Winchester on the 25[th,] when he took on Banks in battle. Soon the enemy was running from the "Mighty Stonewall." On the 29[th,] "Stonewall" acted like he was going to attack Harper's Ferry but found out that the Yankees were coming after him with both barrels loaded. There was Fremont with 15,000, McDowell with 20,000 and Banks with 5,000. "Stonewall" withdrew toward Winchester but couldn't stay there long. Union forces were determined to catch him so "Old Jack" moved south.

Halleck's big army had been surrounding Beauregard's small army at Corinth for about a month. Beauregard saw no way to hold the city and on the 30th retreated toward Tupelo.

Johnston, at Richmond, had been watching McClellan hoping he would make a mistake. As McClellan approached Richmond there were two Union Corps south of the Chickahominy River. If the South could strike these two corps before reinforcements arrived they may win a great victory. President Davis came out to watch the battle not go the way Johnston has planned. Everything was late. The enemy wasn't destroyed. Late in the day, Johnston was badly wounded and Davis had to find someone to take over quickly. His former aid now became commander of the Army of Northern Virginia, Gen. Robert E. Lee. On the 1st of June, the Battle of Seven Pines was over and the armies still sat where they were before the battle began but many a brave lad didn't get to live to see the outcome of the war; about 1,000 Confederates and 800 Yankees died. McClellan again called it a "Brilliant Victory."

Many people were not happy that Lee took command; they remembered Western Virginia. Johnston was recovering from his wounds when a friend came in and said that Johnston's wound meant disaster for the South. Johnston replied, "No, Sir! The shot that struck me down is the very best that has been fired for the Southern Cause yet...." Johnston and President Davis didn't get along; Johnston knew Lee could work with the President.

Because the Yankees controlled Corinth and the railroad, Fort Pillow couldn't be re-supplied; it fell on the 3rd. The North took control of more of the mighty Mississippi. With Pillow gone, the Federal fleet moved on Memphis, Tennessee. On the 6^{th,} they were there but so were Capt. Montgomery and his Confederate River Defense Fleet. The battle opened at 5:30 A. M. and big crowds watched from the bluffs. Smoke and fire were upon the river as outnumbered, out-armed and outgunned Southern vessels took on the fleet. One after another, Confederate craft were damaged and sunk; only one Southern boat survived the battle. By 7:30 it was all over. By 11 A. M. the mayor had surrendered the city. The people wept because the boot of the tyrant was upon their neck.

Back in the Shenandoah, "Stonewall" lost his great cavalry commander, Turner Ashby, in minor rear guard action near Harrisonburg.

On the 7th, Federal troops took Jackson, Tennessee; an important rail center.

The Yankees had been chasing "Stonewall" south through the Shenandoah for miles. At Cross Keys, Jackson turned on Shields' Army. Outnumbered, "Stonewall's" foot cavalry gave Shields a licking on the 8th. Without rest, Jackson threw his army into pitched battle with Fremont near Port Republic on the 9th. Fremont did no better than Shields; now the Yankees retreated north. In the last 48 days, Jackson's men had marched 676 miles; fought five major battles against superior enemy forces and won all five battles! The Shenandoah was clear of Yankees and Lincoln worried that Jackson may come and visit the White House.

The Confederate star general, Turner Ashby, had passed from this life on the 6th. James Ewell Brown Stuart's star was about to rise. From the 12th through the 16th, JEB rode around McClellan's Army. He picked up big news, the Union flanks were weak. He also destroyed supplies and captured wagons. During the raid his father-in-law, Brig. Gen. Philip Cooke, tried to catch JEB but the Yankee never caught his son-by-law.

As Stuart was ending his drive, Brig. General H. W. Benham attacked the works at Secessionville, South Carolina. With everything on his side, he was sure to win but N. G. Evans wasn't on his side. Evans won fame at 1st Manassas. Due to drink, he didn't rise in ranks but he was still ready for a scrap with the Yankees. Evans' 2,500 handed Benham's 6,600 a big defeat and stopped, for now, further Union moves on Charleston.

Beauregard hadn't done well against the massive Union Army so Gen. Braxton Bragg replaced him on the 17th.

The Federals had been taking over in Kentucky and Tennessee. There were more Yankees than Rebs and on the 18th the Cumberland Gap (where Virginia, Kentucky and Tennessee meet) fell into Union hands; another major blow was dealt to the South.

In Washington, Lincoln signed a law stopping slavery in the territories on the 19th.

Things were heating up around Richmond. McClellan with his massive army was closing in. McClellan told Lincoln that he faced a larger Confederate Army and needed the troops of Irvin McDowell (30,000 men). Lincoln said he couldn't have them. Old "Stonewall" might attack Washington at anytime. Although McClellan said he was outnumbered by the Rebels, he didn't act that way. He was sure that Lee would stay on the defensive and not attack him. He had plenty of time to plan and attack Richmond. McClellan loved his army which he had built but an army is made to destroy the other army. When two armies fight, both armies lose men and supplies. McClellan thought of his men as his "Children" and didn't want to harm his "Children."

Lee was far outnumbered, with 60,000 men to McClellan's 100, 000 men. According to the rules, Lee should have remained on the defensive. Lee, who knew all the rules of war, broke all the rules of war. Lee did build defensive works but he did it for two reasons. He knew that spies would tell McClellan and McClellan would take his time before attacking. With works up, fewer men could defend Richmond while the rest of the army attacked. Lee pretended to send reinforcements to "Stonewall" to make Abe think an attack on Washington was coming but Lee ordered Jackson to Richmond. When "Stonewall" came there would be about 78,000 Confederates.

Lee was waiting to attack but McClellan didn't. To tighten the noose about Richmond McClellan attacked at Oak Grove or King's School on the 26th. It cost McClellan one of his "Children" for each 10 yards of advance; this was the start of the Seven Days Battles (Campaign).

Lee had ordered D. H. Hill's, James Longstreet's, A. P. Hill's Divisions plus reinforcements from Jackson to attack Union Major General Fitz-John Porter's V Corps. The Corps was on an exposed flank; the attack was to start at 9 A. M. on the 27th. About the time the attack was supposed to start a message arrived for Lee at

Mechanicsville. The mighty "Stonewall" and his "Foot Cavalry" were still 13 miles away at Ashland. So everyone waited on "Stonewall." They waited and waited. At 3 P. M., A. P. Hill had decided he had waited long enough; surely Jackson was very near. Without orders he attacked. After a short advance, his men were pinned down by dug-in infantry backed by 36 cannons. Jackson's Foot Cavalry took 14 hours to move 13 miles. When they got to Mechanicsville, "Stonewall" lay down and he and his men went to sleep before the sun set. Hill's men were dieing within their hearing. Lee, the President and some Congressmen were watching from near by and couldn't believe what they were seeing. Lee lost 1,484 men to McClellan's 361 men in their first meeting. Maybe Davis was wondering if he had picked the right man.

D. H. Hill

McClellan sent Lincoln a message "Victory…against great odds" but McClellan was shaken. Lee knew the rules, he was supposed to defend, not attack. McClellan decided to shift his base. He had Porter retreat back four miles, during the night, to the farm of Dr. William Gaines. By morning Porter was dug-in behind Boatswain's Swamp, a stream that flowed toward Gaines' Mill.

Lee found Porter's new line and ordered A. P.'s boys forward. Units didn't attack all at once, as Lee had ordered but were sent in piece meal. Longstreet joined the battle. Again, Jackson was missing. Lee went to see "Stonewall" and told him he must attack very soon. Hours passed and it was 7 in the evening before Jackson's men moved forward. Porter's Yankees had taken a beating that day and "Stonewall's" charge was too much. The Union line collapsed and the flight was on. Because "Stonewall" was so late, there wasn't enough daylight left and complete victory was lost. In the dark both sides called the roll and 6,837 Yankees didn't answer and there was no response from 8,000 Rebels. Lee's losses were high and victory not complete but President Davis breathed easier. Richmond was saved! That night Porter's boys fell back across the Chickahominy and McClellan made it official; the Union was moving back toward White House Landing, where gunboats could protect his army.

On the 28[th,] Lee received reports that the Yankees were gone but where? Late that day, Stuart reported that they had left White House. Lee also got information that they had left Fair Oaks. Magruder, who had done so much to fool McClellan, found the Federals dug-in at Savage's (railroad) Station. Magruder's little army couldn't attack McClellan's big army so they waited and waited and waited for Jackson. While they waited, they saw the Federals burning supplies they couldn't carry. At 5 P. M. an invention of Robert E. Lee arrived; a 32 pound (very large) navel gun on a rail road car. This is the first time in history that "railroad artillery" was used. The gun did little damage. So with little daylight and no "Stonewall," Magruder attacked. It wasn't a big fight but Magruder's boys took heavy causalities from Union artillery. McClellan panicked; he left 2,500 of his wounded for the Rebels to care for as he retreated. McClellan felt lucky that Lee hadn't attacked in force.

The two best roads for McClellan to use to escape from White Oak Swamp came together at Frayser's farm. Lee ordered the "late" "Stonewall" to attack there early on the 30th. Jackson didn't get to the bridge over White Oak Swamp until noon. By then the Yankees had burned the bridge and were safely over. When Jackson did follow at 2 P. M. Union artillery caused him to retreat in haste. Jackson wasn't Jackson and after a couple attempts to cross over, the mighty "Stonewall" lay down at 3 P. M. and took a nap! While "Stonewall" napped other columns, including one led personally by Lee, were late moving on the Federals.

It wasn't until 5 P. M. that the Southerners could attack and then it was Longstreet that carried the burden. The Federals poured artillery shells, some from gunboats in the James River, onto Longsteet's men. This slowed but did not stop the attack. The Union line was broken! In hand-to-hand fighting, the South took most of the Yankees' cannons. Each side sent more and more troops into the battle. Late in the day, A. P. Hill led a gallant attack and the Yankees took flight. The Battle of Frayser's Farm was over and Lee took 3,300 casualties to the North's 2,853. Lee gained some land and some cannons but lost the chance to catch McClellan.

On July 1st, the Union army was dug in along the top of Malvern Hill. There were 250 cannon and cannon on the Union gunboats just waiting for the Rebels. D. H. Hill took one look and told Lee "...we had better leave him alone," but by noon Hill, A. P. Hill, Jackson, Magruder and Longstreet were preparing to attack. Lee wanted 60 guns to start the attack but his 80 gun reserve was lost somewhere to the rear, so the South opened with only 20 cannons. The Federal artillery made quick work of them and the attack failed.

At 4 P. M. Lee got two wrong reports. One Confederate commander reported that the Yankees in front of him were retreating but they were just changing positions to better receive an attack. Magruder sent a report that Gen. Lewis Armistead was pushing the Yankees back. Armistead did push some Yankee skirmishers back but when he hit the main army body he was stopped cold. Lee believed the two reports.

Lee sent word for Magruder to attack but Magruder wasn't where Lee thought he was. When Magruder's boys started the attack, D. H. Hill threw his men into battle. That was a big mistake! Union artillery cut Hill's boys to pieces. Magruder didn't attack all at once but with small groups of men. Each attack failed. Jackson tried to reinforce D. H. Hill but that failed too. By 9 P. M. it was over; McClellan had a clear cut victory. Over 5,000 brave Confederates had fallen compared to less than 3,000 Union boys and McClellan held his ground.

During the dark, as July 2nd approached McClellan ordered his army to retreat. Many of his commanders told McClellan he should hold the strong position but it was "retreat." When he started the retreat, McClellan's Army began to fall apart. Many men threw their guns and knapsacks away; this wasn't a retreat, it was a route! It rained hard and that saved McClellan's Army. Southern forces couldn't get over some streams as both armies moved toward Harrison's Landing. When the armies did stop moving, Lee looked at the Federal line and decided not to attack. Lee could not stop McClellan from retreating. The Seven Days Battles were over. McClellan telegraphed President Lincoln to blame him for the loss; Lincoln hadn't sent all the troops requested.

In the South, the newspaper reporters did not know of Lee's battle plans that didn't work out; they didn't know about the "late" "Stonewall" Jackson; they didn't know about the very high causalities that Lee's Army had suffered. They did know that Richmond was safe and Lee had done it. Lee was a hero!

Lee had the greatest military mind on either side during the war. He knew well of the problems. General Lee knew that time was a factor in war. The longer the war lasted, the less likely the South would win. The Yankees had too many men and resources for the South to stop. England had not come rushing to the Confederacy's aid. (The commissioners, Trent Affair, had given an excuse to England to join the South but they hadn't. One of the reasons they hadn't was that Egypt was now producing much cotton and factories in England were not closing.) General Lee wanted to attack not defend before the clock ran out for the Confederacy.

During the time of Seven Days, the Yankees were working on the problem of Vicksburg. A cannel was being dug. The town shelled. On the 28th, some Union gunboats passed the city in the night.

Back in Washington, on the 1st of July, Lincoln signed a bill creating the Union Pacific and Central Pacific Railroads. It was

George "Shanks" Evans

Lincoln, himself, that selected Council Buffs, Iowa as the starting point. It was only a coincidence that Lincoln owned land there and expected to make a big profit.

John Floyd

States Right Grist

William Loring   Simon Bucker

CHAPTER 6 JULY 2-AUGUST 31, 1862

On July 2nd, President Lincoln signed a number of bills that affect us to this day. He signed the anti-Mormon bill that outlawed marrying more than one person. He signed the Morrill Act which started land-grant colleges in each state. He signed a Loyalty Act, which said all government officials, elected or appointed, must swear loyalty to the Federal Government.

Confederate cavalry general, John Morgan, celebrated Yankee Independence Day, by starting his first raid into Kentucky.

McClellan, who had failed to take Richmond and blamed Lincoln for it, now wrote the President a letter that became known as the "Harrison's Bar Letter." He told Lincoln that getting rid of slavery was not the military thing to do.

In Virginia on the 10th, Gen. John Pope changed the rules of the war. Confederate Partisan Rangers were citizen-soldiers. When called upon, they fought in the area where they lived. Many did not have uniforms and that made it difficult for the invading Yankees to tell who to shoot at. Pope said that Partisan Rangers were not really soldiers; they were "guerillas." When the Federal Army was attacked by these guerillas that U. S. citizen's (remember the official Union line was that there was no Confederacy) houses and/or towns would be burned. Anybody caught in the area where an attack was made on the Union Army "…would be shot without civil process." One Yankee wrote, "…pillage and arson ceased to be crimes."

On the 11th, Maj. Gen. Henry Halleck was appointed General-in-Chief for the Federal Army. Most believe he was a good administrator.

Confederate cavalryman, Morgan took Lebanon, Kentucky on the 12th and another Confederate cavalryman, Forrest, took Murfreesboro, Tennessee on the 13th.

On the 15th, the *Arkansas*, a Confederate ironclad, made it to Vicksburg. This changed things because it would make it much harder for Union gunboats to pass the city.

The Yankees had stopped the Confederate Commissioners for a while but on the 16th, Slidell met with Napoleon III of France. He asked Napoleon to say that the Confederacy was a nation and send help. Napoleon did not make a reply. President Lincoln knew of the meeting and was afraid that both France and England may help the South.

On the 17th, Lincoln signed the Second Confiscation Act; only the "Radicals and the ultra-abolitionist forces (wanted it)..." It said that slaves could be stolen from their Southern masters. After stealing the slaves they were not to be set free but be made "slaves" for the North and forced to work in the Union Army (but not as soldiers). The Act also provided for shipping Negroes out of the country.

Also on this date, Confederate, Morgan, took Cynthiana, Kentucky and Yankee, Pope, took Gordonsville, Virginia. The next day, Morgan crossed the Ohio River and took Newburg, Indiana. Yankee, Pope, continued changing the rules. He said his army would "subsist upon the country;" that is steal food or anything else from the citizens (U. S. citizens living in the South).

Lincoln was very worried about England and France helping the South. He believed that by saying the war was about slavery, he could keep other countries out of the war he had started. In a private meeting with his cabinet (advisors) on the 22nd, he told them he was going to issue an Emancipation Proclamation. Everyone was "surprised"! They all knew how he felt about the Negroes. He had said over-and-over that the war was not about slavery. He had refuted the Proclamations his military commanders had made and then fired those commanders. They all knew how he called the Negroes an "inferior race" and wanted to ship them all to Africa or South America. No wonder the advisors were "surprised." The cabinet also worried that if Lincoln went through with it, that the people would say that "Honest Abe" was a "big liar." They worried how the army and citizens would react because so few people wanted slavery done away with. They knew that the Proclamation was not about morality but because of military need. If issued now, it would make the Union look like it was losing the war? They told the President, if he were going through with his scheme, he should wait until there was a big Northern victory before making the announcement. Lincoln agreed and told them not to talk about it. Meanwhile, he would still tell the people that the war was not about slavery. Also on this date, Morgan's Raiders returned safely to Livingston, Tennessee.

Pope bragged to his army, "I have come to you from the West, where we have always seen the backs of our enemies." He told them that he was a tough fighter and on the 23rd he continued his war, on civilians. Anybody that refused to take the loyalty oath "…would be shot and his property confiscated (stolen)."

On the 29^{th,} Confederate spy, Belle Boyd was caught and sent to Old Capital Prison. She was held for a month without charges.

The "Beast of New Orleans" had heard about Southern churches giving their bells to be made into cannons. Butler defiled the places of worship and stole their bells which he sent to Yankee foundries. He took that which was Holy and used it for his unholy purposes. Now many Southerners would find out, "For whom the bells tolled."

On the 31^{st,} President Davis reacted to Northern atrocities. He said he had to "retaliate" (get back at) because Pope's acts were "…indiscriminate robbery and murder." He said, if any of the officers of Pope's Army were captured, that they would be considered "felons" (criminals); not prisoners of war.

McClellan knew that his boss, Lincoln, was mad at him, so on the 2nd of August he advanced from Harrison's Landing and re-took Malvern Hill. It was too little, too late. On the 3rd Lincoln's order arrived that, in effect, demoted McClellan. McClellan was to move what army he had left on the peninsula and fight under Pope. Lincoln liked the way Pope bragged but McClellan didn't want to be his second.

On the 4th Lincoln admitted that not enough people wanted to fight in his war so he was going to draft (force) 300,000 men. A delegation of Negroes met with the President and told him that they could help with the need for more men. They would raise two regiments of Negro soldiers. Lincoln said "no." He would take the Negroes into the army but only to work along beside the stolen Southern slaves. To Lincoln, free Negroes were the same as "Yankees slaves." In New Orleans, Ben Butler said he would force the citizens to give $350,000 to help the "...poor of the city." Butler and his top officers must have thought of themselves as poor; they lined their pockets with stolen loot.

Maj. Gen. John Breckinridge decided to attack Baton Rouge, Louisiana and take it back from the Yankees. To help him the *Arkansas* was to sail down the Mississippi but her engines kept breaking down so Breckinridge attacked on the 5th without her powerful guns. In a dense fog, the Rebels attacked and at first pushed the Yankees back. The attack ran out of steam and Union gunboats poured lots of cannon fire on the

South. Breckinridge retreated, he had lost 84 killed, 315 wounded and 57 captured or missing. The Union also lost 84 killed, plus 266 wounded and 33 missing but they held the town.

The *Arkansas* arrived one day too late, to help Breckinridge. Now that she wasn't protected by the big Confederate cannons on the bluffs at Vicksburg, five Union vessels attacked her. The *Arkansas* was badly damaged and caught on fire. She couldn't be saved so the crew sent her to the bottom.

On the 8th at Huntsville, Alabama, the Federals again made war on Southern religion. The Yankees controlled the town but Southern Partisans kept blowing their trains up. So the Federals arrested "...ministers and leading churchmen..." and placed them on the trains. That way, Southern fighters would blow their own religious leaders up along with the trains.

Lee knew that McClellan was leaving the peninsula. General Lee decided to attack Pope before McClellan could reinforce him. As the armies grew in size around Gordonsville, Pope's and "Stonewall's" armies met at Cedar Mountain or the Battle of Cedar Run on the 9th. At first Pope's Army pushed two divisions of "Stonewall's" Army back but A. P. Hill arrived in the nick of time and turned the battle. Pope withdrew leaving 314 dead, 1,445 wounded and 622 missing. All the Southern losses totaled 1,341. This was the opening battle to what would be called the Second Manassas Campaign.

On the 11th, Partisan Rangers took Independence, Missouri and on the 12th, Morgan and "his terrible men" took Gallatin, Tennessee.

Lincoln let his feeling show when he received a delegation of free Negroes at the White House on the 14th. He blamed the whole war, all the deaths and destruction on them when he said, "but for your race among us there could not be war…It is better for us both (both races), therefore, to be separated." He meant, shipped back to Africa!

Maj. Gen. Edmund "Kirby" Smith, Confederate Army of Kentucky, pushed toward the Cumberland Gap on the 16th. This pass, where three states met, was very important to both sides.

Turner Ashby

John Morgan

The next day, JEB Stuart took over command of all of Lee's cavalry.

This day, the Sioux Indians who were anti-United States; which made them pro-Confederate, started an uprising. They broke out of their reservation in southwestern Minnesota trying to regain lost freedom. They fought against soldiers and settlers and killed up to 600 before they were forced back on their reservation on the 23rd of September. An unknown number of Sioux were killed and on December 26th at Mankato, Minnesota 38 more were shot for their part in the uprising.

On the 18^{th,} Pope pushed Lee's Army back toward the Rappahannock and waited for McClellan to reinforce him. The 5th New York Calvary almost captured JEB but they did capture orders that told Pope of Lee's campaign plans.

President Davis sent a message to Congress about the bad things that Ben Butler was doing in New Orleans. Also on this date, Col. R. Mason surrendered Clarksville, Tennessee to the Rebs without a fight. Later Mason was thrown out of service for "…cowardice in the face of the enemy."

Breckinridge didn't win the battle but he put so much pressure on them that the Yankees withdrew from Baton Rouge on the 21st. President Davis proclaimed Generals David Hunter and John Phelps to be war criminals and placed a reward on their heads for arming slaves. On the day that Davis made him a war criminal;

Phelps resigned the army because Lincoln also opposed arming the slaves.

Horace Greeley was a very powerful newspaper editor and he had written in his newspaper that abolition of slavery should be a central part of the war policy. Even after Lincoln had talked to his cabinet, on the 22nd, Lincoln wrote Greeley back in his own newspaper, "If I could save the Union without freeing any slave I would do it, and if I could save it by freeing all the slaves I would also do that…what I do about the Negro race I do to save the Union." In New Orleans, Ben Butler was not listening to his boss and started a Negro Union regiment. Its purpose was to insult the people of that city. Also, on this date JEB captured Pope's supply train which set Union efforts against Lee back. JEB rode off with Pope's dress uniform.

Lincoln did not have a mandate (right) to rule. Less than half the people voted for him. Thirteen states left the Union rather than have him as President. His military commanders ignored his policies. They blamed the boss for their failures and told the boss what to do. Lincoln couldn't even control his own cabinet. On the 25th, Secretary of War, Edwin Stanton said the army could take in 5,000 Negroes to be made soldiers for guard duty. Lincoln must have shouted, "I am the President! I am important!" But no one was listening.

George McClellan   Jacob Cox

Things were starting to heat up near Manassas. By the 21^{st,} Pope was in a good defensive position along the Rappahannock River. He was waiting on reinforcements from McClellan but McClellan was in no rush to become second in command.

Lee had placed Jackson in temporary command until, he, Lee could come from Richmond. Even after Jackson's mistakes in the Seven Days Campaign, Lee had confidence in "Stonewall".

Pope thought he saw a weakness and sent Franz Sigel's Corps over Freeman's Ford after Jackson. However, soon it was the Yankees who were running back over the ford. "Stonewall" sent Jubal Early's Brigade over the ford to put pressure on Pope but heavy rains caused the river to rise and cut Early off. Pope tried to move against Early but didn't move fast enough. Early re-crossed to safety on the 24th.

When Lee arrived, he called "Stonewall" to meet him on the 25th. Lee let Jackson know the facts. Pope's position was too good to try and attack. The first of McClellan's (Little Mac's) army was arriving. Soon the Yankees would have all the advantages. Lee told "Stonewall" of his daring plan. Lee would stay with his small army and act like he wanted to attack Pope. However if Pope attacked; Lee would probably be destroyed. While Pope would be watching Lee, Jackson was to take his army and march west and north away from Popes army and then swing south and east. If Jackson could hit the rear of Pope's Army hard enough, Lee believed that Pope would fall back from the fords over the Rappahannock.

This time Jackson was not late. At 3 A. M. on the 25th, his army of 24,000 started moving. In two days they covered 50 miles. The army moved passed Salem (Church) then turned east by Thoroughfare Gap. Jackson broke Pope's supply line, the Orange and Alexandria Railroad at Bristoe Station and captured some supply trains. While most of the army rested that night, "Stonewall" sent Gen. Isaac Trimble's Brigade to Manassas Junction. Jackson hoped to capture Pope's main supply base. The next day all of Jackson's Army was at Manassas enjoying much needed Union supplies. Pope thought that Jackson's troops were only a few cavalry boys and he sent George Taylor's New Jersey Brigade to run them away. Taylor was hit hard by Jackson's Army and took great causalities.

When Pope found-out that Jackson was in his rear, Pope wanted to trap and destroy the Mighty "Stonewall."

Pope sent messengers to all of his commanders to move at once on Manassas. Lee was right and Pope moved away from the fords. Now it was Jackson who was in trouble. If Pope could strike Jackson now, Jackson would be outnumbered two to one and doomed. Lee with Longstreet's Division was on its way but would they reach Jackson before Pope did?

Jackson fell back to a position on the old battlefield of 1st Manassas. However, Jackson sent his army units in different directions so that the Yankees weren't sure where they were heading. "Stonewall" took a good position along an unfinished railroad bank.

By early morning of the 28th, Pope had learned that Lee was coming by way of Thoroughfare Gap and sent Brig. Gen. James Ricketts to seal the gap. The rest of his army he moved toward Jackson.

When Lee and Longstreet came to the gap, Ricketts was ready and a sharp fight broke out. It was very late in the afternoon when Lee got through the gap. When the Confederates came through the gap they heard the sound of battle. Jackson was under attack! Could they get to him in time?

It was Jackson who was trying to pick a fight. He sent men to attack part of McDowell's column marching toward Manassas Junction. When the Yankees drove Jackson's men back, McDowell decided it was just a bunch of pesky Rebels trying to slow him down. Therefore, he did not follow Jackson's men but continued to march.

Because "Stonewall" sent troops in different directions to get to Manassas, Pope was confused. He decided that Jackson was moving toward Centreville. He sent McDowell orders to move toward Centreville. McDowell started his column moving and then rode off to talk with Pope. McDowell's second was Rufus King. King was an epileptic and he had seizures and couldn't command anything. However, few people knew of the seizure. As the strung-out column marched, it was just what Jackson had been waiting for. It was past 6 P. M. when Confederate artillery broke loose on the column. Then Ewell's and Taliaferro's Divisions hit the confused Yankees. Without a leader some of the units froze, some ran and others stood their ground. "Stonewall" outnumbered the Yankees but could not break their line. It was a bloody, up-close fight. Taliaferro said the Yankees fought with "…true valor." Then Taliaferro was shot as was Ewell. As the twilight left the sky, the noise of battle decreased. Jackson's losses were very great. The two divisional commanders were seriously wounded, two regimental commanders dead, 40 of the 45 men with the 21st Georgia were casualties as were 72% of the 26th Georgia. Both Rebel and Yankee casualties were about the same 1,300 but "Stonewall" had failed in his attempt to destroy a sizable part of Pope's Army.

King was out of his seizure by now and didn't want to fight "Stonewall" again. He didn't know that Pope had ordered McDowell to Centreville; the last order he knew of said to go to Manassas. "Stonewall" wasn't there and there was where King wanted to go. Pope, of course, did not know that King was off to Manassas Junction but he did know for sure where Jackson was. Pope wanted Jackson. Pope started his forces toward Jackson and had King to start marching back. By some large mistake, Pope was not told that Lee and Longstreet had broken through at Thoroughfare Gap and was heading toward Manassas with 30,000 men.

Jackson knew that the Federals were closing in, so he formed to receive battle and hoped to see Lee very soon. It was the Yankees he saw first. In late morning, part of Sigel's 9,000 moved from Jackson's position at the first battle on Henry House Hill toward Jackson's new position on the railroad cut. In two spirited attacks, the Yankees were thrown back but "Stonewall" knew he couldn't hold out long. At about 10 A. M. "Stonewall" breathed easier, the first units from Lee and Longstreet were arriving!

When the great general arrived he was looking the Union line over when a Yankee sharpshooter's bullet glazed his check. It didn't seem to worry Lee. He was thinking that soon he would have 50,000 men there and could attack Pope.

General Pope, himself, was on the battlefield at 1 P. M. Although McDowell knew that Lee was there, Pope still had no idea that he was facing more than just Jackson.

At 3 P. M. Pope ordered Maj. Gen. Joseph Hooker to attack. With bayonets fixed the Yankees screamed as they struck "Stonewall's" line. The Georgia boys gave way and were being pushed back hard when A. P. Hill's boys saved the day!

Next Pope sent Col. James Nagle to attack at the railroad gap. At first the Union was winning but Confederate forces pushed back in a fearsome counterattack. Part of the Union's artillery was taken before reinforcements stopped the Confederates.

At 5 P. M. Pope sent Maj. Gen. Philip Kearny to attack where Sigel had nearly broken through earlier. Hill's boys were there to receive the Yankees. Because of the earlier fighting Hill's boys were low on ammunition. Just when it looked like a Union victory was at hand, "Stonewall" sent Early's men into the battle. The last attacks stopped as darkness set in. It was at this time, that Pope realized that Lee-Longstreet were there.

At dawn on the 30[th,] Pope was informed of a considerable amount of movement on the Rebel side during the night. Lee was making ready to attack but Pope decided he was seeing the "backs of his enemies;" the Confederates were running! To make sure this was so, he sent fake attacks forward. When there was little action from the Confederate line, Pope was sure that he had struck the rear guard of Lee's Army. He ordered two corps to catch the fleeing enemy. When the Yankees came close, Southern cannons spoke and the

Federals fell back. Pope decided to launch a massive attack. As he was preparing for the attack, Pope was told that there was a very large Confederate force on his left flank. Pope did not believe the report and kept getting ready to attack.

At 3 P. M. Pope launched his big attack. The cannons of Lee and Jackson found their mark and tore big holes in the enemy's ranks. When the Federals got in range, Jackson's men at the railroad cut, cut loose but the Yankees kept coming. "Stonewall" sent all the troops in the area to stop the Yankees but it appeared that the enemy would break-through. Some Southerners were out of ammunition and started throwing rocks at the Blue Bellies. Again Hill came to the rescue and the Yankees retreated taking heavy causalities as they fell back.

McDowell ordered Reynold's Division from the already weak side to reinforce the Union attack on "Stonewall." General Lee was watching and at 4 P. M. knew the moment had arrived. The Yankees had no chance as Longstreet's 25,000 men hit them! In less than 10 minutes, Col. Gouverneur Warren's 1,000 man regiment was wiped out! Longstreet's men caught the last of Reynolds men moving off line and tore through them and captured the Union artillery in that area.

Longstreet was rolling up the Union left until his men ran into 1,200 brave Ohioans under Col. Nathaniel McLean. They stopped the Gray Backs for 30 minutes until Kemper's Virginians arrived. These 30 minutes, bought with Ohio blood, gave time to Pope. He now realized that there was indeed a big Rebel force on his left. He gave orders to McDowell to send reinforcements to the Ohio Boys. Pope, himself, went to Henry House Hill to set up a line of defense.

By 6 P. M. Longstreet had broken through the line of Ohioans and their reinforcements. That part of the Union Army was routed and running for their lives. "Stonewall" was slow to attack and let the Yankees run back to Henry House Hill. Here the Union line held until dark when the beaten Federal Army "showed their backs to the enemy" and retreated. The beaten, demoralized army was in full route back across Bull Run just like they were after 1st Manassas. Fresh troops coming from McClellan's Army saw Pope's beaten army and "jeered" their own men. Pope believed, and rightly so, that McClellan had not moved fast enough to help him. Confederate cavalry was unable to stop the retreat so that Pope's Army was not totally destroyed!

Second Manassas was much more bloody than the First. Federal losses were 1,724 killed, 8,372 wounded, and 5,958 missing or captured. Southern figures: 1,481 killed, 7,627 wounded and 89 missing.

Though the battles were bloody, the word "Manassas" has two meanings. In the North it will forever mean shame and mourning. To the South it will always mean rejoicing!

Ambrose Burnside

George Crook

James Longstreet

JEB Stuart

By the fall things were changing in favor of the Confederacy. Because of the *Arkansas*, the Union river fleet was either below Baton Rouge, Louisiana or above Helena, Arkansas and not at Vicksburg. Confederate forces were back in Kentucky and Tennessee and Federal forces were being shifted north to oppose them. Lee had stopped McClellan, defeated Pope and now threatened Washington. Yankee abolitionists were demanding Lincoln make this a war about slavery and a peace movement was starting in the North. Those who wished to have peace and let the South go its own way were called "Copperheads."

On the first, as Pope moved his wounded army toward Washington, Lee struck again at Chantilly also called the Battle of Ox Hill. "Stonewall" attacked and Philip Kearny defended. When the smoke cleared, Kearny was dead and the Yankees continued running.

On the 2nd, McClellan was no longer number two. Lincoln placed McClellan back into command of the whole army. Pope demanded to know where he fit in. He didn't. Lincoln sent him out west to fight the Sioux. Pope was being sent into exile.

"Meditation of the Divine Will" was written by Lincoln. He said both sides say that God is on their side but Lincoln said God could only be on one side; not both. Lincoln now was telling God what to do. On this date, Kirby Smith re-took Lexington, Kentucky. On the

3^{rd,} the Confederacy re-took Winchester and Gen. Albert Jenkins raided to Point Pleasant, Ohio on the 4th. General Lee was not unhappy that Lincoln had put McClellan back in charge; Lee's Army started to move over the Potomac singing "Maryland, my Maryland Virginia has come to claim you." That is to say, "allow her to leave the Union." Thousands of recruits were expected; hundreds came.

On the 6^{th,} Fredericksburg, Maryland was occupied by "Southern Gentlemen." There was no burning, looting or insulting the people. President Davis wrote that the South did not wish to conquer the North but only wanted to live in peace and would help other states to leave the Union, only if they wished to do so. In a statement made in the Maryland newspapers, Lee reflected President Davis's words. "The people of the Confederate States have long watched with the deepest sympathy the wrongs and outrages that have been inflicted upon the citizens...." As Lee's Army moved north, the State of Pennsylvania sent its treasury and archives to New York City. McClellan didn't move very fast when he started to Richmond from the peninsula. When he faced Lee this time, he didn't start his pursuit until the 6th.

On the morning of the 13^{th,} Union cavalrymen found some cigars at Fredericksburg. Around the cigars was wrapped a copy of Lee's order number 191. Soon McClellan was reading Lee's battle plans. Lee's plan called for Jackson taking Harper's Ferry, thus protecting

Lee's rear. Then "Stonewall" would move to join Lee and the rest of the army at Boonsboro, Maryland. McClellan believed that if the garrison at Harper's Ferry would hold out that he could move and crush Lee. He planned to force-march his army and control the mountain passes on Lee's right flank.

With Lee's order and timetable, McClellan moved too slowly. "Stonewall" surrounded Harper's Ferry and on the 14th began his attack. While Jackson was attacking; Lee moved north. To guard the passes on his right, Lee left D. H. Hill. Lee with Longstreet continued to Hagerstown. When Lee learned that McClellan was approaching the gap at South Mountain "in great strength" Lee and Longstreet moved back south to help Hill.

Before Lee-Longstreet arrived, McClellan's columns struck Hill at both Turner's and Fox's Gaps in what would become known as the Battle of South Mountain. At 9 A. M. Gen. Jacob Cox sent his 3,000 men to attack the 1,000 men of Gen. Samuel Garland's North Carolina brigade at Fox Gap. Garland fell dead and the Rebels were routed. Then Cox moved on Turner's Gap. Hill sent two cannon and a few troops to slow the Yankees. The boys fought hard and slowed the Union. As the Yankee attack lost steam, more fresh troops arrived on the Southern side and now the Yankees were falling back. It was now the Yankees turn and they poured more men into the gap. IX Corps Commander General Jesse Reno arrived to take command of the

Union attack but he was greeted by a Rebel bullet near the spot where Garland had died earlier that day. Soon Reno joined Garland in death. If McClellan had of moved faster and struck harder, almost for sure, Hill's Division would have been destroyed. With Lee's plans in hand, McClellan blew it. It was late in the day before Longstreet arrived to reinforce Hill but by nightfall the Federals held the gaps. Little Mac wired Washington of his "glorious victory." Lee was not happy with the day's events, "The day has gone against us...." Lee had lost 2,000 brave men but not Hill's whole division.

In the dark, Lee withdrew from South Mountain and moved towards Sharpsburg and set a defensive line along Antietam Creek. McClellan followed.

Lee knew that Federals, under General William Franklin, were moving toward Harper's Ferry. Lee was concerned that the Confederates on Maryland Heights (north of the Potomac), 8,000 men under Gen. Lafayette McLaws, may be cut off; so he ordered them to move toward his position. Lee did not know how the Mighty "Stonewall" was doing.

On the early morning of the 15[th,] Lee received Jackson's messenger. Harper's Ferry had fallen with the catch of 12,500 Federals and 73 cannons. Lee was delighted that his rear was covered. He sent an order to Jackson, "leave A. P. Hill to take care of the prisoners and move the rest of the army to him near Sharpsburg." After Hill finished paroling (letting them go on their word that they would not fight against the South anymore) the prisoners, Hill too would join the whole army.

Jackson had three divisions over the Potomac near Shepherdstown by noon of the 16th. Jackson's men had fought a hard battle and forced march; many had not slept in two days. Both Lee and McClellan brought forces forward; shots were exchanged but no battle occurred on the 16th. Late in the day, McLaws' men came in and even later, A. P. Hill arrived. Even with most of his army near Sharpsburg, Lee knew he was vastly outnumbered. Some of Lee's generals advised Lee that he should not take on the Yankees in these numbers and on these grounds. Lee was a gambler and said he would fight here and now!

At dawn of the 17th in a dense fog, McClellan "opened the ball." Hundreds of artillery shells flew through the skies and the ground shook. Gen Joseph Hooker's I Corps struck Jackson's line of tired men in a cornfield, near a Dunker Church. The Dunkers were against all wars. By 7 A. M., "Stonewall's" line was near breaking. That is when Hays' Louisianan Brigade of 500, called the "Tigers" arrived. When the Tigers showed up so did Ricketts' Federals and 323 of the Tigers went down. John Gibbon's Iron Brigade struck Jackson's left and started toward the center at the church. As Gibbon ran out of steam, Confederate, William Starke, attacked the Union. He died in the corn but his men kept pushing the Yankees back. Then Union resistance stiffened and Jackson's line again was near collapsing. "Stonewall" send his last troops, Gen. John Bell Hood's Texas Brigade into the enemy. There was savage killing in the corn but Hood's men pushed the Yankees out of their field. 82% of Hood's Boys were causalities before the day was done.

When the Rebels thought they owned the corn, Gen. Joseph Mansfield's XII Corps struck Jackson's right. The attack was not done well and not all the Yankees attacked at one time. Mansfield died along with lots of his men in the east end of the corn field. They were exposed to fire from both Jackson and D. H. Hill but the determined Yankees almost made it to the church.

By 9 A. M. the clamor of attack and counter-attack lessened. McClellan decided to attack a weakened Jackson with Gen. Edwin Sumner's II Corps but they hit Longstreet's Division by mistake. Longstreet's artillery found their mark. The Yankees moved toward the artillery without realizing that Jubal Early was ready to attack their right flank, which was unprotected. Early's boys inflicted heavy casualties and sent the Yankees running into the woods.

As this attack was beaten back, Yankee Gen. William French sent three ranks to attack to the left of where Sumner had been stopped. Hill's and Longstreet's men were dug in along an old sunken road. It was more like murder than war; more like slaughter than battle. Great heaps of Yankees died attacking; great heaps of Confederates died counterattacking. The sunken road was nearly filled with wounded, dieing and dead men. The sunken road is now remembered as "Bloody Lane." Confederate Gen. John Gordon had been wounded four times that day but refused to leave the field. The fifth wound shattered his face, knocked him out; he was taken off the field unconscious. By some error, Confederate artillery was withdrawn from the area and by pure force of numbers the Union began to drive the South back.

McClellan's plan called for Gen. Ambrose Burnside to attack Lee's far right flank but Burnside wasn't there because of a bridge. Each time his massive army of over 8,000 men started to cross Antietam Stream Confederate sharpshooters on the hill fell the infantry and stopped the Yankees dead cold. This had been going on all morning, a few pesky Rebels stopping Burnside's column. Burnside wouldn't quit and finally pushed his columns across the bridge. He became famous as a fighter who wouldn't quit and most of his career was earned at the bridge. He became famous and the bridge was named in his honor. He won fame not because of great generalship but because of the lack of generalship! Antietam Creek is only a few feet deep. Burnside could have easily sent troops to ford above or below the bridge and pushed those pesky 550 Rebs off the hill. The passing over Antietam should have been easy and just a footnote to the battle. Because of the time, fine infantry and perhaps the crushing blow to Lee which Burnside did not deliver, he became a national Union hero!

Even though he was late and had already taken many casualties, Burnside was rolling Lee's flank up until about 4 P. M. Again, it was A. P. Hill who saved the day! He had forced marched his men 17 miles without a rest and threw them into Burnside's attack. Hill's Boys stopped the last hope the Yankees had of breaking Lee's line.

Night fell and the day's work was done. Never in the history of the Western Hemisphere has there been a day of blood letting as was the 17th of September, 1862. Over 75,000 Yankees came to fight along the banks of Antietam; 2,010 were dead on the field of honor, 9,416 were wounded and 1,043 not accounted for. The Confederacy had between 35,000 and 40,000 engaged; now 2,700 were dead, 9,024 lay wounded and 2,000 missing. The losses were terrible and about equal. Lee still held his position on the field against a very superior foe. Through the night and all the next day, the armies glared and prepared to do battle but no battle came. On the night of the 18th, Lee withdrew south; the Maryland campaign was over.

It wasn't a big fight but it was important an action at Charleston, (W) Virginia when the Confederates ran the Yankees out of town on the 13th.

George Meade

John Pope

Bushrod Johnson

Sam Jones

Porter Alexander

William "Mudwall" Jackson

CHAPTER 8 SEPTEMBER 19- DECEMBER 31, 1862

Confederate General, Earl Van Dorn, moved his force from Tupelo to Lula, Mississippi. He was trying to stop Grant and Buell from linking up. On the 19th, Grant sent Rosecrans to attack Van Dorn before Van Dorn could attack. It was about an even contest but Van Dorn learned that Grant was approaching with the rest of the army. Van Dorn broke off contact and moved south. He took 1,516 total causalities to the Union loss of 1,700.

Lee had retreated from Antietam and that was enough of a victory for Lincoln. He was most anxious to keep England and France out of the war. He made a lie of ever public statement he had ever made on the subject. "Honest Abe" showed himself to be totally dishonest. He had no right to amend the Constitution of the United States but he did. On the 22nd, he issued the third Emancipation Proclamation. The other two he had disowned and fired those who made them saying "this war is not about slavery!" His Emancipation made this war about slavery though it freed no slaves. President Lincoln made it very clear that this illegal proclamation applied to Confederate States only. He freed slaves where he had neither political nor military power to do so. He made sure that the slave-holding states in the Union knew that their slaves would never be free. Lincoln was in great fear of what the military and citizens of the United States would think of his new lie.

On the 23^{rd,} partisan rangers took over the Yankee steamer, the *Emma* on the Ohio River and burned her. Southern forces attacked the Union gunboat the *Eugene* on the Mississippi River. Federal forces burned the nearest town, Randolph, Tennessee to the ground as revenge.

President Lincoln decided to further take the citizens rights away. On the 24^{th,} he said there would be no civil trials for "...Rebels and Insurgents, their aider and abettors...all persons discouraging volunteer enlistments, resisting militia drafts or authority of the United States." In other words, anyone who didn't go along with the President was subject to arrest and imprisonment without charges. They would be sentenced by a military court.

In a speech on this day, President Lincoln told a crowd "I can only trust in God I have made no mistake..." (In issuing the third slave Proclamation). However, even God couldn't trust Lincoln.

Buells' Army made it to Louisville, Kentucky before the Rebels.

The manpower needs of the South weren't being met so on the 27th President Davis signed a second draft bill that would call men up to age 45.

Part of this day, President Lincoln "interrogated" Maj. John Key. Lincoln didn't like what Key was saying about his new slavery policy so Lincoln personally kicked Key out of the army. Lincoln also let McClellan know that he was very unhappy because the army was not moving south.

In New Orleans, Butler officially put his Negro unit into Union service to harass the white people of the city.

By the 1st of October, the Northern abolitionist realized that Lincoln's Proclamation freed no one and they were very upset at the President. Southerners said that Lincoln's real war aim was now unveiled, the freeing of slaves and slave revolt. Union recruiters went to the Negroes and told them to join the army and fight against slavery. What they didn't tell the black recruits was that they would never be treated as equals, given $7 less pay a month because they were Negroes and never promoted above private because they were considered stupid and untrustworthy.

On the 3rd, the *Alabama* captured three Yankee cargo ships. Union shippers cried that it was wrong of the South to capture their ships. It was okay for the North to take Southern ships but not for the South to take Northern ships.

By this date, Van Dorn had been reinforced by Sterling Price. Together they attacked Rosecrans at Corinth, Mississippi (Grant was at Jackson, Tennessee). On the first day of battle, Southern forces pushed the Yankees back but the Yankees took good defensive positions. On the 4th, the Southerners attacked again and again. By afternoon, the Confederates knew they weren't going to win and they pulled off toward Chewalla, leaving 473 dead.

Also on this date at the capital of Kentucky, Confederate Governor Richard Hawes took the oath of office. He left town when Bragg's Confederate Army did.

Lincoln wanted McClellan to fight but "Little Mac" wasn't moving. So on the 6th, he received a presidential order, "The President directs that you cross the Potomac and give battle to the enemy...." Lincoln couldn't make it anymore clear.

Weather conditions caused strange happenings during the war. Sometimes battle sounds did not carry near but could be heard clearly miles away. On the 8th, at Perryville, Kentucky the weather played its trick. Parts of Bragg's Army and parts of Buell's fought a major action on Doctor's Creek, which flows below the Chaplin Hills, near the town. There was the terrible sound of battle along the creek as men died. Southern forces attacked and Union forces defended. General Bragg and most of the army was near Frankfort but they heard no battle sounds and sent no reinforcements. Buell was even closer and he heard no sound. It was late in the day before both commanders found out that their armies had fought a major battle. 845 Federals were killed, 2,851 wounded and 515 were missing before Buell knew what had happened. Bragg received the news that 519 of his men were dead, 2,635 were wounded and 251 missing. It was a Yankee victory and Bragg started moving south toward the Cumberland Gap.

On the 10[th,] Rebel-Sioux fought with a boatload of miners near Fort Berthold in Dakota Territory. President Davis asked the State of Virginia to draft 4,500 Negroes to work on fortifications. On this date, Stuart started another ride around McClellan's Army. On the 11[th,] JEB was at Chambersburg, Pennsylvania. Here his men cut telegraph wires, took horses, destroyed military supplies, railroad shops, depots and trains. Union efforts to catch the horsemen failed and Stuart was back on Virginia soil by the 12th. The daring raid cost JEB but one soldier but humbled McClellan.

Lincoln knew the newspapers and people were complaining about the draft. On the 17[th,] rioting broke out in Berkley, Pennsylvania and troops were needed to fight United States citizens! Lincoln made war on his people!

John Morgan's small band of cavalry defeated and captured a much larger Federal garrison at Lexington, Kentucky on the 18th. No wonder the Yankees began to say that "Morgan was the devil, himself."

Because President Lincoln had taken so many of the people's rights away, the citizens in occupied Tennessee listened when on the 21st Lincoln called on them to support the Republican Party in coming elections. The Yankees did not control East Tennessee but President Davis was worried about anti-Confederate activities in the area.

Because Buell had let Bragg escape, Rosecrans took over his boss's job on the 24th.

After Lincoln's order and JEB's ride, McClellan began to move his army over the Potomac on the 28th. Lincoln was still not happy.

On the 31^{st,} Abingdon in Southwest, Virginia became the capital of Kentucky, when Governor Richard Hawes moved his "government in exile" there.

The "Beast Butler" was having the time of his life tormenting the people of New Orleans. On November 1^{st,} he issued orders to take more slaves from owners who he considered to be pro-Southern.

Lincoln became even unhappier on the 4th. In the elections the Republicans kept control of the House of Representatives but Democrats made strong gains. That showed that more people were opposing his war.

There was a Democrat who had been a pain in Lincoln's side for a long time. On the 5^{th,} Lincoln fired McClellan and replaced him with the "bridge hero," Burnside, "...there was truly nothing in Burnside's background to indicate that he would be capable of leading (a big army)...." While he was at it, Lincoln replaced a McClellan supporter, Fitz Porter with Joseph Hooker. McClellan was "surprised, stunned, hurt" when he received Lincoln's order on the 5th. It was a very emotional time on the 10^{th,} when "Little Mac" bid farewell to his army, which he loved and which loved him.

Yankee newspapers had been following Butler and his reign of "…cruelty, speculation, and dishonesty." He was even giving the Damned Yankees a bad name. On the 8th, he gave his last mean order in New Orleans, he closed the breweries. That same day he received news that Maj. Gen. Nathaniel Banks was taking over.

By the 15th, Burnside moved his army toward Fredericksburg. Burnside knew he had to move rapidly over the Rappahannock River and take the town before Lee knew that he was there. About the time the Federal Army arrived, it started to rain hard and the river rose. Burnside had made it very plain that he had to have his pontoon bridges ready to place when he got there. General Halleck had promised Burnside that they would be there but they weren't.

Burnside couldn't get over the river but his cannons could. He demanded that Fredericksburg surrender. The mayor refused and Burnside threatened to shell the town to rubble but there was no surrender or bombardment.

Though he didn't know it, Burnside lost the race when on the 19th Longstreet moved to the heights over looking the city. By the 23rd, Lee knew the Union plan for another "on to Richmond campaign." Lee sent for "Stonewall." Because Federal artillery could shell the town at will, Lee decided to fight the battle of Fredericksburg outside of town. The pontoons arrived on the 27th and Jackson on the 29th. There were 118,000 Yankees ready to take on 78,000 Rebels.

Confederates told the townspeople that they must leave in the cold of November and December! The poor had little to keep them warm and no place to go, so they moved into the woods around their city.

When Burnside knew that at least part of Lee's Army was waiting, he decided to cross farther down river. That plan fell through when Union gunboats were turned back by Confederate cannon. Also the balloon men had seen some of Jackson's men setting at the ford Burnside wished to use. Burnside decided to go with the first plan and cross at Fredericksburg. Other Union commanders had been studying the city and those hills beyond. Col. Rush Hawkens told Burnside, "…it will be the greatest slaughter of the war; there isn't enough infantry in our whole army to carry those heights…." "…your plan will be murder, not warfare," echoed Lt. Col. Joseph Taylor.

Burnside was not the sharpest tack in the box. His army had been setting by the Rappahannock for 26 days and he was still saying he was going to "surprise" General Lee. With the river flowing by, it appears that Burnside had not thought much about how he would get his army over. Those, who were still standing after Antietam, could say that he wasn't much good at getting the army over any stream of water. Burnside had watched the Rebels on the other side of the river watching him. He must have thought that they were going to lay a "welcome mat" out for his men.

Henry Wise   John Echols

At dawn of the 11^{th,} the 50th New York Engineers began laying the pontoon bridge. All was going well until the sun burned the fog off, then William Barksdale's Brigade of Mississippians cut lose on the engineers. The engineers that didn't go down or for a swim, dove for cover. Each time Burnside ordered them back, the Rebels just shot them down and the bridge wasn't getting built.

By noon Burnside had had enough of those pesky Rebels, so he lined 150 cannons up and fired over 5,000 shells into the town. Buildings collapsed and some caught fire but the Mississippians had their holes dug. After the fireworks, they came back out in time to shoot more engineers!

It wasn't Burnside but someone under him who thought of a way to get those Rebels. The Union used parts of their bridge that they couldn't put together, as boats, and flowed infantry over to fight the Mississippians. Enough Yankees came over and ran Barksdale's bunch from the town to Lee's lines on the heights. Even with the Rebels gone, Burnside's orders were so confusing that Union troops did not march over any bridge until the 12th.

Now that he had his army over the river, Burnside stopped to figure out what to do with it. Without orders or any place to go, the Yankees decided to visit town. There were no shopkeepers in that day so the Yankees stole at will, smashing what they didn't steal. They then went to call on the townspeople but they weren't at home either. The Yankees entertained themselves by stealing and destroying. Burnside must have wondered what had happened to his army when he saw so many of his men in women's clothing. Some Union commanders tried to stop their men's privations but most just joined in the looting. There was a moral difference in the men of the armies.

Lee and his Southerners watched in great anger from the heights. While the Yankees were destroying the town, Lee extended and strengthened his line as more of Jackson's men arrived.

Burnside sent written orders to William Franklin to take his "Grand Division" and strike Lee on the right flank at dawn. Had Franklin followed Burnside's orders to the letter, he would have marched completely past Lee's right and fought nobody. Franklin realized that his orders were wrong so he too made a mess of things by turning his army "...directly into the teeth of two of (Jackson's) divisions."

By luck, Franklin was attacking in a gap (hole) between the two divisions but Rebel artillery tore through the Union ranks as they attacked. For a little while Franklin was pushing Jackson back but "Stonewall" sent more reinforcements and plugged the hole. Jackson lost almost 3,500 to Franklin's 5,000 but Lee's line remained unbroken.

At midmorning, William French got his turn to attack. It wasn't easy. His men had to march out of town, cross a canal over three shaky bridges, and cross 350 yards of open ground except for one small bluff. Then they would have to attack up a very steep and muddy hill. While they were on their way, Rebel artillery on the hill rained shell down on them. Southerners waited behind a stone wall at the base of the hill. When the Yankees were 125 yards away "a sheet of orange flames flashed..." and then another and another. Yankees, by the hundreds, went down. Those that could; ran for the bluff. More of French's brave men marched toward the wall and more went down. This wasn't battle; it was butchery!

Burnside couldn't think of anything better to do so he ordered more men forward. Burnside watched Winfield Hancock's three brigades disappear in the smoke. He watched as the divisions of Oliver Howard and Samuel Sturgis did the same.

Joseph Hooker didn't like Burnside much before the battle started and even less now. He went to see the boss and Burnside ordered Hooker to attack with his Grand Division. Hooker said it was a "...useless waste of life" but Burnside was stubborn. Hooker obeyed his orders. One Billy said, "The grass was slippery with their blood." When his first brigade got into the same trouble that all the Union units had encountered, Hooker stopped the blood letting. No progress had been made and 7,000 Federals lay wounded and dead at the foot of the hill. Lee looked down on the fields filled with blue clad bodies and with great pity said, "It is well that war is so terrible. Otherwise we should grow fond of it."

Burnside said no retreat; that the men had to hold their positions. As it got darker, it got colder. The dead and wounded couldn't leave the field and those living were ordered not to do so. To get protection from Rebel bullets and icy winds, the living stacked the dead around them. During the night corpses froze "like logs." The wounded cried for help; help to live or in some cases, help to die. Stretcher bearers got some wounded off the field. Some Confederates braved the field to strip the dead of their uniforms; they too were freezing. Some, from both sides, risked their lives to help the Yankee wounded.

President Lincoln had demanded a general that would fight! He got one! At headquarters Burnside realized what he had done and wished that his body was now freezing. To that end, Burnside said he would personally lead the charge the next morning. Thinking of their own men, all of his sub-commanders firmly said "No!" Many would have supported his idea if Burnside had proposed a one man attack.

The daylight of the 15th was spent in getting the living off the field. Under the cover of a driving rainstorm that night a defeated, demoralized, destroyed army re-crossed the Rappahannock.

Lee wished to pursue but he knew better. The pontoon bridges were gone. A river lined with 150 cannons was more than Lee would ask his men to face.

President Lincoln got a man to fight his army. He read the reports: 12,653 dead, 9,600 wounded and 1,769 Yankees unaccounted for to the Southern losses of 595 dead, 4,061 wounded and 653 missing. Lincoln listened to an eyewitness account to the horror and replied, "If there is a worse place than hell, I am in it." Lincoln read Burnside's report; in his report, Burnside rightly blamed the Chief-of-Staff, Halleck, for not having those pontoon bridges there on time but also, blaming himself for attacking.

While the campaign at Fredericksburg raged, on the 21st of November, President Davis named James Seddon as Secretary of War. Lincoln was having his troubles; Unionists from Kentucky demanded that he take back that anti-slavery proclamation. President Lincoln said, "I would rather die than take back a word...."

The power of the press showed itself again. First Butler was removed and on the 22nd Union Secretary of War, Stanton released most of the hundreds of "political prisoners" Lincoln was holding, illegally.

At Cane Hill, Arkansas on the 28^{th,} James Blunt attacked the Confederates under John Marmaduke and drove them back as both sides struggled in the Trans-Mississippi.

President Lincoln spoke to his Congress on December 1st. He knew that people were beginning to learn the truth about his fake slave Proclamation. "You can't fool all the people..." He asked Congress to work on three amendments to the Constitution. First, all "states" that would abolish slavery by 1900 would receive money for slaves released. Any slave that got their freedom during the war would stay free after the war. If the slave belonged to a "loyal (to the Union) master" the master would be paid for the slave. (According to Constitutional law, if the government takes property {slaves were property under the law} the government must pay the value.) Thirdly, the government would send any "...free colored persons..." to Africa or South America (but only if they wanted to go).

Off of North Carolina, three Southern vessels were seized in one day, the 3^{rd,} as the blockade tightened. The anger against the Rebel Indians was shown in Mankato, Minnesota when helpless prisoners were slaughtered by the citizens. Lincoln liked the idea so well that he got in on the action by having 38 savage-Sioux hung on the 6th. They weren't considered to be "real" Confederate soldiers.

It was a cold December 7th when Confederates attacked the Federals about twelve miles southwest of Fayetteville, Arkansas. Southerners under James Blunt and Francis Herron hoped to do battle before the separate Yankee forces could come together but they were too late. So they fought the whole bunch and lost. It cost the Blue Bellys 1,251 casualties to the Gray-Backs' 1,317.

The South hoped that fast moving cavalry could hit isolated positions, destroy supplies and stop Union invasions. In Hartsville, Tennessee Morgan's, bigger than life, character grew when he defeated a much larger Union force and made 1,800 of the 2,100 prisoners.

On the 10^{th,} the South reclaimed some of its land by defeating the enemy at Plymouth, North Carolina. A Confederate "mine" or "torpedo" exploded under the *Cairo*, a Yankee gunboat, on the Yazoo River close to Vicksburg on the 11th.

More Rebel cavalry under Forrest moved behind enemy lines on the 15th.

Grant thought that Lincoln's Proclamation was nothing but politics. He said, "If I thought this war was about abolition, I would resign my commission and carry my sword to the other side." Grant, through his wife, was slave owner. In fact, there were more slave owners in the Union Army than there were in the Southern

Army. Of course, there were more soldiers in the Yankee Army also. As he watched from his headquarters in Holly Springs, Mississippi, Grant saw cotton disappearing and knew that big profits were being made. He decided to do something about it. So on the 17th he issued his infamous Order No. 11. "The Jews, as a class violating every regulation of trade established by the Treasury Department and also (this) department orders, are hereby expelled from the department within 24 hours...." When Lincoln read Grant's order he must have thought of all the troubles he had had with so many generals. How dare Grant take the people's rights way; that was the President's job, so Lincoln "rescinded" the order. As soon as Lincoln finished with the Jew hating general, he got caught in another battle. Half the people in his cabinet hated the other half. Secretary of the Treasury, Chase; Secretary of State, Seward and his son, Frederick Seward told the President, "We quit." Lincoln asked them to stay until he could work something out.

Forrest soundly beat Federal cavalry at Lexington, Tennessee on the 18th, as he continued to attack Grant's supply line. On this day, President Davis visited Chattanooga on his Southern trip.

On the 19th, Lincoln was trying to deal with his cabinet crisis as Forrest was destroying Grant's supplies at Jackson, Tennessee.

While Grant was watching Forrest destroy his supplies, he didn't see Van Dorn coming. Van Dorn gave Grant a bad whipping when he captured 1,500

Yankees and most of Grant's supplies at Holly Springs on the 20th. When Grant learned about Forrest hitting the railroad at Trenton and Humboldt, he knew he would have to delay his operations. Back in Washington, there was another stormy cabinet session. After a big blow-up, everyone told Lincoln they would stay at their post and stay mad at each other!

President Davis visited Vicksburg. John Morgan left Carthage, Tennessee on a Christmas visit to his home state of Kentucky on the 21st.

On the 22^{nd,} Lincoln sent a message to be read to all of Burnside's troops. He "congratulated" the army for its "bravery" and called Fredericksburg an "accident." That must have started the soldier's scratching their heads.

Dateline; Vicksburg, December 23: President Davis called for long-range heavy guns to be sent to this city. He also called "the Beast Butler'...a felon, an outlaw, a common enemy of mankind; if captured...he should be hanged immediately."

On the day before Christmas, Morgan captured Glasgow and on Christmas he fought the engagements at Greens's Chapel, and Bear Wallow, Kentucky in Kentucky. President and Mrs. Lincoln spent part of their day seeing a product of Lincoln's war; they visited soldiers in the hospital.

On the 26^{th,} Morgan fought more Yankees in Kentucky as Forrest began to withdraw back toward his

Mississippi base. These two cavalry leaders had up-set Union time tables.

Gen. John Pemberton moved his army into Vicksburg on the 27th at the same time Morgan captured the whole garrison at Elizabethtown.

On the 29^{th,} Sherman attacked Vicksburg from the north. A few Confederates cut the Yankees to pieces. Sherman took 1,776 casualties to Confederate losses of 207. The loss ratio was similar to Fredericksburg.

The *Monitor* went to the bottom in a storm near Cape Hatteras. Sixteen sailors drowned on the 30th.

Showing his deep love for the Negro race, Lincoln ended his year by signing a contract to ship Negroes to Haiti.

A. P. Hill

Kirby Smith

Jubal Early

John Breckinridge

CHAPTER 9 JANUARY 1- MAY 6, 1863

The New Year was greeted with confusion and bewilderment in the Southland. Nothing that was supposed to happen had happened. In '61 everybody knew that after a battle or two the Damned Yankees would let the South live in independence and peace. That hadn't happened. In '61 everybody knew that if a blockade were tried, England and/or France would come to the aid of the South and Southern Independence would be assured. That hadn't happened. How long would Northern mothers send their sons to fight and die against a people that only wanted to be free? Although the struggle may be longer and more painful than believed in '61, everybody knew that the Confederacy would survive. There had been over 2,000 fights and still nothing was settled!

As the year dawned, there was outrage in the North and South because of Lincoln's Emancipation. The South said it just unmasked Lincoln's true reason to start the war. It was to destroy the South and cause the Negroes to rise up. Anyone living in Dixieland, who still thought there was reason to hope that the two nations could become one again, now knew that would never happen. It was now "victory or death." The Southern people pointed to the lying Lincoln and his proclamation. He freed slaves where he had neither political nor military authority. He kept slaves in bondage in the North, where he could try to free them. It was still felt that a president couldn't amend the Constitution by himself. Lincoln was cursed but Butler now had a $10,000 reward placed on his head.

Some people in the North thought the reason for the war should be changed to freeing the slaves. These were mostly abolitionist. Most people did not wish to die to free slaves. By the end of January, fully one quarter of the Union Army would desert! The soldiers would risk imprisonment and maybe death not to fight for the Negro. In one Illinois regiment, the officers and all deserted, except for 35 men.

When word reached Norfolk, Virginia about Lincoln's third emancipation, free Negroes, with the help of Union soldiers, organized a march through that city. The Yankee flag flew above the marchers.

John Magruder and make-shift gunboats attacked Galveston, Texas. After four hours the South reclaimed their city!

Burnside filed his report on Fredericksburg. He rightly blamed Halleck for not getting those pontoon bridges to him on time. He blamed himself for the attack. In a talk with Lincoln, Burnside asked permission to attack General Lee again. Burnside had only left town when General Franklin was with Lincoln telling him not to let Burnside attack. Franklin told the President that no senior officer under Burnside had confidence in Burnside or his plan. It may have been said that at some point Burnside would have to get the army over a stream. Lincoln thought about what

Burnside had done to the army. He thought about what Franklin had said, before he gave Burnside the go ahead to attack "Bobby Lee."

On the 2nd, Breckinridge attacked Murfreesboro, Tennessee with almost 35,000 men. On the northeast side of town ran a stream and many men would fall at the Battle of Stone's River. At first, the South was wining but Rosecrans had more men and he retook that hill. Charge and countercharge ensued and both armies lay in line of battle. Each believed the other would either attack or retreat. Neither did and with a combined casualty figure of over 24,000 names, Breckinridge withdrew.

On this same day, both Morgan and Forrest began to move back to Southern held territory after successful raids and John Marmaduke began a raid into Missouri and Arkansas.

On the 5th, President Davis returned from his western trip to a tremendous welcome in Richmond. The crowd "serenaded" him. He gave an up lifting speech saying the Confederacy would survive and the Yankee invaders would be expelled.

Marmaduke fought at Linn Creek, and Fort Lawrence, or Beaver Station in Missouri on the 6th and captured Ozark, on the 7th. On the 8th, he attacked Springfield, but did not take it. Also on the 8th, another Confederate cavalryman, Joseph Wheeler, started a raid in Tennessee. A Yankee general, McClernand, wrote the President that his proclamation was illegal and amended the constitution. Lincoln wrote back the people "...of course...did have rights in the *Union as of old*." (Under Lincoln, slave owners {or anybody he decided} had no rights.)

On the 9th, Marmaduke attacked Hartville and the Yankees destroyed a salt work at St. Joseph, Florida. Before refrigeration, salt was needed to store and transport meat. The South didn't have enough to meet its needs.

Combined navy and army forces attacked the Confederate Fort Hindman, in Arkansas. Yankees, Porter and McClernand, were successful. Also on the 11th, the *C. S. S. Alabama* sunk the *U.S.S. Hatteras* off Galveston.

On the 12th, President Davis predicted that the Lincoln proclamation would lead to Negro uprisings and the "extermination of the Negro race."

On the 13th, Wheeler's cavalry captured the gunboat, *Sidell*, at Harpeth Shoals in the Cumberland River. They also captured three transports with many wounded enemy on board. Wheeler was a Southern Gentleman General; the wounded were placed aboard one transport and sent north, while the other two burned. In North Carolina, the *U. S. S. Columbia* ran aground. It would sail no more. It was captured and burned.

Lincoln wanted to keep England out of the war. He sent an answer to the people of Manchester on the 19th. They had written Lincoln saying the blockade was stopping the cotton and that they were out of work because of his blockade. Lincoln said the fault was the South's "our disloyal citizens." That is like blaming the victim for being raped.

On the 20th Marmaduke took Paterson. Lincoln placed David Hunter back in command of the Department of the South. He had fired Hunter earlier because Hunter had dared to issue an Emancipation.

A Federal "forage" wagon train was captured while stealing from the Southern population near Murfreesboro, on the 21st. At Sabine Pass, Texas two Federal blockaders were taken by Confederate steamers.

Lincoln knew how much the people of New Orleans missed "The Beast, Butler" so on the 23rd he thought about sending Butler back but never did. However, Burnside's Army was coming back. Burnside went to attack General Lee but had to fight "General Winter" and "General Mud." Winter storms turned the roads to mud. After six days, the deaths of many horses and mules, the exhausted army shivered back toward home. The infantry called it a "Mud March."

On the 25th Marmaduke's raid had reached Batesville, Arkansas. Also on this date, Burnside set across from Lincoln and gave the President two options; either fire all the commanders under him or fire the commander! It took several minutes for Burnside to receive his orders to report to the Department of Ohio. Lincoln liked Burnside's idea and did fire that tattle-tale, Franklin. Old Sumner was too old, so he was fired also.

Joseph Hooker had made no secret that he wanted Burnside's job. He had also said, "that what his country needs is a Dictator" and that he was suited for that job also. On the 26[th,] Lincoln appointed Hooker to run the army and wrote him a letter that only confirmed what Hooker had been saying. After making him the head general, Lincoln wrote, "...I am not quite satisfied with you." That was like shaking Hooker's hand and at the same time slapping him in the face but Lincoln was just getting started. "...during Burnside's command of the Army, you have taken counsel of your ambition, and thwarted him as much as you could, in which you did a great wrong to the country...." (He accused Hooker of disobeying orders, causing the loss of battles, and the deaths of many fine men. Why would Lincoln want a man like that to run his army?) Lincoln continued, "I have heard that you said '...both the Army and the Government needed a Dictator.'" (This may have hurt Lincoln's feelings because he thought he was doing such a good job of taking the people's rights away.) Lincoln wrote on, "Only those generals, who gain successes, can set up dictators. What I now ask of you is military success, and I will risk the dictatorship." (Is it any wonder that his Secretary of War Stanton called Lincoln a "buffoon?" Hooker, who would be dictator, now commanded the most powerful army near Washington.) The following grew out of the war:

"Jeff Davis rides a dapple gray,
Lincoln rides a mule.
Jeff Davis was a gentleman,
Lincoln was a fool!"

On the 27th, a U. S. Naval fleet attacked Fort McAllister near Savannah but was driven off. The U. S. Government was still afraid to let their citizens read the truth and so they closed the Philadelphia *Journal*.

Federal troops defeated the Confederate-Bannock Indians at Bear Creek, Utah Territory on the 29th. On the 30th, Grant took command of all forces against Vicksburg.

The Federal gunboat, the *Isaac Smith*, was captured and burned near Charleston, South Carolina on the 30th. The next day Confederate gunboats *Chicora* and *Palmetto State* rammed and shelled their Yankee counterparts the *Mercedita* and *Keystone State*. One was captured; one was sunk. It made Southern people happy that something was being done about the blockade.

On the 1st day of February, the Union navy was back attacking Fort McAllister; losing and sailing away.

On the 2nd, the Yankees destroyed another salt work this one at Wale's Head, Currituck Beach, North Carolina. At Vicksburg on the 3rd, the Union vessel the *Queen of the West* took three Confederate boats with prisoners, including ladies. General Forrest attacked Fort Donelson but was beaten back. On the 4th, Marmaduke was forced out of Batesville. On the 8th, the

Yankees caught the Chicago *Times* telling the truth and closed it down, "His truth (does not) go marching on."

Lincoln was upset to find out the Confederate Commissioners to England were at the "Lord Mayor of London's Banquet" on the 11th. On the 13[th,] President and Mrs. Lincoln received Gen. Tom Thumb and his bride at the White House. Tom was a circus midget.

The *Queen of the West* captured the Confederate gunboat the on the Red River but Southern shore batteries caused the steam pipe on the *Queen* to break. The Yankee crew of the *Queen* deserted her and boarded the *No. 5*. Then they set the *Queen* on fire to destroy her but Southern heroes boarded the vessel and put the fires out. On the 17[th,] the Federal gunboat the *Hercules* met her end by Southern Partisan Rangers near Memphis. On the 24[th,] it was the Union vessel the *Queen of the West* but under a new flag, that attacked the Federal fleet near Vicksburg. The South used the *Queen* and other gunboats to ram and force the *Indianola* to surrender. This was a serious blow to Grant's efforts.

What started as fun at Fredericksburg on the 19[th,] culminated in the biggest snowball fight ever on the 25th. It snowed on the 19th and some North Carolina troops attacked some Georgia troops. It snowed again the 25th and by then everyone had taken sides. The Army of Northern Virginia fought itself. Units operating in regimental strength, with officers mounted on horses, fought with the white stuff. It was said that "Stonewall" watched 10,000 men at war and at play.

Calling it a war move, Lincoln took over the banking system by creating a Currency Bureau of the Treasury on the 25th. The Admiral, Charles Wilkes, who got Lincoln in trouble in the 'Trent Affair" was back at his old tricks when he captured the English ship the *Peterhoff*. The English ship had Confederate supplies but was headed to Mexico. Once in Mexico, the supplies could be shipped safely to the Confederacy. Her Majesty's Government was very upset!

The Yankees were winning the war against the Indians. On the 26th, the Cherokee Nation rejoined the Union. Partisan Rangers burned a Union freight train near Woodburn, Tennessee. At Vicksburg, the Yankees decided to play a joke on the defenders. They rigged up an old coal barge to look like a very big gunboat and sent it flowing down stream. The Southern crew of the *Queen* saw "the monster in the night" and warned the crew of the *Indianola* that she was about to be boarded. The Southern crew set the *Indianola* on fire. The Federal joke, a floating pile of junk, cost the South a captured prize. On another river, this one near Savannah, a Union monitor, the *Montauk*, sank the C. S. S. *Rattlesnake* (*Nashville*) on the 28th.

On March 3rd, Lincoln was busy signing bills. The Draft Act forced Union men to join the army. Or they could pay $300 and let someone else do the dieing for Lincoln. During the war 162,535 were drafted and 116,188 bought their way out. Lincoln also changed the draft rules. From now until the end of the war, state troop requirements were met first by volunteers. If not enough men volunteered then "all Negroes were to be drafted" before the first white boy was drafted. Now when Union armies invaded the South, they captured military age Negroes and took them with them. The Negroes could either volunteer to join the army or they were drafted. Seldom were Negroes ever promoted above the rank of private; the Yankees did not think they were capable. (Thus the Yankees, in effect, made Negroes into "slaves." Now when the Union Army came to "end slavery," military age Negroes ran away from that army.) By thus taking Negroes, the State of Kentucky drafted no white boys during the war. Also, Negro soldiers received $7 less a month because of their skin color. Lincoln also signed a bill to "stack" the Supreme Court. Before, Lincoln had just ignored the court when it told him he was acting illegally. But now Lincoln could appoint four new justices so that nothing he did was illegal. Also, he signed another bill that showed his policy toward the South was stupid. Lincoln claimed that there really was no "Confederate States of America" but he signed a bill to make it legal for the Union Government to take control of any property or supplies belonging to the Confederacy, "which did not really exist." This day, the Union Navy attacked Fort McAllister and lost again.

On the 4[th,] Forrest and Van Dorn teamed up to give the Yankees a thrashing at Thompson's Station or Spring Hill, Tennessee. After a heavy engagement the Blue

Belly cavalry ran for their lives leaving the infantry to surrender on the 5th. Also on the 5th, Yankee soldiers heavily damaged the newspaper the *Crisis* in Columbus, Ohio. When were those editors going to learn that they couldn't print the truth, in the "Land of the free?" Even singing was too much for the Northern Government. In Baltimore on the 7th, it became illegal to buy Southern songs, "secession music." The conquerors of Maryland didn't like the popular new tune, "Maryland, My Maryland." There was something about that last verse that called them "Northern scum" that upset them.

The Yankees called them "Rebel Guerrillas" and Southerners called them Partisan Rangers. On the night of the 8th, Capt. John Mosby and twenty-nine of his men, wearing raincoats, simply rode through Union guard post after guard post. Finally they arrived at the house where Union General E. H. Stoughton lay peacefully sleeping in Fairfax Court House, Virginia. Mosby roused the general asking if he had ever heard of Mosby. The Yankee asked, "Have you captured him?" "No," was the reply, "He has captured you." Together they rode into Rebel lines: Mosby to eternal glory; Stoughton to eternal embarrassment. When word spread of what the courageous Mosby had done, there were squeals of delight in the South and "chagrin" in the North.

The Yankees at Vicksburg liked their joke so well that they repeated it on the 9th. Another "Quaker" gunboat flowed down stream. Much to their delight Confederate cannons roared.

To insult, humiliate, and terrorize the citizens the Federals sent "mostly Negro" troops to occupy Jacksonville, Florida on the 10th. President Lincoln was embarrassed and humiliated because over 25% of his army deserted after his proclamation. He needed those men back so he offered "amnesty" (no punishment) to soldiers who would return before April Fools Day.

Grant was finding it very hard to even approach Vicksburg. On the 11th, he was stopped again. Union gunboats were still 90 miles from the city on the Yalobusha River when they ran into a quickly constructed Confederate fort. Grant had been outgeneraled and outfought.

On the 14th, Admiral Farragut decided to steam his fleet up the Mississippi River passed the batteries at Port Hudson, Louisiana. The *Monongahela* and the *Richmond* were badly damaged and the *Mississippi* exploded before his eyes. For a while it seemed the deadly accurate Confederate fire would destroy his whole fleet.

On the 18th, Lincoln wrote Congressman Henry Davis, "Let the friends of the government first save the government and then administer it to their own liking." Again, Abe showed he had no regard for the law and he was trained as a lawyer.

Partisan Rangers did their duty again on the 21st when they took out a Union train near Grand Junction, Tennessee. On the 22nd, part of Morgan's Boys under Basil Duke captured the Federal garrison at Mount

Sterling, Kentucky. On the 24^{th,} Grant was stopped again; this time at Steele's Bayou north of Vicksburg. At Vicksburg itself, on the 25^{th,} the Union gunboat, *Lancaster* was sunk and her sister vessel, the *Switzerland* disabled when they tried to pass the city.

Although it was not an official Yankee state, West Virginia, was acting like a state when on the 26th the people voted to get rid of slavery, sometime. That day Lincoln wrote to the man he made Military Governor of Tennessee, Andrew Johnson, "The bare sight of 50,000 armed and drilled black soldiers on the banks of the Mississippi, would end the rebellion at once."

On the 27^{th,} the people and soldiers of the South bowed their heads in prayer and went without food for the day. Near Pattersonville, Louisiana on the 28^{th,} Confederates captured the Federal gunboat the *Diana*.

After his failure north of Vicksburg, Grant set Sherman's men to digging yet another ditch on the 29th. On the 30^{th,} Morgan's Boys were fighting at Dutton's Hill. When Lincoln heard about the South's day of prayer and fasting, he hollered, "Me too, me too," and declared April 30th to be the same as Davis had done. The people of Jacksonville didn't like the way the Negro troops were acting so on the last day of the month, they ran them out of town.

On the 2nd of April at Richmond, there was a "Bread Riot." Everything, including food was getting into short supply in the South. Thugs started stealing food and anything else they could get their hands on when they smashed into shops. President Davis got in a wagon and headed toward the looters. From the back of a wagon he spoke to the crowd and even threw all the money from his pockets to them. The people listened and most went back home; a few went to jail.

At Reading, Pennsylvania four men were arrested because they spoke favorable of the South. If Lincoln had of read the Constitution and Amendments, he would have found something about the "Freedom of Speech." On the 6th, Her Majesty's Government took a vessel being built in England for Confederate use. Lincoln's Emancipation was starting to work.

There was a special place of hatred in the Yankee heart for Charleston, South Carolina, where the war began. On the 7th, the Federals decided to attack the city. A very large fleet sailed in to the harbor. Cannon from Fort Sumter and Fort Moultrie sent over 2,000 shells flying through the air. Most ships that came in range were struck. The *Weehawken* was hit 53 times, the *Passaic* 35 times, the *Montauk* 47 times, the *Nantucket* 51 times, the *Patapsco* 47 times. After 40 minutes of iron from the sky, the fleet limped out of the harbor.

After the "Bread Riot," President Davis sent a message to Congress on the 10th, asking the people of the South not to plant cotton but to plant food. He went on to condemn "...the lust of conquest (in trying for the) ...subjugation of a free people. (He went on to say)...the unholy purpose...has thus far been defeated."

Lafayette McLaws

Stephen D. Lee

Fitzhugh Lee

Custis Lee

This day Van Dorn attacked Franklin, Tennessee but was forced to retreat.

The next day six Yankee vessels chased the blockade runner, the *Stonewall Jackson,* to shore near Charlestown.

On the 13[th,] an unhappy Burnside issued orders for the people of Ohio. Anyone caught speaking good about the Confederacy would be sent south. Anybody caught helping the South would be put to death (The Land of the free and the brave).

The death of a queen: on the 13[th,] the Yankees attacked Fort Bisland in Louisiana. That night Confederates left the area but before they did, they burned the former Yankee vessel the *Queen of the West* to keep it from becoming a Yankee vessel again.

By the 16[th,] Grant had decided to cross his army over the Mississippi below Vicksburg and attack the city from the landside to the east. To cross over, he needed the fleet. During the night Porter moved the Federal fleet toward Vicksburg. Southern scouts saw the fleet and lit bonfires on the west side of the river so that Confederate gunners on the east side could see the Yanks in the night. Though some vessels were damaged and one sunk, the fleet was now south of the city.

On the 17[th,] Col. Benjamin Grierson led 1,700 Union cavalrymen out of La Grange, Tennessee headed for Mississippi to take pressure off Grant. The same day Marmaduke left Arkansas to raid the Yankees in Missouri.

Another salt work was destroyed on the 18th near New Iberia, Louisiana. On the 21[st,] Confederate raiders, under Brig. Gen. William "Grumble" Jones, struck the Baltimore and Ohio Railroad. On the 22[nd,] more Union boats attempted to pass Vicksburg. One transport and six barges didn't make it but Grant was still reinforced.

Crazy Mary Lincoln was involving more high officials in her nutty "séances." This time the President, Secretary of War and Secretary of the Navy were there. All left saying they had felt the presence of the "spirits."

There was much shouting in the English Parliament on the 25[th,] as they debated the U. S. taking one of their ships on its way to Mexico. On the 29[th,] Porter's gunboats shelled the town of Grand Gulf to help Grant's Army get over the Mississippi. They failed.

Back in Virginia Gen. Joseph Hooker, "Fighting Joe," had been reorganizing Burnside's old army. Hooker was always proud of himself and always willing to tell others just how great he was. He wrote Lincoln, "I have the finest army on the planet." Hooker liked the bottle and the broads. Though married he liked the ladies-of-the-night and always kept a number near him. Thus, prostitutes are called to this day "hookers."

Even though Lee had given Burnside a sound beating, Lee's Army was not in good shape. There was no bread in Richmond or in Fredericksburg. Horses didn't have much to eat and there was a great shortage of wagons. There was a shortage of clothing and shoes in the cold winter. Lee had sent one of his divisions under

- 163 -

Longstreet to operate near Norfolk. Hooker had Lee outnumbered, out-supplied and outgunned. There were less than 60,000 Confederates to Hooker's 130,000. There were 410 Federal cannons to Lee's 210.

The first move toward the big Battle of Chancellorsville started in a classroom at West Point. Two classmates were rivals then and rivals in the spring of '63. Fitzhugh "Fitz" Lee was the nephew of General Lee and headed one of the cavalry divisions. On a raid over the Rappahannock, Fitz took 150 Yankee cavalrymen from William Averell as prisoners. Fitz left his old classmate a note challenging him to even try to cross over the river; and if Averell did come, for him to "please bring some coffee with him." Coffee was in short supply and Fritz bragged that when he captured Averell he wanted a good cup of coffee. Averell didn't think the note to be funny at all. On March 17th, he accepted the challenge as he approached the Rappahannock with 3,000 men plus artillery. Fitz had a small welcoming party ready to receive Averell. At Kelly's Ford Fitz had a barricade setup. About 20 brave Yankees went into the cold water with axes but before they could cross the stream to start cutting, they were cut down by Confederate cavalrymen. Averell brought his artillery forward and blasted those Rebels off line. His men began to cross the stream.

Fitz was at Culpeper and surprised to find out that Averell had accepted his invitation. Fitz with 800 men rode hard to receive his old classmate and his 3,000. As he came close to the ford, Fitz was surprised again; Averell had not pressed the attack but was digging in.

By pure chance Stuart and Major John Pelham were in the area and had come to see what all the shooting was about. Pelham was an artilleryman both skilled and brave. In an earlier battle report, he was referred to as "Gallant." It was his "Stonewall" name; the "Gallant Pelham." He was young, single and made many a Southern Belle's heart beat faster. Though an artilleryman, Pelham joined the first charge of Fitz's cavalry. Though an artilleryman, he was now a cavalryman and a Yankee artilleryman fired a piece of artillery that killed the "Gallant Pelham," and the South mourned the loss of a hero.

Fitz's invitation said nothing about JEB Stuart being there. After Averell found out that Stuart was there, he decided to leave. On a large sack of coffee, Averell left this note: "Dear Fitz, Here's your coffee. Here's your visit. How do you like it?"

Hooker thought his plan "…as brilliant as the battle plans of the great Napoleon himself." Before the first man marched, Hooker was a legend in his own mind. He was sure it would confuse Lee, and keep Lee pinned in place until he was ready to destroy him. "God have mercy on Bobby Lee; for I will have none," said Hooker. To confuse and hold Lee, Maj. Gen. John Sedgwick would cross the Rappahannock south of Fredericksburg as if getting ready to attack "Stonewall." Maj. Gen. Dan

Sickles would stay in camp but act like he was ready to ford and attack at anytime.

The real attack would start when about one third of the army, under Maj. Gen. Oliver Howard, marched up the Rappahannock and crossed at Kelly's Ford. Then they were to turn toward Fredericksburg and move to a crossroads. At the crossroads was the plantation house of the Chancellor family, know as Chancellorsville. At Chancellorsville, they would meet up with Maj. Gen. Darius Couch's II Corps. There would be over 70,000 men ready to strike Lee's exposed flank (more men than Lee had in his whole army).

It was warm on April 27th, when Hooker started his troops moving. Because they had been in camp and not on the march, many Yankee soldiers became footsore and fell out of ranks. As they became hot and tired on the march, many soldiers threw away their tents, overcoats and sometimes even blankets. All went well and by 2 P. M. on the 30th the first units began to arrive at the Chancellor house. Hooker was more than pleased with his troops and himself; he said of Lee, "...the enemy must either ingloriously fly or give us battle on our own ground, where certain destruction awaits him."

At that moment in time, Lee would probably have thought Hooker's opinion was correct. If fact, Lee did not know Hooker's strength or intent, he just knew something big was happening.

When Sedgwick crossed the river toward Jackson, "Old Jube" Jubal Early took up position in front of him. Hooker's plan was working perfectly.

By the 30th, Lee was still guessing. Stuart's scouts were bringing in information but it was too vague. On the 30th, Maj. Gen. Richard Anderson was at Fredericksburg and he saw the Union troops headed toward Chancellorsville and sent Lee word. Lee now knew where Hooker was heading. Lee sent word to Jackson to leave only Early to watch Sedgwick and move his army as fast as possible to join him. Lee knew that if Sedgwick attacked, Early couldn't hold. Lee echoed President Davis' words, "It must be victory or death..."

"Stonewall" was not late this time. He started his men marching at 2 A. M. by 11 he was in front of Hooker's Army. For reasons that are not clear, Hooker did not order his troops forward, until past noon. As they advanced, they ran into Jackson's men. Sharp skirmishes broke out all along the front but with overwhelming manpower the Yankees were pushing the Rebels back. Though winning, Hooker called a halt to the Union advance and ordered his troops to fall back on Chancellorsville. His commanders at the front were very angry. One Federal general said, "Nobody but a crazy man would give such an order when we have victory in sight!" The man who would take the offensive to Lee, now went on the defense; later Hooker would say, "...I lost confidence in Hooker."

As the sun was setting, Lee and Jackson talked under some pine trees. They had stopped the Union advance but what to do now. Lee had looked the land over and decided that an attack on the center would cost many lives and not succeed. As the two talked, Stuart rode up and he had "hot information." Oliver Howard's Corps was far to the west away from all action and they were expecting none. The Yankees weren't dug in nor was there any natural defense line, like creek or hill for them to hide behind. Stuart said their flank was "in the air." Lee and Jackson saw a place to strike but how could they move enough forces that far undetected and strike? The famous mapmaker for the Confederacy, Jed Hotchkiss, made a map showing a route. Lee asked Jackson, what do you propose? Only Jackson would have told the senior commander that he, Jackson, would take nearly the whole army, march around and attack the enemy. What should Lee do? With a little force Lee was to act like he was getting ready to attack but if Hooker struck first, Lee would be wiped out. Basically Lee said, "It sounds good to me" and off Jackson went into the night.

By 7 A. M. on the 2nd, "Stonewall" had his army moving. Union pickets and scouts sent word to Hooker through the day of sighting a large movement of Confederates. At one point Hooker guessed that they could be moving to his right flank in the west and sent a warning to Howard. Dan Sickles struck the rear of Jackson's column and rolled it up. Hooker now decided that "Bobby Lee" was doing what Hooker always thought he would do, retreat!

It was a long march but at 5:15 the Rebels came screaming out of the woods upon the unsuspecting Yankees. They struck Howard's flank that was "in the air." Some tried to form lines but most Federals just ran for their lives. The Union right flank had been smashed and a rout was on. By dark the Confederates had driven the terrified Yankees two miles. Because of the chase, the army had separated and scattered. Southern commanders didn't know where their units were. All the Rebels were very tired and hungry. Everybody was ready to call it a day, but Jackson.

"Stonewall" wanted a night attack to destroy the enemy. He and his staff rode into the dark woods looking for the enemy. At 9 P. M. some of the boys with the 19th North Carolina thought they saw a Union cavalry unit riding toward them in the dark. They fired and a number of the mounted men were hit, including "Stonewall" Jackson. Two bullets shattered his left arm. A litter (stretcher) was found and Jackson placed on it. There was more fire incoming as they carried Jackson. The litter bearers dropped the "Mighty Stonewall." In the fall one or more of Jackson's ribs broke and probably punched little holes in his lung. During the night "Stonewall" was carried to a field hospital where his arm was amputated. He seemed to be recovering so the next day, he was transported by bumpy ambulance toward

Guiney Station From this station, "Stonewall" could be sent to Richmond and the best hospitals the South had.

When Lee received the news about Jackson he was much saddened but couldn't quit work. Lee at once turned Jackson's infantry over to the cavalry commander JEB Stuart with orders to hit them with all you got in the morning.

During the night, more Union forces crossed the Rappahannock; now Lee faced more than before, 76,000. Hooker could have still attacked Lee's separated forces (Jackson's old command now under Stuart) but Hooker was only thinking defense. He ordered Dan Sickles to pull back for the higher ground. Porter Alexander, Lee's chief of artillery saw the move and said, "…rarely has there been a more gratuitous gift of a battlefield." The Yankees gave Alexander's cannons good ground.

Stuart had worked hard through the night to find and reform "Stonewall's" units. The sun came up at 5:30, by six o'clock Stuart had Archer's Brigade attacking. They took the ground that Dan Sickles had just given up. Porter Alexander started shelling Hooker's line near the Chancellor house. A. P. Hill had also been wounded so it was his replacement, Henry Heth, who sent five brigades slamming into, II, III and XII Corps. For two and one-half hours it was bloody and sometimes hand-to-hand battle. Both sides took 50% casualties in some units. Colston's Southern Brigade went through four commanders that morning. Despite heavy losses, Stuart wouldn't let the attack fizzle. When the advance slowed, he sent in more troops as they drove the Yankees back toward Chancellor House. At the house, Hooker was knocked senseless when one of Alexander's cannon projectiles hit the house and part of the house hit Hooker. Though addled, he did not give up command for some time. He did, later, turn over command to Darius Couch with orders to "Retreat."

About this time, Lee gave orders to his smaller part of the army to attack. As "the fierce soldiers with their faces blackened with the smoke of battle (saw Lee, they gave) one long, unbroken cheer (hailing) the presence of the victorious chief."

During the night of May 2nd, Hooker had sent orders to Sedgwick to move toward Chancellorsville but Early's men stood in the way. Early's position was where Burnside had been so badly beaten on the heights near Fredericksburg. After very heavy fighting, Sedgwick's men came over that famous stonewall and chased Early back. When Lee received the news, he had to lessen his attack on Hooker and send troops under Lafayette McLaws so that Sedgwick couldn't attack Lee's main force.

Sedgwick attacked McLaws at Salem Church. Both sides advanced and retreated until the sun went down. Because Sedgwick had a smaller force and was so far away from Hooker's main force, Lee decided to destroy him on the 4th. To do so, Lee ordered McLaws to attack from the front, Early to hit him from the rear while Richard Anderson would march all the way around Sedgwick to attack him on his exposed southern flank. It took a lot of marching and a lot of messengers to make an attack at the same time; thus it was 6 P. M. before the battle opened.

Early struck first and started rolling up Sedgwick's rear. When Anderson's men attacked, they didn't hit the enemy straight in the side, as planned, but moved toward the sound of Early's battle and went toward the rear of Sedgwick. McLaws' men got lost in the woods and didn't do much. Sedgwick realized the he was in a hard place and he slipped Lee's trap and re-crossed the Rappahannock on the 5th.

When Lee realized that Sedgwick had slipped the trap, he turned his attention again to Hooker and planned an attack for the 6th. By now Hooker was back to his right mind and realized that he too was in a pickle, so he ordered his army back across the Rappahannock also. Federal losses were 1,606 killed, 9,762 wounded and 5,919 missing for a total of 17,287. Confederate losses were 1,665 killed, 9,081 wounded and 2,018 missing for a total of 12,764. Southern losses were much higher than the Union loses on a percentage basis; also, they were much harder to replace.

By the 6^{th,} Lee knew he had won a great victory but was unhappy that he had failed to destroy either of the Union's main bodies. Now he could turn his attention to a more personal matter; he sent a message to

"Stonewall." "Tell him...he has lost his left arm but I have lost my right."

When "Stonewall" had gotten to Guiney Station his personal doctor, Hunter McGuire, examined the stump where his left arm had been. It appeared to be healing. Jackson seemed to be recovering until pneumonia started in his lungs because of the fall from the litter. Anna, Jackson's second wife, was there with their little daughter. (His first wife had died due to childbirth.) Anna talked to Dr. McGuire and then told her husband "today...you will be with the Savior." Jackson expressed thanks that he would die on Sunday. In the last hours, he slept and sometimes roused and gave orders to soldiers that weren't there. Before the sun sat on May 10th, Thomas Jonathan "Stonewall" Jackson seemed to find peace and he spoke his last and perhaps most famous words, "Let us cross over the river and rest under the shade of the trees." President Davis declared a "national day of mourning." Jackson was buried next to his first wife in Lexington on the 15th. "Stonewall" Jackson's school, Virginia Military Institute, has never forgotten that date.

"The Confederate troops treated the Federal prisoners kindly...." But by now too many reports were being heard to ignore. After the Yankees had overrun Early's line at Fredericksburg there were lots of bodies on the ground. The Yanks had won and they were the only ones standing. The Federals knew many of those Rebels were dead or very badly wounded. They also knew many were only slightly wounded or not at all and just pretending to be dead. The Southerners on the ground knew if they moved too lively, the Blue Bellies may put a bullet through them. To put an end to this situation, the victorious Union soldiers began to shout that if any Reb who could stand, would stand, that they wouldn't be shot but treated fairly as prisoners of war. Many, not all, of the Confederates who could, did. After as many stood as would stand, the Damned Yankees opened fire and murdered them. There was the sound of body thud and blood splash as surrendering Confederate soldiers were once again on the ground. Some of the lively Confederates on the ground found themselves under bodies of their comrades and awash in their blood. Some of these men escaped in the night and told of the massacre.

Safely back over the river, Hooker began to blame everyone but himself; he fooled no one. From the private to the President all were downcast, that a man with so much could lose so badly, to an army with so little. Lincoln was worried. A quarter of his army had deserted, newspapers were still printing the truth about his war and there was a growing peace movement. When the people of the North learned about Hooker, "Bobby Lee" and Chancellorsville, there would be hell to pay! In the White House, Lincoln wrung his hands and kept repeating, "My God! My God! What will the country say?" On the 5[th,] the leader of the "Peace Democrats or Copperheads," former Congressman

Clement Vallandigham was arrest in Dayton, Ohio. On the 6th, he was tried by "a military commission for expressing treasonable sympathies." (One of the things the Copperheads wanted was the removable of the word "Liberty" from all United States money.) Burnside meant what he said; so much for free speech and the Constitution.

In the South, church bells were ringing because the great General Lee had given the Confederate States of America another great victory. In the South, church bells were ringing because the Confederate States of America had suffered another great defeat; the "Mighty Stonewall" would never make a stand again.

𝔘. 𝔖. 𝔊rant

𝔚illiam 𝔖herman

Edwin Stanton

John Fremont

CHAPTER 10 MAY 7 – JULY 9, 1863

(Note to Reader: Two major events will occur in this chapter. Gettysburg and Vicksburg took place during the same time period. Each will be covered separately.)

On the 7th of May, Grant and Sherman combined their forces as they decided on a plan to attack both Vicksburg and Port Hudson. These were the South's last links over the Mississippi River to the rest of the nation. Grant wanted to take them and split the Confederacy. Instead of attacking from the river, they would move inland and attack Vicksburg from the east. It was also decided to steal all the food that the army could from the citizens.

Emigrants from other countries, who weren't U. S. citizens didn't believe they should have to fight in Lincoln's war. Lincoln cared nothing about the domestic law, why should he care about international law? Those people were here and they too became subject to the Union draft on the 8th.

President Davis trying to do something about the Mississippi area assigned Joseph Johnston to command the area on the 9th.

Lincoln and his Secretary of the Treasury, Salmon Chase were back at each other again on the 11th. Chase said he wanted to resign but Lincoln would not let him.

On the 12[th,] there was an engagement; it wasn't a very big engagement, each side took about 500 casualties but it sealed the fate of Vicksburg. At Raymond, Mississippi the Confederates were pulled back toward the state capital, Jackson. After Grant took Jackson the next day, Pemberton's forces at Vicksburg were cut off from Johnston's outside of the city. The two armies could not unite to attack Grant. During this time, President Davis was dealing with North Carolina Governor Zeb Vance. A confederation of states did not have a strong central government like Lincoln had. Davis had to ask the states for help, not demand it. Vance didn't want to help the central government as much as Davis thought he should.

At the Battle of Champion's Hill on the 16th, Grant kept Pemberton and Johnston from joining forces. The following day at Big Black River, Grant had Pemberton pinned against the river but Pemberton burned the bridges and moved into Vicksburg. On the 18th, the Siege of Vicksburg began!

Also on this date, the House of Lords in England basically said, that even though the Yankees were seizing their ships on the high seas that England didn't want to get involved in the American Civil War. This showed that the English people were buying "Honest Abe's" lies. They now thought this was a war to end slavery. The fact that no Yankee slaves were released was something they did not know.

On the 19th, Grant made his first attack on the city but the South had strong defenses; 1,000 Yankees fell before the Southern guns.

Burnside had arrested Vallandigham one day, tried and sentenced him the next. Lincoln was probably proud of the way Burnside acted but Vallandigham was a former congressman and he still had some political power. So on this date, Lincoln ordered the former congressman released and sent south.

On the 21^{st,} part of Grant's force, under Nathaniel Banks, lay siege to Port Hudson.

On the 22^{nd,} Grant made an all out assault on Vicksburg. Some called it "suicidal" others said it was "butchery." Grant lost 502 killed, 2,550 wounded and 147 missing. The Southern casualties numbered less than 500. One of the generals under Grant, McClernand let Grant know in no uncertain terms what he thought of Grant's generalship. In England this day, the British and Foreign Anti-Slavery Society voted strong support for Lincoln's war.

On the 23^{rd,} Lincoln was still hearing from Ohio in the form of petitions. Many people there signed to protest "the arbitrary arrest, illegal trial and inhuman imprisonment of Hon. C. L. Vallandigham." On the 25^{th,} he was handed over to Confederate authorities but this wasn't something that President Davis wanted. The peace movement in the North had to be independent of the South or otherwise people would say that it was started and supported by the Confederacy. True the South liked the movement but it had to be a Yankee peace movement not Southern. So on June the 11^{th,} President Davis had Vallandigham sent to Canada.

Banks attacked Port Hudson on the 27th. Banks used the gunboat the *Cincinnati* in his attack but it was sunk. He placed his Negro troops in front and they took very high casualties. He did no better than Grant had done at Vicksburg.

On the 28^{th,} the governor of Indiana sent a letter to Lincoln saying the illegal treatment of Vallandigham was increasing anti-war protest in his state. If Lincoln wished to keep his war going, he would at least act like he wanted to uphold the law. Burnside offered to resign because of the Vallandigham affair but Lincoln wouldn't hear of it. Burnside was a chip off the old block!

Burnside was so glad to find out the President backed him that on June 1st he closed the *Chicago Times*. The mayor of Chicago wrote to Lincoln protesting the closing.

During this time period, Lee went to Richmond to meet with President Davis. Lee saw two uses for his army. One he could protect Richmond or he could invade the North. By going north it would allow Virginia farmers time to raise crops. Also, Lee's Army could feed off Yankee farmers like the Yankee Army had been doing in the South. If a big victory could be won on Northern soil that would aid the Union Peace Movement and maybe get England or France to come to the Confederacy's aid. Some of Davis's advisors wanted to send a large part of Lee's Army to help at Vicksburg but Lee felt that his invasion into the North would relieve pressure on that city, also. Others worried that if

Lee started north, then Hooker would march between Lee and the capital. Lee had won too many great victories to be ignored; his plan was approved. What nobody knew then but many historians now believe is that General Lee had a heart attack before starting to move north. The doctor called it the "fever" but General Lee wasn't General Lee at Gettysburg.

On the 3rd, Lee started moving his army northward. This could be considered the beginning of the Gettysburg campaign. As Lee moved north, New York Mayor, Fernando Wood called a meeting to urge peace. Enough Northern boys had died trying to stop the South from being free. Lincoln was hearing the message. On the 4th, he ordered Burnside to let the *Times* print again.

As Lee marched north, JEB Stuart decided to have a fancy dress review of his proud cavalrymen at Brandy Station, Virginia. 8,000 horses and flashing blades made a beautiful sight.

On the 7th, Confederates at Vicksburg took the offensive by attacking toward the African Brigade. They drove the Negroes to the bank of the river before Union gunboats came to save them.

On the 8th, Stuart gave another review; this time for Lee and most of his top generals. Everyone seemed to have a great time.

On the 9th, Stuart had some unexpected and unwanted guests at his cavalry review. Union General Alfred Pleasonton brought his cavalry and some infantry and for 12 hours the air at Brandy Station was filled with the sound of horse charge, pistols, cannon and sabers. JEB won but it was a costly victory. He felt very bad that he had been taken by surprise. The Battle of Brandy Station was the biggest cavalry battle ever fought in the Western Hemisphere. This day, the Federals at Franklin, Tennessee hanged two Confederate soldiers; said they were spies.

The people of the South were religious. Their leaders and generals were, by-and-large, Christian. As the war deepened the people knew that if they were to stay an independent nation, God's help was needed. More and more of the people gave their hearts to Jesus. On the 10[th,] Gen. Braxton Bragg joined the Episcopal Church.

Even though he had been shipped to Canada, Vallandigham's name was placed in nomination for the Governorship of Ohio on the 11th. Lincoln was feeling the heat on the 12th when he addressed the issue of illegal arrest and trials. He said that "...he regretted" (having to arrest so many people and stomp on the Constitution) but that he would "continue... (for) public safety."

During the week before, Lt. Charles Read and his crew of the *Clarence* had captured six Union vessels off North Carolina. On this day, he captured the *Tacony*. It was a better ship than his, so he transferred his crew and sunk the *Clarence*. He started raiding north.

On the 14[th,] Hooker started moving his army north following Lee. Maj. Gen. R. H. Milroy was at

Winchester and didn't believe the reports he had received that Lee was moving north. This day he became a believer. It is called the 2nd Battle of Winchester. Milroy's 7,000 were beaten badly by Richard Ewell, who now commanded most of "Stonewall's" Army. He sent troops north of Winchester to block Milroy's escape route. The next day the 2nd Battle of Winchester ended at Stephenson's Depot, about four miles north of the town when Milroy ran into Ewell. The South took some prisoners and killed about 100 Yankees. The big prize was the 300 wagon loads of supplies and 23 cannons the South now had to help with its northern invasion.

While this was going on, Partisan Rangers fired on the Union gunboat the *Marmora* near Eunice, Arkansas. The Damn Yankees left their boat and went into the undefended town and burned everyone's homes and businesses.

On the 15^{th,} the Yankee Naval Department sent many ships looking for the now *C. S. S. Tacony*. Also today, Lincoln learned of draft protest in Boone County, Indiana. The men grabbed a draft officer and held him while the women threw eggs at him. The next day there was an anti-draft protest in Holmes County, Ohio. Also, the citizens of the capital of Pennsylvania began to flee the city, fearing Lee's Army.

On the 17^{th,} the Confederate ironclad the *Atlanta* fought two Yankee vessels and lost. She surrendered off the Georgia coast.

On the 20th, President Lincoln signed a document that shouts to the world that "Honest Abe" was among the most dishonest of men to ever live in the White House. It said that everyman, who fought, labored or died, did it for a Lincoln lie. On this date, President Lincoln signed a bill making West Virginia the 34th State to enter the Union. In the bill, which passed both the House and Senate, it says very specifically that a part of a state has the right to "secede" from that state. If a part of a state can break away from its union then a full state can break away from its union. Also, Lincoln again showed that he had no regard for the Constitution. One part of the Constitution says very clearly that the Federal Government can not change the internal boundaries of a state. Thus the illegal State of West Virginia will for ever stand as a monument of shame to Abraham Lincoln!

Despite the great navel fleet chasing him, Lt. Read and his crew of the *Tacony* took five more Union vessels off New England on the 22nd.

To keep the South from sending troops to fight against Grant, William Rosecrans left Murfreesboro, Tennessee on the 23rd. This campaign was more about marching than fighting. Rosecrans drove and Bragg retreated in the "Middle Tennessee Campaign." There were some skirmishes fought as Bragg was forced back south of the Tennessee River by early July. Just as importantly, he could send no soldiers to fight Grant. On this date, about 1,000 Yankees surrendered at Brashear City, Louisiana.

On the 24[th,] the main force of Lee's Army began to cross over the Potomac at Shepherdstown and later at Williamsport. The bands played, "Maryland, My Maryland" and the "Bonnie Blue Flag." Lee gave orders that his men were not to act like Yankees, stealing everything that wasn't tied down, burning or raping. Some of his soldiers did steal food and chickens as they traveled. Because Lee had given the Yankees the slip, Hooker's Army was marching fast to try and get between Lee and Washington.

To keep the Federal Army off balance and guessing, Lee told Stuart to "pass around" Hooker's Army and do as much damage as possible. Stuart was still feeling bad because of Brandy Station; he decided to ride completely around Hooker.

All was going very well for General Lee. Ewell had taken York, and Carlisle, Pennsylvania. Most of the army was near Chambersburg, and Harrisburg, was within Lee's grasp. All that changed late on the evening of the 28th. A scout with Longstreet's Division reported that Hooker's Army was at Frederick, Maryland less than 40 miles away. Lee's forces were scattered and Hooker could attack and destroy any one of them; the army must consolidate. Lee chose Cashtown, not far from Gettysburg, as a point to meet. Later Lee learned that he no longer faced Hooker's Army of the Potomac but now it was Gen. George Meade's Army. Lincoln had fired Hooker.

There was a rumor that there was a shoe factory in the little town of Gettysburg. Gen. James Pettigrew was given orders to check out the town but if the enemy were to appear he was not to fight. Meade wanted to find Lee so he sent his cavalry under Gen. John Buford; the armies found each other on the 30th.

As ordered, Pettigrew withdrew to Cashtown. Lee was not there yet which made A. P. Hill the ranking commander. After hearing Pettigrew's report, Hill was sure that any force at Gettysburg was small. He gave orders for Gen. Henry Heth to take his whole division to the town tomorrow.

Buford saw that Gettysburg could be important. There were twelve roads leading into the small town; it would be a good place for either army to concentrate. Buford sent word to the nearest Union infantry division to move at once toward Gettysburg.

At 5:30 A. M. on July 1[st,] Lt. Marcellus Jones with the 8th Illinois Cavalry fired his carbine at the column of Maj. Gen. Henry Heth's Division and the Battle of Gettysburg was on. Heth thought his 7,500 men could easily push the few Yankees there aside and take the town. When he saw large numbers of Union Cavalry take the high ground in front, he knew he would have to fight to get those shoes. Heth did not order a strong attack and both sides exchanged shots until about 9 A. M. when Maj. Gen. John Reynolds 1st Federal Corps began to arrive on the field. Reynolds was there for the opening but he wouldn't see the end; a Rebel bullet tore through his head. The weak Confederate attack was stopped and there was a quiet from 11 to 1 P. M. During this time both sides moved troops on to the field. Maj. Gen. Oliver Howard took command for the North while General Lee came onto the field.

At 2:30, Lee felt he had enough men and attacked. He did and many a good man was killed, wounded, or captured. Some units took 70% casualties; there were 14 flag bearers for the 26th North Carolina that went down. Though taking heavy casualties the Southerners wouldn't quit and the Union line began to fold under the pressure. By 4 P. M., it was Howard's Boys that were dieing or flying or surrendering. It was almost a rout as the Union Army fled into the town.

Lee's keen eye saw that a small rise, Cemetery Hill, was a key to controlling the area. He told Richard "Dick" Ewell to take that hill "...if you think practicable." Ewell was used to "Stonewall" who would have only said, "Take that hill." Ewell did not take the hill. Many Confederate veterans believed that if "Stonewall" were there, the hill, Little Round Top, would have been taken. During this same time, Maj. Gen. Winfield Hancock brought his Union troops up and stopped the rout.

By midnight, the Federal Commander had arrived at Gettysburg. Maj. Gen. George Meade hadn't been in command long and now he was in a major battle!

Throughout the night, more and more Union troops were arriving; this allowed the Yankees to occupy the higher ground. Meade sent troops up Culp's Hill southeast of town; and put more troops on Cemetery Hill and along Cemetery Ridge. However, the left flank of the line on Cemetery Ridge was thinly manned. After the night march most Yankees were very tired.

While the Yankees marched and Meade generaled, Lee didn't sleep well; he was thinking of his plans for the next day's battles. Lee was up at "early dawn" (one hour before sunrise). He was happy to hear that part of Longstreet's Corps had arrived in the night. These were the troops Lee wished to use to give the knock out-blow to the Yankees. Lee's plan called for the troops to use Seminary Ridge to block the enemy's vision and march until they could attack the Federal left. Then part of Hill's Boys would attack the center. To keep the Union from moving troops to their left, Ewell would strike their right flank. Lee felt he was attacking "blind." The "eyes" of the army is the cavalry and JEB Stuart was out riding, God knows where. Lee needed his "eyes."

Longstreet listened to Lee's plan and liked none of it. He advised Lee to side step Gettysburg and find better high ground and let Meade attack him. Lee said, "No." Then Longstreet said he didn't want to attack until all his troops arrived, which would be another day. Lee said, "Today!" Longstreet went off to start the attack but he didn't do the job he should have. Lee had called Longstreet his "War Horse" but this time the

"War Horse" didn't seem to want to fight. It was four in the afternoon before Longstreet made his advance. By this time, Longstreet faced a different situation. Instead of a weak force to his front, he would find an entire Union Corps. However, not all was going against the Confederates. A Yankee-politician-general, Dan Sickles, decided that he didn't have a good enough position and without orders moved two of his divisions toward "the Devil's Den," Longstreet and danger.

At 4 p. m. line after line of Gray Backs slammed in to Sickles exposed divisions. The Rebel yell and Southern shot was too much for the Blue Bellies and Sickles Boys fell back. Meade's mapmaker saw that Little Round Top was not well defended. Without waiting for orders, he sent men and cannon to the hill. The 20th Maine arrived on the hill only minutes before the 15th Alabama struck. At times it was desperate hand-to-hand combat. This is where Col. Joshua Lawrence Chamberlain became a Yankee hero by holding the hill.

While the fighting was going on, on Little Round Top, part of Hill's Division under General T. J. Anderson moved to attack the center. As soon as Anderson's men moved out of the woods, Union artillery cut loose a galling fire. Other Federals, protected by a rock wall, cut loose with rifle. The attack was broken-up about as soon as it started. Some of the Yankees were running low on ammunition, when Joseph Kershaw's South Carolina Brigade joined the fight. Kershaw's men took heavy casualties from Union artillery as they came along side Anderson's men. Together they began to push the Yankees off the hill. The Yankees began to panic; it looked like a Southern victory in the making, when Brig. Gen. John Caldwell brought his division to stop the Union retreat. The Federals retook the Wheat Field which had bodies, both gray and blue lying upon it. As soon as the Yankees took the field, Hill sent two more brigades under McLaw and took the field back. More Union units came to fight and die in someone else's wheat field but the Southerners just chewed them up in "a whirlpool of death." At 6:30 P. M., Barksdale's Mississippians, 1,600 strong, attacked. The Union line was collapsing; artillery and infantry were fleeing the field. The Confederates were taking the center toward Cemetery Ridge. Meade seemed to be elsewhere so General Hancock threw everything he could at the advancing Rebels. Col. William Colvill's 1st Minnesota hit Barksdale's weakened attack and started the Southerners in retreat. As the Southern troops fell back, they came to a range where Southern artillery could cover their retreat. The artillery did a fine job and stopped the Union counterattack. Colvill lost his head to a Confederate artillery shell. Barksdale lost his life to Union bullet wounds to his chest and leg. Many brave men bled and died that day. It was a Union victory because the Yankees still held the center.

Ewell did attack on the right at Culp's Hill. It was to be only an attack to attract the Union's attention while the real attack occurred on the left. It wasn't a good attack. Units fought as individuals not as an army. The Federals were able to hold Culp's Hill.

The town of Gettysburg was occupied by Confederate soldiers and would be for the next day and one half. There was a big difference in the character of the fighting men. While occupied by Southerners, not one home was burned, not one home was looted, not one person was robbed, not one citizen was assaulted, not one woman raped; only food and water were taken by the Confederate soldiers.

Meade was new to his job and had done little generaling. That night the air was full of moans, groans, and screams from those who couldn't leave the field after the battle. Meade called a meeting of his subordinate officers and asked them what he should do. Should he stay or run? They all said "Stay."

JEB Stuart finally came into Rebel lines. Lee was not happy that Stuart had been out riding around Meade and not where Lee needed him. Stuart said he was proud of the fact that he had burned the Union barracks at Carlisle, Pennsylvania and captured so many wagons. Lee needed his "eyes" more than wagons but now that Stuart's cavalry was here, Lee could use JEB in the next day's attack. Stuart was to circle the Union Army and attack them in the rear toward their supplies. Lee knew the Union center had taken a beating that day. Maybe another push and it would fold? Lee issued orders. Again, Ewell was to divert the Federals attention by attacking Culp's Hill while Longstreet hit the center.

More of Longstreet's troops under General George Pickett had arrived. These men would spearhead the attack after a massive cannonade softened up the Union line. Meade held a conference. Lee was too tired to talk; he issued orders and went to bed. This shows that General Lee wasn't as energetic as Lee normally was.

Thus ended July 2, 1864:

Lee's plans for the 3rd didn't go as planned. Ewell was to attack when Longstreet did but the Yankees attacked Ewell at dawn. Ewell had to start fighting then and not as a single unit, as planned. There were desperate struggles but neither side did much more than die. The lines barely moved by noon, the Battle at Culp's Hill was over.

Longstreet wasn't happy about anything at Gettysburg and the frontal charge Lee had ordered didn't change his attitude. He told Lee that he felt it was unwise to attack. Lee wouldn't listen so Longstreet went and talked with the three commanders who were to lead the attack. They were Virginians, George Pickett and Issac Trimble, and North Carolinian, Johnston Pettigrew. Because Pickett was senior, he was the top field commander.

At 1 P. M. the barrels of 170 Confederate cannons belched smoke and iron toward the Union line on Cemetery Hill. Federal artillery replied. The cannonade went on for almost two hours. The Confederates thought they were pounding the Blue Line but most of their shells were going over the Yank's heads and doing little damage. The Southerners saw some Union artillery pull off line and thought the Yankees were running low on ammunition. This is when the infantry attack began.

At 3 P. M. about 12,500 Southern soldiers stepped on to an open field. Lee had ordered 16 to 18,000 to attack but Longstreet said he couldn't get them all ready by charge time. The cannons on both sides went silent after the barrage; it seemed to be very quite indeed. It was a slow walk of men who seemed to be in a parade more than going to battle. They were saving their breath and energy for what was to come!

The Yankees weren't out of ammunition. They had plenty of long range solid shot and exposing shell and short range canister or grapeshot. When the Rebels got in range, Union cannon spoke. Solid shot tore big holes in the ranks while shells exploded over head. Many men fell; the walk became a charge (run). Southern men moved together to reform the ranks that the artillery had blown open. Near the Emmitsburg Road the pace slowed as the army either pulled down a rail fence or climbed over it to get to the Yankees. Yankee infantry knew that the Gray Backs were now within range and they loosed their muskets on the Rebels. The Confederates were now at close range and Union artillery switched to canister. Canister is a big can filled with lead or iron balls. It makes the cannon like a big "shotgun." The air was filled with balls and the ground with dead and dieing Southern soldiers. The noise was deafening. Smoke made it so they could neither see nor breathe. Death was everywhere. Each cannon report was followed by parts of men's bodies flying through the air. The losses were too great and the confusion too much to maintain a united attack. Now it was small groups of men, leaderless; unsure they groped toward the Yankees line. Despite unbelievable losses the Southern Boys pushed forward. Lewis Armistead took his hat off and put it on his sword so his men could see something to follow. He and about 200 other men went over the wall; the first line of the Union center was broken! Again it was Hancock, not Meade, who was there to stop the Rebel breakthrough. The bravest of men fought, Armistead was killed, the Union line restored. Those Confederates, who could, ran, stumbled, crept, and limped back toward their lines. What is known as Pickett's Charge was over. Lee met the remnant of men he had ordered to charge into hell. Here again Lee showed he stood above other men. In defeat, he still stood tall. Unlike so many who blamed others, Lee said over and over, "It is all, my fault."

Stuart did no better. He was intercepted and defeated by cavalry under George Custer.

Both armies stared at each other on the Union's birthday, the 4th of July; neither side attacked. Late on the 4th, General Robert E. Lee and his Army of Northern Virginia began to move toward the fords on the Potomac. The wagon's Stuart had captured were filled with wounded. The wagon train snaked out over 17 miles in length. Each bump, and there were many, brought forth cries of pain from the wounded; for there were many. The wagon floors were covered by blood and the rain washed the blood to the ground. Many, who were wounded when placed on the wagon, were dead when the wagon stopped.

United States figures are more accurate. There were 3,070 killed, 14,497 wounded, and 5,434 captured and/or missing. Confederate States of America estimate the dead at 2,592, 12,706 wounded and 5,150 captured and/or missing. Both armies were in very bad shape but Lee's had taken a far greater percentage loss. The total body count was over 43,000; this was the biggest battle ever fought in the Western Hemisphere. This battle is the one that is most often re-fought. Veterans on both sides wrote and spoke and argued about this battle. Historians still do. The biggest "what if" factor is, "what if "Stonewall" Jackson were there?" The most questioned decision is Lee's order that sent Pickett across that open field." There were many factors that led Lee to that command decision. He believed the South's best chance to win the whole war was the center of the Union line. He could have reasonably expected more damage to the Federals from his cannon fire. He could have reasonably expected several more thousand men to attack than did. Even without those reasonable expectations, the Union's first line was broken; only a little push more and the Battle of Gettysburg would have been a Southern victory! Almost to a man, Lee still had the trust of every man under his command. His soldiers called him "Marse Robert." That is to say, Master Robert, as if he were their good owner and they his good slaves. If questioned, most would just said, "What ever Marse Robert ordered us to do; it was the best thing to do."

Neither Lee nor the pursuer, Meade, made great speed as they headed toward the fords on the Potomac. Lincoln urged Meade forward! Davis sent out desperate appeals to his army to send troops to protect those fords.

The rain that fell on the armies and on the land raised the level of the Potomac. It was a slow and difficult process to cross over the river. At Williamsport, Meade had Lee with his back to the water and no place to go and both generals knew it. Lee prepared for attack. Meade counted the cost of attacking Lee and decided not to do it. Lee had to leave some of the wounded who had groaned in those wagons since Gettysburg at the fords. They were made prisoner of the Union Army. By the 15[th,] Lee's beaten army was back in Virginia.

When the third day's battle at Gettysburg was coming to a conclusion; things were also coming to a conclusion half a country away at Vicksburg. It took the Confederate Army a month to reach Gettysburg; it took the Federal Army a year to reach Vicksburg. Why Vicksburg? The Union Navy and Army had been working north from New Orleans, Louisiana and south from Cairo, Illinois. By July 1863, the only place where a Southern railroad crossed the Mississippi, the only place that the two parts of Dixie was held together was Vicksburg. President Davis said it was "...the nail head that held the South's two halves together." Without Vicksburg the Department of the Trans-Mississippi (Texas, Arkansas, Louisiana and the territories) would be cut off from the rest of the country. Both countries knew that food, primarily beef, and wool for uniforms came from Texas over the rails of the Southern Mississippi through Vicksburg to the Confederacy. Also, manufactured goods and the raw materials of war flowed to the country via Mexican ports. A primary need was mercury. The South had no such deposits but for the rifles to fire they needed a mercury-fulminate percussion cap. Southern weapons wouldn't fire without mercury and the Spanish connection was the main way it got into Dixie.

Grant lost many a good man trying to take the city from the water but the bluffs where Vicksburg was located and the strong Rebel positions had stopped him dead. So as was seen, he put his army south of the town, drove east over land, took Jackson. Then he turned west to attack the city from the land side from the west. The commander of the department was Joseph Johnston and the commander of Vicksburg itself was John Pemberton. Together their armies didn't match Grant's in numbers or strength and their armies weren't together. After the Battle of Champion's Hill on May 16[th,] Pemberton fell back to the city and Johnston was outside. Pemberton couldn't fight his way out and Johnston couldn't fight his way in. This is when the Siege of Vicksburg began.

On the 19th, Grant stormed the city. 1,000 Yankees fell and the city stood. On the 22nd, Grant pounded the city with 200 field pieces by land and Admiral Porter threw 200 pound shells by water. After hours, thousands of Yankees charged with bayonet fixed. They fell in "windrows" (Like hay raked into rows to dry in the wind.) Grant could easily see that his soldiers were falling and going nowhere, so he ordered more of his men to bleed and die. Over 3,000 of his men became casualties, while "Grant (was) glumly sitting his horse and whittling a piece of wood...." His army numbered over 70,000 so he didn't worry; he still had 67,000 to go.

Grant decided that if he couldn't outfight them, he would "out camp the enemy." A road was made around Vicksburg and to the Mississippi so that plenty of food got to his army. All roads to Vicksburg were cut so that no food got to the city. The city was shelled by day and by night. Trenches were dug as close as possible to the defender's lines. The lines were so close the soldiers shouted insults or jokes and sometimes swapped tobacco, coffee and newspapers. Vicksburg was under constant pressure. Time was Grant's ally and the South's enemy.

Grant's artillery rained iron on the town until virtually every home was damaged or destroyed. The citizens left the comfort of home and dug caves into the muddy hillsides. The Yankees began to call Vicksburg,

"Prairie Dog Village." Soon the food supply for army and citizens was all but gone. There were peas growing on the banks and dead horses and mules in the street so the people ate those. There were some frog, snakes and rats so they ate those. There were even reports of boiling the leather from shoes until it too could be swallowed. Soldiers and citizens watched the eastern sky for a sign that Johnston was coming to save them.

Grant called upon those who had mined coal before they had learned to kill. They tunneled under the Southern line, packed the hole with 2,200 pounds of gunpowder and lit the fuse. There was a great hole made in the earth and the sky filled with dirt and smoke but few Rebel defenders died. They had heard the Yankee diggers, and formed a new line from which to kill the attacking Yankees. More Union soldiers fell but the line held!

Grant didn't mind wasting gunpowder and lives so he ordered an even bigger tunnel, even more gunpowder and an even bigger attack. Those who fought didn't like wasting their lives and their officers talked Grant out of another tunnel.

Grant didn't need a bigger tunnel. General Time and General Hunger were winning the Siege of Vicksburg. As Lee attacked on the first day at Gettysburg, Pemberton called his senior commanders together. "Can we fight our way out?" he asked. "No" was the answer. The men are too weak from hunger to march and fight. Two days later on the 3rd of July,

Pemberton sent a message, under flag of truce, to Grant. The note said, let us end "…the further effusion of blood." Pemberton asked for terms of surrender.

At first Grant wanted to keep the name the newspapers had given him and said, "Unconditional Surrender only." Later in a face-to-face meeting with Pemberton, Grant said he would allow the Southern soldiers (not officers) to be paroled on the spot instead of being sent to Yankee prison camps. Pemberton knew he had the best deal he was going to get. Pemberton was born in the North and some called him a "Northern man." On July 4th the city, "the Gibraltar of the west," fell to the Yankees. To the credit of the common Union soldier there was no celebration. To the credit of the City of Vicksburg there was no celebration of the 4th of July until the end of World War II.

Those first days of July sealed the fate of the Confederate States of America. The country had lost too many men at a small town in Pennsylvania; the country had lost a crucial piece of real-estate on the Mississippi.

George Pickett

CHAPTER 11 JULY, 10- SEPTEMBER 21, 1863

Because the prisoner-of-war issue spanned the entire war, an incident that happened on July 4 was held for this chapter. Vice President Alexander Stephens risked his personal safety by climbing on board a gunboat at Richmond and moving down the James River. He wished to talk to Yankee authorities about this great military-humanitarian issue. The South had taken more prisoners in battle than the Union had. The Confederacy didn't have enough food to feed its own army. It was very hard on the South to provide food, clothing and shelter to enemy prisoners. Men captured alive on the battlefield were dieing in prison. Stephens wanted to talk about an increase in the exchange rate of prisoners and maybe even terms to end the whole war.

Lincoln was well aware that the South had little and it was much harder on the South to hold the prisoners than the North. Lincoln did not want his war to end until the people of the South were in bondage to the North. He sent word to Hampton Roads, before Stephens arrived, not to meet with the Vice President. When the war did end, many Southerners were imprisoned and at least one executed because Yankee prisoners died in camps Southerners ran. When, in fact, it was Lincoln who refused to save these men.

During the first part of July, Gen. John Hunt Morgan continued his raid heading north through Kentucky toward the Ohio River. Pro-Southerner, Pro-

Peace, Copperheads took over much of Huntington Indiana. The Union Army had to come and take the town back from its people. The Federal leaders feared that Copperheads may rise up and help Morgan if he got to Ohio. Also, Lincoln's Draft Act was starting and the Union citizens did not like it.

On the 10th of July, Union troops landed on Morris Island near Charleston, South Carolina. The Yankees were determined to take Fort Sumter. The next day they attacked, Fort Wagner and the Yankees invaders fell; the fort held.

On the 11^{th,} the names of those to be drafted were drawn. On the 12^{th,} those names were published in the newspapers. On Monday the 13^{th,} the North exploded in riot! The biggest riot, with the most press coverage, was the riot in New York City. The worst civil violence in the history of the country had just started! There were many reasons the people rioted. Lincoln had changed the war from one to "Save the Union," to "Free the Slaves." As seen, one fourth of the army had deserted because they weren't willing to die to "free the niggers." The Draft Act also allowed those with money to buy their way out of service. This was also playing on a background of a strong peace movement, "too many men have already died to force the South back into the Union." There was also a strong Copperhead movement that would fight the United States Government to stop this "unjust war."

In New York City there was "seething unrest." The draft headquarters was taken and burned. Draft officers were beaten and killed, their houses burned. Businesses were looted. Police, fireman and soldiers tried to stop the crowd but they were outnumbered. "...crowds tore through the streets spreading destruction and death." Many in the crowd were yelling, "hooray for Jeff Davis." The seething hatred of the Negro came to the surface. A Negro church and orphanage were burned, houses set afire and Negroes shot or lynched. Troops that fought the enemy at Gettysburg were sent to fight the enemy, their own people, in New York. Lincoln needed some one who would deal with the citizens ruthlessly; the Beast Butler, would command. Over 1,000 people were killed or injured and over $1,500,000 in property damage was done. The rioting continued until the 16th, when enough troops arrived to put down the revolt. Lincoln then announced that the draft was suspended until August 16th. By that date, enough troops would be in the city to stop the will of the people. Riots also took place in Troy, Boston, Portsmouth, (New Hampshire), Rutland, (Vermont) and Wooster, (Ohio).

Also on the 11th, Lincoln had the *Missouri Democrat* in St. Louis closed because they wrote some bad things about him. Morgan crossed the Ohio River at Harrison and headed towards Cincinnati. Union troops occupied Natchez and Yazoo City.

In far off Japan on the 16th, the *U.S.S. Wyoming* was trying to catch the Confederate raider the *Alabama*. The Japanese were in an anti-foreign mood and attacked the Union man-of-war. The *Wyoming* fought off the attackers and the first naval engagement between the two countries was won by the United States. At Jackson, Mississippi Johnston had to leave the city to Sherman because the Yankees outnumbered and outflanked him. Sherman wrote Chief of Staff, Halleck, the "United States has the right and power...(to) take every life, every acre of land, every particle of property, everything to us that seems proper...I fight for one purpose, a Government independent of niggers, cotton, money...."

At Honey Springs, in Indian Territory, on the 17th, Union General, James Blunt, attacked Confederate General, Douglas Cooper. Part of the Northern Negro troops fought Southern Indian troops. The South ran out of ammunition and had to retreat.

For months the Union had wanted to attack the South's only source of lead (bullets) at Austinville, or one of the last places where the South could get salt (food preservation) at Saltville, Virginia. However, it was believed that the Confederate forces were too strong to make such a raid. Because of Southern newspapers, Union commanders knew that troops were being shifted from the area to cover the fords at the Potomac. The time had come! Col. John Toland left his camp near Charleston, (W) Virginia with about 1,000 mounted troops and headed toward Saltville. After he realized that his column was discovered and Saltville readied for an attack, Toland decided to hit the Virginia-Tennessee Railroad at Wytheville and then the lead mines.

The South had little to send. Two small companies and 130 civilian employees from the headquarters, at Dublin, were sent by train to Wytheville on the 17th. Here 40 "old men and young boys" joined them. The whole force was less than 300 weak but when Toland's thousand came to town; they were greeted with a hail of bullets. Even women fired on the Yankee column from their windows. Toland was killed, his second in command seriously wounded as the Yankees took the town. A number of citizens including at least one "faithful slave" were shot dead. The Courthouse and many homes were burned. Women were insulted. The town looted. Even though the Yankees won the battle, the third in command decided to retreat north and not hit the lead mines. When the barbaric Yankees left town, they left their wounded to the care of the very citizens they had defiled. The wounded were well taken care of.

In order for the Yankees to get to Fort Sumter they had to take Fort (Battery) Wagner on Morris Island. The 54th Massachusetts Colored Infantry was used as "cannon fodder" as the white officers led the Negro troops to their deaths. On the 18th, many Yankees fell but Wagner stood. This loss showed the Union commanders that it wasn't going to be a quick victory. Charleston and the forts were placed under siege. The

"Swamp Angel" a mortar that fired a 200 pound shell was used against the forts and the city.

By this date in Ohio, Morgan was getting into trouble. His path was often blocked and his tired men and horses were constantly pursued.

Despite what had happened in the North, President Davis called for a stricter enforcement of the Confederate Draft Law.

On the 19th, Morgan tried to cross the Ohio at Buffington Island, and 820 of his men were lost. The command was still trapped north of the river.

On the 20th, the Cincinnati Chamber of Commerce expelled 33 members who would not swear loyalty to the Union. In New York City, merchants passed the hat to collect funds to help the Negroes, who had been burned out of their homes.

On the 21st, Lincoln asked Secretary of War Stanton to raise more Negro troops. The more Negroes they could get, the less white boys that would be drafted. The Negro population of the North was 1% but they supplied 10% of the troops.

On the 23rd, Meade tried to stop Lee's retreat by cutting the Southern Army off at Manassas Gap but the army got through before the Yankees could plug the gap.

On the 26th, Morgan and the last of his men surrendered at Salineville, Ohio. His exhausted men and horses numbered 364. Morgan and his top officers were not considered prisoners of war. They had looted and burned almost as badly as had the United States Army.

Morgan's group was placed in the bottom of the Ohio State Penitentiary in Columbus. Here green mold grew on gray uniforms and Morgan vowed that if he was ever free; he would never again be captured.

On the 28th, Meade worried and wondered where the "Gray Ghost," Col. John Mosby, would strike him next. Mosby and his small group of Partisan Rangers liked to take Federal wagon trains and escape before the Union Army showed-up. Meade had to use too many men to guard against Mosby.

While Meade worried about Mosby; President Davis worried about where and how the Confederacy could get more "horseshoes." The South had so little.

The Yankees didn't treat them like full soldiers. Negroes received less pay and couldn't be officers but when Southerners captured, these less equal troops and treated them less equally; the Yankees complained. On the 30th, Lincoln told the South to treat them as real soldiers even though the Union didn't. He didn't want them sent back to their rightful masters. The Union Army had gone to a lot of trouble to steal them. They were Federal slaves now, the Union government owned them. The Southerners knew that some of the Negroes were run-away-slaves, others had been captured and forced to fight. In either case, they were back in the South trying to kill their masters. They deserved to die, like any traitor; to be re-enslaved was a kindness they didn't deserve. Lincoln's decree played well in Europe to make them think the war was about slavery and not about a people who wished to throw off the heavy yoke of an oppressive government. Secretary of War Stanton, with Lincoln's approval, decided to punish the Southern Army by punishing the Southern prisoners. Rations were cut even further, blankets and tents were not given to prisoners and men were placed at "hard labor" and "torture was common."

Torture included "Pointing for corn." Here soldiers were forced to stand stiff legged and bent and touch their toes. They held this pose until they fainted. Some men were "Suspended by their thumbs (but)…remained as dumb as oysters, although suspended until the balls of the thumbs absolutely burst open." Some men were forced to ride "Morgan's Mule." This torture was named in dishonor of the Southern general that they feared and hated. Here a 2" X 4" twenty feet long was suspended at horse's height off the ground with the 2" side up. Men were forced to rock (ride); thus smashing their testicles and they fainted. Some men were so hungry that they bribed guards for the privilege to eat from garbage cans.

Earnest Wart was a Yankee, who was captured early in the war and held in a Southern prison. Later in the war, he was a guard at a Northern prison. He compared both and believed that prison life in the South was much preferable to that in the North. There was a difference in the character of the peoples.

Despite the fact that the South had less to give to their prisoners; the prisoners were treated better. During the war the South captured 270,000 Yankees. The Yankees captured 220,000 Confederates. The death rate was too high for Northern prisoners, 9%. The death rate for those held in Northern prisons was even worse, 12%. The prison with the highest death rate for the whole war was located at Elmira, New York.

By the first part of August, what had happened in July was sinking in. The Confederacy had been dealt heavy blows. The North was rejoicing and a depression was setting in, in Dixie. However, the people of the North knew that Lee wasn't beaten and that Fort Sumter still stood. President Davis gave any soldier who was AWOL 20 days to report for duty. In a speech, he spelled it out to the Southern citizens, "...no alternative is left you but victory, or subjugation, slavery an utter ruin of yourselves, your families and your country."

On the 5th, Gen. William Averell started a cavalry raid from Winchester. The next day, by Lincoln's proclamation, the Yankees had a day of thanksgiving to God for their recent victories. Mosby and his men gave thanks to God for all the food they had captured from a large Union wagon train. England had officially swung against the Confederacy but the subjects of the colony of Cape Town, South Africa cheered loud when the *Alabama* came into port.

On the 10th, Federal forces under Gen. Frederick Steele began a drive on Little Rock, Arkansas.

William Averell   Alfred Duffie

On the 16[th,] Rosecrans and his Army of the Cumberland began to move toward Chattanooga, Tennessee.

The next day, almost 1,000 shells pounded Fort Sumter. There was much destruction but the South held. On the 18[th,] the Yankees did what they did on the 17th and the South still held. In Washington, Lincoln personally tested the Spencer Repeating Rifle.

By the 19[th,] there were enough troops in New York City to stop the will of the people, so Lincoln's draft could start again. In (W) Virginia, Averell destroyed a saltpeter (used in making gunpowder) works near Franklin.

On the 20[th,] Col. Christopher "Kit" Carson began a campaign against the Confederate Navajo Indians. There were many atrocities committed.

The Yankees had bombed Fort Sumter for many days but the fort stood defiantly. Not being able to take his military objective, Gen. Q. A. Gillmore threatened citizen's lives. On the 21st, he demanded the fort surrender or he would shell the city. The fort did not surrender.

It was called "Bleeding Kansas" even before the war began. There were atrocities committed here before the nations knew that they were at war. On this date, William Quantrill with 450 Confederates and some Partisan Rangers took Lawrence. The rangers included a number of people that history would not forget; the Cole brothers, the Younger brothers, the James brothers (Frank and Jessie) and "Bloody" Bill Anderson. The Yankees had murdered many in Osceola, Missouri. On the 15th, the Yankees went after pro-Southern females. They abused some during the questioning period. After questioning them, the Southern women were locked in a rickety old building. Some said it collapsed because too many were inside. Some said it collapsed because the Yankee guards started pushing on the weak walls. What ever the cause, several women were killed and many were injured. After the collapse, Federal soldiers offered no assistance but stood by laughing heartily at the helpless victims. One of the dead was "Bloody" Bill's sister. It was "pay-back" time when Quantrill rode into Lawrence. By the time the raiders left the town, about 150 men were killed, some in cold blood. A great part of the town burned but not one woman was harmed.

Charges were later brought against Quantrill by Confederate authorities. He was accused of acting as badly as the Yankees.

During this time, the Yankees tried a unique and daring raid against the Virginia-Tennessee Railroad. About 30 Yankees traveled by night using a compass (straight line direction) and invaded the Department of Southwest Virginia. They traveled undetected until they were within a few miles of the railroad when they were discovered near Marion. Some were killed, some captured but the railroad kept rolling.

By the 23rd, over 5,000 cannon rounds had hit Fort Sumter. It was a pile of rubble with only one gun in service but it was a Confederate gun!

While Meade, in Virginia, was complaining about Mosby, Gen. Thomas Ewing issued the infamous Order Number 11 in Missouri. "All persons who could not prove that they were loyal" in the counties of Jackson , Cass, Bates, and Vernon, must leave their homes. Over 20,000 men, women and children were forced out with nothing but what they could carry. Their homes and crops were burned. Their hearts and pocketbooks were broken but their defiance of the Union Government grew! Quantrill is branded an "outlaw" to this day. Only the descendants of those who lost everything, remember Ewing's name.

On the 26th, Averell was stopped near White Sulphur Springs. Part of the Confederates, who stopped him, were under the command of Col. George Patton. His grandson was famous in WWII.

In Charleston Harbor, the Confederate submarine the, *H.L. Hunley,* sunk by accident drowning five daring men. Despite the danger and loss of life the boat was re-floated; it would try again.

It was becoming daily routine, Union artillery pounding away at the very symbol of Southern Independence, Fort Sumter. The cost in time and powder far outweighed the military need. The fort may have been in ruins but they were still Southern ruins!

On the 1st of September, Fort Smith, Arkansas fell to the Federal invaders. Knoxville fell to Burnside on the 2nd. In Alabama, the legislature passed a resolution allowing Negroes to enter service in that state. Also on this date, Lincoln admitted what was already known about his Emancipation, it "...has no constitutional or legal justification except as a military measure." He, himself, admitted it wasn't about morality and was unconstitutional.

By the 4th, Rosecrans had passed over the Tennessee River at Bridgeport, Alabama. Bragg's Confederate Army at Chattanooga was threatened from both the south and the west.

In Mobile, Alabama there was a bread riot. In New Orleans, Grant was drunk when his horse fell on him. He was partially disabled for weeks. He should have known that drinking and riding don't mix.

More evidence that Lincoln's lying proclamation was having the desired effect in England came when two ships being built there, for the Confederacy, were seized by the English government. Also, on the 5[th,] there was a skirmish near Tazewell, Tennessee. The skirmish wasn't important but it showed further weakness in the South. The Union Army was closing in on the all important Cumberland Gap and the South couldn't do anything to stop them. On this date, President Davis would read an editorial in the *Charleston Mercury* saying Davis "...has lost the confidence of both the army and the people."

After a massive bombardment of Battery Wagner, which included 6 monitors, on the 6[th,] Confederates withdrew during the night. When the Yankees attacked on the 7[th,] they took an empty pile of rubble. The enemy demanded that Fort Sumter also surrender but it didn't.

Finally on the 8[th,] Dixie got some good news. A mighty fleet of ironclad gunboats and troop transports moved toward Houston, Texas. From a partially finished earth work with few men and few cannon, the Dixie Boys let go. The first two gunboats were hit and forced to surrender. The rest of the fleet ran, "It was a humiliating Federal failure...."

On the 9[th,] Union forces stormed Fort Sumter. Confederate small arms fire dropped 125 of them and the fort still held. In Richmond, President Davis approved a plan to send Longstreet to reinforce Bragg at Chattanooga. What Davis didn't know was that Bragg on this day had withdrawn from that city. Bragg had lost middle Tennessee. He had failed to stop or slow Rosecrans so he blamed his officers for his failures. Bragg had cause to accuse because at times his officers did not attack when ordered to do so. To say the least, Bragg's officers were not a happy crew.

On the 10[th,] Little Rock fell to the enemy.

On Sunday the 13[th,] twenty crewmen from the *USS Rattler* decided to attend church in Rodney, Mississippi. It was the Confederate cavalry that was called upon to take collection that day; the collection included all twenty crewmen.

On the 15[th,] Lincoln, in effect, admitted that the people of the United States had largely rejected him and his war policies, including the Emancipation Proclamation. On this date, he suspended the right of habeas corpus for the entire Yankee nation. This action coupled with the suppression of the Freedom of Speech and the Freedom of the Press shows that the only way Lincoln could stay in power was to destroy the document that gave him right to rule, the Constitution. He could not let the people read the truth, speak the truth and anyone who opposed him would be jailed. Jails were filled with political prisoners. Hooker had said the country needed a dictator; well they had one.

The enemy had cut the country in two by using the Mississippi. Now, it was feared that they could cut the South in two again via the middle Tennessee. Bragg was reinforced. Simon Buckner, John Breckinridge, and William Walker joined Bragg. Longstreet, from

Virginia, was still on his way. Bragg now had enough troops to challenge "Rosy" Rosecrans.

South of Chattanooga runs a river with an Indian name, Chickamauga. Some say it is the "River of Death," others the "River of Blood." At this river, the Union's XXI Corps was detached from the rest of Rosecrans' Army in Chattanooga. Bragg hoped to destroy Thomas Crittenden's Corps before he could get to the city.

The attack was supposed to start at dawn on the 18th but everybody was slow. When they did move, a Union cavalry outfit stopped the Confederate infantry dead at the stream. The reason was the Spencer Rifles Lincoln had approved. The rifle could shoot seven times and very rapidly before being reloaded. It took Bragg all day to get 9,000 men over Chickamauga. That night the most of Bragg's Army crossed over but it was too late. The element of surprise was gone. During the night Rosecrans sent troops to Crittenden.

Neither Bragg nor Crittenden had given orders to attack on the 19th. Both sides were trying to feel the other out. Bedford Forrest's cavalry was looking for the enemy and Yankee, John Brannan, was doing the same, when they met. At first, the Federal infantry was pushing the Southern cavalry back but Gen. States Rights Gist (real name) came to Forrest's aid. Then more Union troops were committed and the second day of the Battle of Chickamauga was on. Throughout the morning each side committed troops piecemeal until thousands of men were engaged. A Union general described it as "...a mad irregular battle...." A private said "...the ghastly mangled dead and the horribly wounded strewed the earth for over half a mile...." At 2 P. M. Bragg sent Maj. Gen. Alexander Stewart to attack the Union center. The Dixie Boys sensed victory. They gave the Rebel Yell and tore into the Union line. It collapsed but the Union commander in that section, George Thomas sent more troops to plug the hole and the Confederate offensive stalled.

"Rooney" Lee   Benjamin Cheatham

As the Longstreet Army traveled, food for men and animals was taken, "impressed," from the citizens along the way. Some citizens didn't give willingly but all gave; and at about 2 P. M. Longstreet stepped from the train. He was met by no one. He and some aids spent the rest of the day searching for Bragg's Headquarters. Longstreet was not a happy chap!

John Bell Hood was a fighter from Texas. He had been waiting for orders from Bragg to attack all day. By 4 P. M. he had received no orders so he attacked anyway. At first his attack was overwhelming. Within minutes, Hood's men had "virtually annihilated" a Union brigade, killing or wounding almost 600 men. Then it was the Federals turn and they turned their cannon on Hood's men. "It was a pity to kill men so," said a Union artillerist. Hood's attack was killed out.

As dark approached, General Thomas was feeling pretty good about himself. The Union line had taken all the South could give and it still held. But the Confederates weren't through. At dusk, Patrick Cleburne's 5,000 hit the Yankees, captured and killed many; they drove the Federals back a mile but still the blue line held.

During the night, both sides moved troops forward anticipating battle the next day. After fighting hard all day, at 11 P. M. Thomas was called to a council of war by Rosecrans. Thomas advised "Rosy" to strengthen the left and stay on the defensive. On the other side of the line, Longstreet finally found Bragg at nearly 11 P. M. Bragg was giving orders for the next day. He would attack the Union center and left flank at dawn.

At 9 A. M., D. H. Hill was still eating his breakfast and reading the newspaper and nothing was happening. About 9:30, Breckinridge struck the Federal's left. At first he pushed them back but more Yanks came and plugged the hole. Then at 10:00 Cleburne attacked and was cut to pieces by dug in Union infantry. Polk sent Cheatham and Walker and they too were stopped dead, by rifle and canister. It appeared that the South was doing little except dieing but Union Commander Thomas thought that there was a hole developing in the line; so a Union brigade was moved to fill the hole. In the den of battle it is easy to misread what is seen. There was no hole to fill but when the brigade was pulled off line and moved; there was now a hole in the Federal lines.

Longstreet's men were rested and they hit that hole. Other Union units in the area were shifting positions at the time. When Bragg saw Longstreet cutting through the middle, he sent John Hood, Bushrod Johnson and Joseph Kershaw to attack. The force was overwhelming. Over 16,000 yelling Rebels smashed through. Union soldiers lay dead or wounded or took flight; almost none stopped to fight. It was a rout in the making! One of the people running was Rosecrans, himself. He was heading toward Chattanooga to save what part of the army he could.

While everything around him was giving way, Thomas held the high ground on Snodgrass Hill. Only Thomas was holding and Bragg threw everything he could at his position. Kershaw, Johnson and Polk lost many men on the slopes while Thomas was still "king of the hill." A future president of the United States was there; Brig. Gen. James Garfield saw Thomas move calmly along the line encouraging his men. He saw Thomas was "standing like a rock" but even the best generals can't fight without ammunition. His army was getting desperate when two brigades joined him; they carried an extra 95,000 rounds with them. Thomas held and the Union Army was not destroyed. Thomas held until nightfall, when he began to retreat. Thomas was still detached from Rosecrans.

The next morning, Thomas was more in the open and without support. This large part of the army was there for the taking but Bragg issued no orders to attack on the 21st. There was a howl that went up at Chickamauga stream that would be heard in Richmond. Longstreet, Forrest and Polk wanted to attack, Bragg. "Why the hell does this man fight battles?" was yelled. Forrest wanted to shoot Bragg.

There was some skirmishing but Thomas was allowed to join Rosecrans in Chattanooga. Estimates put Union loses at 1,657 killed, 9,756 wounded and 4,757 missing. Southern figures were 2,312 killed, 14,674 wounded and 1,468 missing. The Battle of Chickamauga was over and the Siege of Chattanooga was beginning.

When word got back North about George Thomas' stand and how he had saved the Union Army, the people of the North were so proud of him that he received a new name.   From then on, he was "the Rock of Chickamauga!" His parents did not share in his joy. In fact, they had given orders that their son's name was never to be spoken in their presence. He had brought nothing but shame and disgrace on his family. They were Virginians!

Bedford Forrest

Confederate General, Joseph "Jo" Shelby, started a cavalry raid into Arkansas and Missouri. The raid would last until October.

The Yankees were bottled in at Chattanooga. Grant started three divisions from Vicksburg to aid Rosecrans.

On October 1st, Wheeler's cavalry captured a large Union wagon train near Chattanooga. The South controlled all roads into Chattanooga and Rosecrans' food supply was fading fast.

After the Yankees had failed so badly, Gen. Banks launched another campaign into Texas on the 3rd. It took him a month to fail in his second attempt to take Sabine.

The Yankees continued to bombard Fort Sumter and the fort continued to hold. Unable to take their military target, they began to terrorize the citizens of Charleston. They used the "Swamp Angel," a mortar that could fire a 200 pound shell to send "Greek Fire" (a shell designed to start fires) into the city. A great portion of the symbol of Southern Independence was burned.

Efforts to shift war casualties from Union white soldiers to black soldiers were increased. Slaves from Maryland, Missouri, and Tennessee were forced into the Federal Army.

A day of thankfulness for the fall harvest had been celebrated since white men and Indians met in the early 1600's. Lincoln now made it a national Yankee holiday declaring the last Thursday of November to be a day of Thanksgiving.

On the 5th in Charleston Harbor, a small unusual vessel approached the Union gunboat, the *New Ironsides*. The small vessel was steam driven and had a "torpedo" on a long pole. The Confederate, *David*, sent the torpedo into the side of the *New Ironsides*. The ship shook with the explosion. It didn't sink but a new navel weapon was born!

Joe Wheeler's cavalry continued to cut Rosecrans' supply line and more Yankee soldiers were hungry.

Meade had been inactive in Virginia until the 9th when he started the Bristoe Campaign. Lee was not surprised and Meade couldn't turn Lee's flank. There was much marching and skirmishing but Meade couldn't use his bigger army to any advantage. By the 23^{rd,} Meade just gave up.

On the 9^{th,} President Davis visited Atlanta to bolster citizen morale. Here he was greeted by large crowds that cheered him loudly. During this same period, Federal officials were planning the dedication of the National Cemetery at Gettysburg. They were trying to figure out a way not to invite the unpopular tyrant-President Lincoln.

On the 11^{th,} Shelby's cavalry captured Boonville, Missouri.

On the 13^{th,} Clement Vallandigham did not win the governorship of Ohio. He did get many votes. It was a good showing for a man who was deported by President Lincoln for telling the truth.

President Davis met with Bragg at Chickamauga. The President allowed Bragg to fire D. H. Hill.

In Charleston Harbor the Confederate submarine, the *Hunley*, sank for the second time on the 15th. This time the inventor, H. L. Hunley drowned with his invention and seven crewmen.

On the 17^{th,} Grant replaced Rosecrans with Thomas. On the 23^{rd,} President Davis relieved Leonidas Polk from command. On the 24^{th,} William Sherman took command of the Army of the Tennessee; thus relieving Grant.

On the 28^{th,} Confederates attempted to close the only supply line to the Union Army of Tennessee. Confederates often cut the supply line and the Yankees called it the "Cracker line." Longstreet attacked Hooker in Lookout Valley. The South lost 408 men attacking and the North lost 420 defending the supply line. When the sun came up on the 29^{th,} it was still a Union supply line.

During the last third of the month, Fort Sumter was mercilessly pounded by 3,000 shells. After each bombardment, brave Confederates raised the flag over the rubble of what was once a fort.

On the 29^{th,} President Davis approved Forrest's request. He didn't want to ever serve again under Bragg!

By November 2nd, the committee putting the dedication ceremony for the Gettysburg National Cemetery together had come to the conclusion that they had to at least invite the President. They waited until the last minute to send the request, in hopes that he wouldn't come. They asked him to come but not be a big part of the show just, "make a few appropriate remarks." It was hoped that Dis-Honest Abe would be insulted and not come. Dis-Honest Abe had heard of the large happy crowds that had greeted President Davis. President Lincoln hoped that at least one person would clap for him. Lincoln was so unpopular. People were always telling him where to go. It was nice to have somebody to ask him to come and be with them, any place, thought Lincoln. The President accepted.

On this same date, President Lincoln wrote that he was very concerned about "...the possibility of violence at the November elections...." He was afraid that the formerly free people of the United States would get angry because they wanted a free-fair election. More arrests must be made!

In stark contrast this day, "Distinguished citizens, military units, and the general public welcomed President Davis to Charleston...." The Yankees were well aware that the President was in the city so they sent 793 shells of hatred on to Fort Sumter.

On the 3rd, a fierce engagement was fought at Bayou Bourbeau in Louisiana. Neither side won the ground but about 200 more Federals fell than did Rebels.

Knoxville, Tennessee was in Union hands. Old Burnside may be beaten if the South attacked before he could be reinforced. To that end, Bragg sent Longstreet's Corps from Chattanooga on the 4th.

Dictator Lincoln sent a message to General Banks in Louisiana saying that there needed to be "a constitutional government" set up. However, the Constitution of the United States must be ignored because the Yankee Government must "be for and not against the slaves on the question of their permanent freedom." Lincoln was trying to form another illegal state that would vote for him in the upcoming election.

On the 6th, William Averell's Cavalry was on its way to destroy the Virginia-Tennessee Railroad when it ran into Confederates on Droop Mountain east of Lewisburg, (W) Virginia. Averell divided his force and struck the Confederates, under John Echols, from both the front and the rear. The Confederates were beaten.

This day, President Davis toured the fortifications at Wilmington, North Carolina. This was the South's last deep water port.

In Virginia on the 7th, Meade crossed the Rappahannock and attacked Lee at Kelly's Ford . Lee fell back across the Rapidan. Thus both armies were where they had been before Meade's Bristoe Campaign.

On the 9th, Federals tangled with the Choctaw Nation in Indian Territory.

Instead of sitting around the White House waiting for invitations that did not come, Dictator-President

Lincoln decided to attend the theater. On this date, he watched John Wilkes Booth in *The Marble Heart*.

In Virginia "Lincoln's little shadow," Gen. Benjamin Butler issued an order on the 11th. Any person who used free speech, "threatening language" toward any loyal (Yankee citizen) was to be arrested; of course, without charge.

President Davis had been having trouble getting the people of North Carolina to pay their taxes. Because of the lack of cash and the army's needs, the tax was taken in kind. That is to say, a wagon load of corn was better than Confederate script. The people of North Carolina didn't want to pay so Davis, on the 14th, had recommended that force be used to get those taxes.

On the 16th, Longstreet had hoped to catch Burnside outside of Knoxville and defeat him. However, at the engagement of Campbell's Station, Burnside was able to keep his retreat line open and fell back on Knoxville. Like Chattanooga, Knoxville was now under siege.

Lincoln's train arrived at Gettysburg on the 18th. There was no official party to greet the President of the United States. He spoke very briefly to a very small group of unexcited citizens at the Wills Hotel.

The next morning a depressed Lincoln had to go to the livery stable and rent his own horse. There was no carriage or escort for the unpopular President. No gentleman rode to an important event, even church, on horseback. No gentleman of rank or means drove his own carriage. Lincoln ride horse back to the ceremony but then Lincoln wasn't a gentleman. The President may have felt slighted as he listened to Edward Everett's "detailed, colorful, two hour address." Lincoln may have thought, "Why should I listen to this guy? It was me and not Everett that caused the deaths of all these brave men. I am the reason for the cemetery in the first place!"

Lincoln's speech "...seemed to excite few...respectful(ly received)" and got "passing coverage" in the press. Lincoln thought his remarks had "fallen flat" and he was "ill" as he returned to Washington. Only after he was dead, did people start talking about the great Gettysburg's Address. It follows with appropriate comment:

"Four score and seven years ago, our fathers brought forth on this continent a new nation: conceived in liberty, and dedicated to the proposition that all men are created equal. (Here he confuses the Declaration of Independence and the Constitution. An understanding of the Declaration shows that the framers meant that all "descendants of white Europeans were created equal.) **Now we are engaged in a great civil war** (Which I started) **. . .testing whether that nation, or any nation so conceived and so dedicated . . . can long endure.** (The answer is "no, of course" I have destroyed the Constitution that founded the nation.) **We are met on a great battlefield of that war. We have come to dedicate a portion of that field as a**

final resting place for those who here gave their lives **that that nation** (not the free union of Southern people) **might live. It is altogether fitting and proper that we should do this. But, in a larger sense, we cannot dedicate . . .we cannot consecrate . . . we cannot hallow this ground. The brave men, living and dead, who struggled here have consecrated it, far above our poor power to add or detract. The world will little note, nor long remember, what we say here,** (I hope no one remembers that I am an after thought and Everett is the important speaker.) **But it can never forget what they did here. It is for us the living, rather, to be here dedicated to the unfinished work** (destroying the free union of Southern people) **which they who fought here thus far so nobly advanced. It is rather for us to be here dedicated to the great task remaining before us. . .that from these honored dead we take increased devotion to that cause for which they gave the last full measure of devotion. . . that we here highly resolve that these dead shall not have died in vain. . . that this nation, under God, shall have a new birth of freedom** (but no freedom for the Southern people). . . **and that this government of the people. . .by the people. . .for the people. . .** (which I have now become the dictator of) **shall not perish from the earth. "**

The Battle of Lookout Mountain (The Battle Above The Clouds), Nov. 24: as stated, Bragg had sent a great part of the army under Longstreet to attack Burnside at Knoxville.

Bragg had 32,000 half-starved troops. Because of the "Cracker Line" he now faced a now well-fed Union force of three Armies of about 70,000 men. Bragg did not know it but the Yankees had broken the flag signaling code and were reading Confederate messages. On the morning of the 24[th,] Bragg controlled Lookout Mountain and Missionary Ridge, by the evening of the 25th, he had lost both.

Generals Grant, Thomas, and Hooker believed the top of Lookout Mountain was impregnable. It stood 1,100 feet above the Tennessee River. Surrounding the top of the mountain is the Palisades, a sheer rock face 50 to 75 feet high. The top was occupied by two Confederate brigades, Walthall's and Cheatham's brigades with Moore's brigade posted up the summit from them.

Grant used Hooker's Division as a diversion. Hooker knew the Confederates had prepared defensive breastworks expecting an attack up the mountain toward Point Lookout. Hooker knew it would cost a lot of men to attack straight up the summit so he attacked the Confederate positions from the south along the side of the mountain.

The Confederates had pickets stationed to prevent a sneak attack but at 7:30 A. M. Hooker's men crossed Lookout Creek and captured forty-two Confederate pickets without firing a shot. The opening was also the turning point of the battle. The Union force made their

John Buford

George Custer

Don Buell

Nathanial Banks

way straight up the mountain because the pickets didn't warn the main army. About 9:00, the line started toward the north end of the mountain. Yankees had to climb huge boulders, cross deep ravines, and go through dense thickets of brush and timber.

Low clouds and fog significantly reduced visibility (Battle above the Clouds). As a result, the Yankees weren't detected until they reached the Confederate breastworks near the north end of the mountain.

The Confederate force of 1,500 defending the western slope was commanded by Gen. Walthall. Walthall's men were thinly spread in a defensive line. The breastworks were made of rocks, boulders, dirt and timber.

Grant thought Hooker's attack would be a diversion but with no shots fired from the Rebel picket, it had turned into the main attack. Sherman was scheduled to cross the river and attack that afternoon. Grant thought Hooker's attack that morning would confuse the Confederates and take some of the pressure off Sherman. It was not to make a major breakthrough.

At about 10 o'clock, a sharp fight took place around Craven's Farm ("the White House") as Hooker moved up the mountain "... A heavy fog covered the scene as both sides brought up reinforcements." About noon the defenders were driven from Craven's Farm to a new position about 400 yards away. Here they were reinforced by the two brigades from the plateau and held this position from 2 o'clock until after midnight, when they were ordered to withdraw.

Reacting to the assault on Orchard Knob, Bragg ordered a third of his troops on Lookout Mountain to Missionary Ridge. This left only 4,000 thinly spread Confederates to defend Lookout Mountain.

When the Yankees arrived at the breastworks about 11:00 am, they outflanked the Confederates. At the same time, another Union force of 3,400 troops crossed Lookout Creek and attacked the lower breastworks. The 15 minute battle at the breastworks netted the Yankees 850 Confederate prisoners. Under heavy artillery fire, the remaining Confederates retreated to the Cravens House.

The breastworks were built to defend against an assault up the mountain. Because the Yankees advanced along the side of the mountain, they were able to easily outflank and enfilade (shoot into from the side) the breastworks.

Union forces reached the Cravens House about 1:00 p. m. where the heaviest fighting took place. The South had a two cannon battery at The Cravens House but the Confederates couldn't use them without killing their own men. The Yankees forced the Confederates from the Cravens House, capturing it and the two cannon. With reinforcements from the top and the eastern side of the mountain, the Confederates established a battle line about 400 yards beyond the

Cravens House. This line, which prevented the Yankees from capturing the Summertown Road (the only road up the mountain), was held until 2:00 a. m. on the 25th. By this time, the Rebels on the mountain had withdrawn toward Missionary Ridge.

The Confederate artillery on Lookout Mountain was ineffective due to cloud cover and the steep angle of fire. The Confederates fired 33 times on the western side and 30 times toward the Cravens House.

It started raining about 4:00 p. m. on the 24th and the night was cold. Wet soldiers on both sides spent the evening shivering and doing their best to stay warm. Before daylight on Nov. 25, not knowing if the Rebels had withdrawn, Union volunteers scaled the Palisades at Roper's Rock and found the Confederates gone from the top. The 8th Kentucky Infantry planted the Stars and Stripes on the mountain top. The Battle above the Clouds was over. Chattanooga was relieved; the Yankees had another victory and the South another loss. Northern losses about 190 men; Southern about 1,250.

On the 25[th,] Grant wanted to stop Bragg from retreating so he ordered an attack at Missionary Ridge. Gen. Patrick Cleburne's Confederates fought like tigers! Hooker and Sherman attacked repeatedly but the Confederate line held long enough to let the Southern Army fall back over Chickamauga Creek. Bragg was able to retreat south with most of his army toward Georgia. The battle for the retreat was much more costly than the Battle for Chattanooga. Union losses were 5,824 to Confederate losses of 6,667.

The Southern siege of Knoxville continued; the Northern pounding of Fort Sumter continued.

With almost double the forces that Lee had, Meade thought he should be able to do something. On the 26[th,] he attempted to cross the Rapidan and turn Lee's flank and make for Richmond; Lee would have none of it. On the 27[th,] Meade headed toward Mine Run Valley but Lee saw him coming and strongly posted the valley.

John Morgan didn't like being a guest of the Ohio Penitentiary System so he and his officers had a coming out party on the 27th. It is believed that Morgan and some of his "Terrible Men" tunneled through granite to breakout. It is also possible that enough money was used to bribe the guards so that the Confederates walked out. Either way, once outside, the Copperheads supplied money, clothes and railroad time schedules, so that

Morgan, "The Devil Himself," rode out of Yankeeland (also called "Yankeedom") and toward Canada.

November 27th, "Death of the Boy Hero:" Sam Davis and his faithful slave, Coleman Smith Davis, were riding south near Smyrna, Tennessee when a group of fellow Confederate soldiers rode along side. These fellow Southerners were, in fact, Kansas Jayhawkers dressed in Rebel uniforms (Jessie Scouts). Sam knew about these cutthroat spies; they even stripped women looking for information and anything else they could see. Sam and his slave were now Union prisoners. Sam was a spy and had information for Braxton Bragg. Sam was taken to the Yankee commander, Grenville Dodge. When Dodge saw what Sam had in his sack, Dodge almost soiled himself! There was an accurate and detailed description of the defenses of Nashville. This was closely held information. Dodge rapidly concluded that he had a spy operating in his headquarters. He told Sam that he would get a fair trail after which he would be hung as a spy; unless Sam told him two things. Who and where was this "E. Coleman" and where did he get those papers? Dodge knew that E. Coleman was operating a spy ring against him. What he didn't know was that E. Coleman's real name was Capt. Henry Shaw and that Shaw was, at this moment, under arrest and setting in a Union prison cell in Pulaski. Dodge tried to scare and bully the nineteen year old but Sam gave not an inch. Respectfully Sam replied, "I would die a thousand deaths before I would betray a friend or my country."

Sam was given a fair trail and sentenced to death. Dodge had Sam placed in a cell so that he could watch his gallows being constructed. The general sent officers and even the Chaplain to try and get the information in exchange for his life. Yankee spies in Confederate uniforms were sent to jail; Dodge had to know who the spy on his staff was! No one got a bit of information from Sam. Sam's slave, Coleman Davis, was in the cell with him. Coleman said he would give the information to save his master's life. Sam said, "No." Watching with interest from one of the other jail cells was Shaw (E. Coleman) and other Confederate spies.

Everyone, Yank and Confederate, in the jail compound knew of Dodges demands and of Sam's refusals. One Federal said, "He showed no fear...." To a captor Sam said, "I know I am in a tight place...never expected to live through the war...life was sweet."

With a noose about his neck and his feet upon the trap door, Dodge's deal "Life for information" was made again. In brief conversations with the officer in charge and the Chaplain, Sam said, "... you may hang me a thousand times and I would not betray my friends or my country...I am doing my country's bidding but that all heaven is sanctioning the act I am about to take..."

The trap door opened, the body writhed, Sam died and the Chaplain led all (North and South) in fulfilling

Sam's last request. They sang in unison, "On Jordon's Stormy Banks I Stand." The veterans of many a bloody battle, wept.

Coleman Smith Davis accompanied his master's body back home. Yankees who caught and killed this Confederate spy helped and showed every kindness as the body was borne back to his home in Smyrna.

General Grenville Dodge went to his grave thinking he had a traitor on staff. The source of the information was another slave-spy, Robert English. He got a job at headquarters as a "porter." After an ink copy was made, he stole the original pencil copy of the Nashville defenses and gave it to E. Coleman's spies.

Being a member of Coleman's Scouts was hazardous duty. Many were captured, many were killed; two were executed without a trial. One, Dewitt Jobe had his "eyes gouged-out and tongue pulled-out."

Elsewhere, Longstreet now knew that Chattanooga was safe for Yankees and that Grant would be able to send reinforcements to aid Burnside and Knoxville. In was raining and sleeting and darn cold but Longstreet had to attack before those Yankee troops could be sent. On the 29[th,] Longstreet hurled attack after attack against Burnside's Boys. At one point the South posted its flag inside the Union breastworks. More Yankees came and the flag went. Longstreet could not take Knoxville.

In Virginia, Meade spent the day pronging Lee's line for a weak spot; he found none. By the last day of

November, Meade had concluded that his big Mine Run offensive against Lee was going nowhere. Lee would stand and Meade retreat.

This last day of the month, was Bragg's last day. He relieved himself from command of the Army of the Tennessee and turned it over to Lt. Gen. William Hardee.

By December 1st, Meade had given up and was pulling his army back into Northern Virginia. Longstreet had given up on taking Knoxville and was pulling his army toward Greeneville, and winter quarters.

Grenville Dodge

On the 7th, the Confederate Congress met in Richmond. President Davis delivered his message. He spoke of battlefield reverses, financial demands, and lack of progress on the foreign relations scene, lack of supplies and men for the army, and regrets that the Yankees refused to exchange more prisoners, and the loss of the Trans-Mississippi. He spoke of the fury of war, the atrocities against the Southern people, especially females and Negroes. He concluded his realistic assessment with, "The patriotism of the people has proved equal to every sacrifice demanded by their country's needs." Davis was a religious man. He knew without Divine interference that it was unlikely the South could stay an independent nation. He was aware of a religious revival, the likes of which had never been seen in North America that was starting to sweep the country.

On the 8th, President Lincoln delivered his message to the United States Congress. He offered "Amnesty" to any and all who had fought against his government if they would but take an oath of allegiance to the Yankee nation. (This, of course, did not apply to the hundreds and hundreds of political prisoners he had jailed.) He again stated that the constitutional right to own slaves was gone. Lincoln could brag that the "lying proclamation" had fooled other governments into thinking the war was about freeing slaves. It had stopped Confederate efforts to get international support. He was proud of the destruction of the Indian Nations, though more remained to be done to them, he said. He was happy the blockade was creating such want for both Southern military and civilians. He was very proud of the military gains and Southern losses. He said, "The crisis which threatened to divide the friends of the Union is past...." He believed the country, indeed the world, should be indebted to him because he had destroyed constitutional freedoms "...for the home of freedom...."

Lincoln's disregard for citizen's rights and heavy handed treatment of the population did keep him in power. It sometimes hurt the Yankee nation but it kept Lincoln in power and that was all that was important to him. A good example of Lincoln's oppression policy going even further wrong came from the border state of Kentucky. Here Lincoln appointed a tyrannical despot by the name of Stephen Burbridge as Military Governor. Being a good Lincoln-ite, Burbridge closed newspapers, burned homes, and arrested anyone he darn well pleased. His mistreatment of the civilian population made the job of Southern troop recruiters easy. One writer put it this way, "It was as if Kentucky seceded after the war was half over." Burbridge deserved and received much criticism but he was often overlooked for something he did do. When Lincoln rewrote the draft rules, where Negroes went before white boys, Burbridge took full advantage of those rules. As Kentucky troops invaded the South, they took any military age Negro, free or slave, prisoner. Each prisoner was now a "volunteer" for the Union Army. Once the draft rules were changed, not one Kentucky white boy was ever drafted! It was a new form of slavery where the slave may be called upon to die!

Elsewhere, Averell continued his raid against the Virginia-Tennessee Railroad. Off of Cape Cod pro-Confederates seized the merchant ship the *Chesapeake*. It was recaptured on the 17th.

On the 9th, Federal troops were called out to suppress a rebellion. The ones who rebelled and the ones who were killed were Union Negro troops. The hatred of being forced to fight, the hatred of being paid less, the hatred of being used as cannon fodder to save white soldiers, the hatred of their new masters, (the white officers) exploded at Fort Jackson, Louisiana. Their revolt was ruthlessly crushed by the Northern Army!

On the 10th, Union forces in Florida destroyed a salt works at Choctawatchie Bay. On the 19th, another salt works at St. Andrew Bay, Florida was destroyed. On Christmas day, Federal gunboats destroyed another salt work, this one at Bear Inlet, North Carolina. The Federals knew that the lack of salt to preserve food was a major bottleneck in the South.

On the 27th, Dictator-President Lincoln and Southern prisoner-torturer, Secretary of War Edwin Stanton, went to see their handiwork first hand with a visit to an infamous prison camp at Point Lookout,

Maryland. They both seemed pleased at the amount of preventable suffering and death at the prison.

The Confederate Congress passed a bill outlawing the "substitution" system on the 28th. Many Southern soldiers had complained that the system made it "a rich man's war and a poor man's fight."

President Davis had, had troubles getting Governor Zeb Vance of North Carolina to collect taxes. The governor didn't want his troops, supplies or food sent out side his state. On the 30th, he wrote the President that he wanted his demands met or he may make "...some effort to negotiation with the enemy." Any words like these between a Northern governor and the Yankee President would have resulted in immediate arrest of the governor.

On the last day of the year, the Richmond *Examiner* summed it up, "To-day closes the gloomiest year of our struggle."

So much had changed in so little time. Both South and North, men were away from home. Families missed their loved ones; loved ones missed their families. Many healthy teenagers or young adults in 1860 were now dead, disabled, imprisoned, deserted and some soldiers who marched off to war simply vanished without a trace; their families never knew of their fate. Women, who had been protected from hard work and had not been in the business world, were now in new roles. At the first of the war, many women encouraged their men to enlist; toward the end of the war some women encouraged their

Lewis Armistead

Richard Ewell

men to desert. Often there wasn't enough food to eat at home; often there wasn't enough food for the soldiers in the field. "If the diet of the Union soldier was bad, that of the Confederate was wretched." The Southern soldier's main course was cornbread, fried in a pan and salt beef or "salt horse" as the soldiers called it. There were fewer acres in crop production and fewer workers. The slaves did a great job and there was never a single slave revolt during the entire war. There were a very few women who moved into completely different roles because of the war. Some became soldiers; some became prostitutes; some became nurses; some Yankee women joined the Sanitation Commission to help improve camp life. The Federal blockade made life harder on both soldiers and civilians. It seemed that everybody in the South missed their coffee. Many blends of roasted nuts, berries and grains were tried to find an acceptable substitute. Southerners seemed to blame their government for this inconvenience because they nicknamed these substitutes, "Jeff Davis Coffee." Confederate soldiers often traded with the enemy swapping tobacco for coffee. The hulls of blockade running ships often contained coffee when war materials were so very short. Salt became so scarce that it was brought in by sea. Many Southern cities, towns and villages were burned and/or were under the harsh rule of the invading enemy. Two sleepy Southern towns in '61 were now bustling, overcrowded world capitals, Richmond and Washington.

Stephen Burbridge

CHAPTER 14 JANUARY 1- MAY 3, 1864

On January 1[st,] the Confederate soldiers got some good news. The privates pay was raised from $11 a month to $18. With an inflation rate of 300% during the war, it was but a small help.

Because the Yankees controlled the Cumberland Gap, they sent troops to Jonesville, to threaten the big salt works at Saltville the last days of '63. The 16th Illinois Cavalry planned to march against the salt works but Gen. Sam Jones attacked them with the 8th Virginia Cavalry and the 64th Virginia Infantry at Jonesville on the 3rd. Most of the 16th was captured along with three cannon and the wagon train. Some of the wounded froze to dead on the field that night. Confederate soldiers gave the captured Yankees their blankets, in some cased their only blanket, because they knew their enemy would freeze to death in the open air boxcars they would ride to prison camp, in Richmond.

To bolster enlistment, Lincoln raised the sign-up bonus to $300 on the 4th but this created an additional problem for the Federal Army. Now many men signed up, got their bonuses, deserted and signed up under a different name in another unit. From this point to the end of the war, new recruits were placed under armed guard so that they wouldn't desert before they got to training camp.

On the 6th, Partisan Rangers successfully attacked the *Delta* on the Mississippi River and many beaten Navajos, "in sad condition" were sent to a reservation at Bosque Redondo.

One lieutenant and one private with the 21st North Carolina captured 25 Yankees at Waccamaw Neck, South Carolina on the 7th.

On the 8th, at Little Rock, Arkansas David Dodd was executed because he was thought to be a Confederate spy. This same date, John Morgan was welcomed back into the Confederacy at a reception at the White House in Richmond. President Davis replied to Gov. Vance in North Carolina. Davis was the head of a Confederation and did not have the powers Lincoln wheeled as head of a Republic. However, Davis let Vance have it because of the remark in Vance's last letter. "...this struggle must continue until the enemy is beaten...not until then will it be possible to treat (talk) of peace."

On the 10th, William Smith's Union cavalry started operations from Memphis toward Meridian, Mississippi. General Forrest didn't like the Federal cavalry one bit and he was driving Smith back by the 25th.

Also on the 10th, the *USS Iron Age* was sunk by Confederates at Lockwood's Folly Inlet, South Carolina. Despite some Southern successes, the blockade continued to tighten.

On the 11th, Sen. John Henderson of Missouri introduced a bill that would be the basis for the 13th Amendment. This bill proposed outlawing slavery in the entire country. The representatives of the slave holding border-states were upset.

Politics was always on Lincoln's mind. On the 13th, he wrote General Banks in New Orleans to start a "free state" of Louisiana. Since the official policy was that no state was out of the Union but only in rebellion against the Union, this violated Lincoln's own policy. Lincoln thought he may need those votes in the next election, so dirty politics overruled policy. Lincoln told Banks that only "unquestionably loyal" (Lincoln voters) citizens could vote in the new "free state" and that the "free state" had to be abolitionist. Freeing slaves was not a moral aim but an economic aim. "Loyal citizens" would own no slaves. By taking the property of slave owners, it would take their wealth. Slave owners wouldn't vote for Lincoln anyway. This was the first Southern State where the President set up a "free state" to help him politically, it was not the last. Arkansas and Tennessee would soon follow. During this time, it was noted that considerable anti-draft protests were taking place in the mountains of Western North Carolina.

Lincoln wanted to rid the country of all black people but some of them hated being sent to San Domingo, so Lincoln sent a ship on the 1st of February to bring them back.

On the 2^{nd,} the South captured and set fire to the *Underwriter* at New Berne, North Carolina.

On the 3^{rd,} the campaign to take Meridian, Mississippi began. The Yankees wanted to destroy the railroad, supplies, offices, arsenals, warehouses and even the hospitals in this important Confederate city. Sherman left Vicksburg with 26,000 men and was opposed by Leonidas Polk's ill-equipped, ill-fed army of less than 20,000. William Smith left Memphis with his 7,600 cavalrymen. He was opposed by a very small ill-equipped, ill-fed cavalry outfit under a mighty leader, Bedford Forrest.

Sherman skirmished with Polk at Champion's Hill and was back in Jackson by the 5th. By the 9^{th,} he was in Yazoo City. Sherman skirmished at Hillsborough on the 10th and at Holly Springs on the 12th. Sherman took the city on the 14th and destroyed it. He, of course, encouraged his soldiers to become looters, burners and rapists.

Smith was headed to Meridian also but he ran into a Forrest. His bigger, better equipped force was out generaled and outfought at every turn. He turned tail and ran back to Memphis.

During the time the Meridian Campaign was underway, the "Beast of New Orleans," Ben Butler, decided to free some Union prisoners. Ben was now east of Richmond on the Peninsula and he was going after the Federals at Libby Prison on the 6th. Butler was good at treating unarmed citizens badly but bad when it came to armed soldiers the Beast wasn't very good. Ben lost a lot of men and failed badly in just three days.

By the 7th, George Pickett had failed to make any gains against the enemy at New Berne and returned to Richmond. Also on this date, the Yankees re-took Jacksonville, Florida.

France had been mostly neutral in the American conflict but Confederate money talked. The *C. S. S. Florida* left a French port on the 10th.

Harry Gilmor and his Partisan Rangers laid waste to the Baltimore and Ohio Railroad at Kearneysville, (W) Virginia on the 11th.

On the 14th, Federal forces took Gainesville, Florida. On the 16th, the Indians were hammered at Walla Walla, Washington.

Naval warfare had changed when the first armor plated battleship the *C. S. S. Virginia* steamed out of Norfolk. On the 17th, naval warfare changed again. The *U. S. S. Housatonic* became the first vessel in history to be sunk by a submarine. At 8:45 P. M. the *C. S. S. Hunley* rammed a torpedo into the *Housatonic*. The torpedo was on the end of a long pole so that when the torpedo exploded the *Hunley* could pull off safely. The torpedo exploded but the *Hunley* went down. The seven brave Confederates did not live to see how they had changed history.

President Davis had argued that he needed the same type powers that Lincoln had been using so effectively. On this date, the Confederate Congress gave Davis the right to arrest and imprison citizens without a trial.

As the Yankees burned Southern towns and plantations, they made many, many people homeless. Lincoln's Army was glad to see white Southerners suffer but these same towns and plantations were homes to Negroes also. With no place to live and nothing to eat, the Negroes made their way into Yankee Border States. There was no place or jobs for them. They ate and stole and caused all types of problems. The Yankee states that bordered the South made an outcry. "Do something with these niggers." Lincoln thought the factory owners of Massachusetts would want this cheap source of labor. So, on the 18th, Lincoln wrote Gov. John Andrew, if "...Massachusetts wishes to afford a permanent home within her borders, for all, or even a large number of colored persons...I shall be only too glad to know it...." When word hit the street in Irish communities that the "niggers" were coming after their jobs, small riots broke out. Newspapers lambasted the idea. No, Massachusetts does not wish....

On the 19th, President Davis expressed his official concern about the defense of Mobile.

The Yankees had been advancing in Florida, looting and destroying as they went. At Olustee, on the

20^{th,} their advance was stopped. 5,000 Confederates tangled with 5,500 Yankees including the 8th U. S. Colored Troops. The white Yankees said the black Yankees ran first. Soon they were all running and they didn't quit until they reached Jacksonville. This was the major battle fought in Florida. It was a smashing Southern victory! The Yankees were driven back with a loss of 1,861 men to the Southern loss of 934 men.

Tyrant Lincoln had 25% of his army desert when he announced his Proclamation. They thought he was doing too much for the Negro. On the 22^{nd,} Lincoln got wind of a "traitor in his own camp." The "Pomeroy Circular" was published. In it some "Radical Republicans and violent abolitionist" said they didn't think Lincoln was doing enough for the Negro and that they would oppose Lincoln's re-election. Lincoln, of course, thought about arresting the whole lot of them and throwing them in jail with all the other political prisoners he had arrested. Lincoln realized he couldn't take care of the problem by jailing everyone when he found out who was encouraging this group and who they wished to see as President. It was his own Secretary of the Treasury, Salmon Chase!

Bedford Forrest is considered among the toughest fighters the Confederacy produced. On this date, Union General Sooy Smith would have agreed. Forrest's Boys hit Smith near Okolona, Mississippi and just wouldn't quit. The fighting raged for over five miles. Much of the fighting was hand-to-hand. Forrest was the only man on either side to go from a private to a lieutenant general during the war. He personally killed 31 men and had 30 horses shot from under him by those who would kill him. He was a successful slave trader before the war and when he went to war he took most of 50 slaves with him. Because of his training, they became very able cavalrymen. Smith's 6,000 rallied and ran from Forrest's 2,500. When the fight was over 388 Yankees couldn't answer the roll call. Forrest had lost about 110.

Also, on this date George Thomas started his Army of the Cumberland toward Johnston at Dalton, Georgia.

Braxton Bragg blamed everyone except himself for every failure. He seemed to enjoy the confidence of no one except the President. On the 24th, Davis made him Chief-of-Staff for all Confederate Armies.

Lincoln, who wanted no Negro in his army except as a slave at the first of the war, was now always looking for any way he could, to get more Negroes in the army. On this date, he signed a Congressional Act that would pay the enlistment bounty to the master of any slave that joins the army. Once the slave joined, then he became a freeman. Naturally the master only tried to enlist slaves that were more problem than they were worth. The act also allowed those who objected to military service, on religious grounds, to serve in non-combat jobs.

On the 25th, Johnston repelled one of Thomas' attacks on Dalton and sent the Yankees scurrying.

This day, Gen. Sam Jones was relieved of the command of the Department of Southwest Virginia by a man of much note. He was a Kentucky lawyer, a member of that state legislature, Vice President under Buchanan, a presidential candidate in 1860 and now a Major General in the Confederate Army, John Breckinridge.

On the 26[th,] Lincoln commuted all the death sentences of deserters and confined them in prison until the war ended.

On the 27[th,] the first Federal prisoners began to arrive at the new prison camp at Andersonville, Georgia.

Gen. Judson Kilpatrick thought his Yankee cavalry band could make a quick strike on Richmond's Libby Prison before the South could react. On the 28[th,] he started his raid. Kilpatrick moved passed Beaver Dam Station, on his way to Richmond on the 29th. Another cavalry unit under George Custer moved toward Charlottesville, and the University of Virginia. If Custer had of known how weak the forces that opposed him really were, he could have burned "Mr. Jefferson's College." Another Union cavalry did destroy a saltpeter work near Franklin, (W) Virginia.

By March 1[st,] the warning rang through Richmond, "the Yankees are coming." Old men and young boys of the home guard manned the lines. Those who could stand came from the hospitals. Office workers laid down the pen and picked up the pistol. When Kilpatrick realized that the empty works were filled and that he had lost the element of surprise, he took off running. Federal cavalry under Col.Ulric Dahlgren ran into Custis Lee's Confederate cavalry. They didn't make it into the city either.

Also, Maj. Gen. U. S. "Unconditional Surrender" Grant took over field command of all Union forces on this day. Many Northern people objected to "the drunk" but Lincoln only asked what he drank, so that he could send it to all of his commanders. According to Col. Isaac Stewart, Grant preferred to get plastered on "Old Crow Whiskey."

By the 2nd, Kilpatrick was running to the safety of Ben Butler's Army on the Peninsula but Dahlgren was being run like a rabbit into a trap. Custis Lee was chasing him toward Fitzhugh Lee's cavalry. Dahlgren ran into the box but he didn't run out. At Mantapike Hill , Dahlgren was killed and over 100 of his men captured. Dahlgren had orders on him to kill President Davis. The Damn Yankees thought it was okay to assassinate the Confederate President and was directly involved in trying to kill President Davis.

While Dahlgren was dieing, Custer rode back to the Union lines. None of the cavalry raids had accomplished anything of note.

To the west, Sherman's men returned to Vicksburg after destroying Meridian.

To get at least part of what little was coming through the blockade, the Confederate Government decreed that one half of all cargo must be for the military.

On the 6th, Rebel forces forced the Yankees out of Yazoo.

On the 7th, President Lincoln gave the go ahead to building a transcontinental railroad, the Union Pacific. He also told the governor of Maryland that he could release the slaves either at once or over a period of time.

Grant was doing some reorganizing in the Shenandoah Valley. He fired Ben Kelley and replaced him with a German, Franz Sigel.

On the 12th, General Nathaniel Banks with a land army and many gunboats started up the Red River toward the heart of Louisiana. The campaign was as much about stealing Southern cotton as fighting the Southern Army.

It appears that the two Presidents were reading each others news releases. After Davis prayed, so did Lincoln. After Lincoln commuted the sentences of deserters, President Davis did the same.

President Lincoln was so unpopular that he couldn't find enough "unquestionably loyal" people to vote for him in the new state he created, the "Free State of Louisiana." Something had to be done. Some of the "very intelligent" Negroes were given the right to vote.

Lincoln was already stuffing the ballot box in a big way with new states and new voters. His main opponent was shaping up to be a military man, who wanted only peace with the South, Gen. George McClellan.

By the 15th, Banks army was floating toward Alexandria.

Confederates hit the Nashville and Chattanooga Railroad near Tullahoma, and Forrest began another raid on the 16th.

Lincoln wanted to punish those pro-Southern Marylanders; he had written to the governor to free their slaves. It wasn't going fast enough for Lincoln so he wrote a representative on the same subject and called for speed on the 17th.

The people of Georgia saw the Damn Yankees pouring in from everywhere and they thought that Georgia may soon have to welcome the unwanted guest. On the 19th, the legislature sent President Davis a suggestion that "after each victory, make an offer of peace...." They wanted to end the war before Georgia was destroyed.

On the 20th, the *C. S. S. Alabama* pulled into Capetown, South Africa. The English fleet surrounded the ship to keep Federal warships from firing on it. These English were neutral on the side of the South.

Lincoln signed a bill on the 21st to make Nevada and Colorado states even though they didn't have enough population to rate statehood. He hoped that those people in the far west didn't know what a bad president he was and may vote for him.

On the 22nd Lincoln tried to justify his Proclamation by saying, "I never knew a man who wished to be himself a slave." Most people would wish themselves health, wealth and happiness. Few would wish for less than the best in life, for themselves.

A Yankee column left Little Rock on the 23rd headed toward Banks on the Red River. If the two armies could meet they would cut the Confederate Trans-Mississippi in two. Back in Washington, pressure was being brought to fire Meade. He had taken so long to do so little.

On the 24th Forrest took Union City, Tennessee back into the Confederacy. The next day he was on the border of Yankeedom, the Ohio River. Here he attacked Paducah, Kentucky.

President Davis was embroiled in ranker with governors of both, North and South Carolina over enforcement of Confederate Government policy.

The people of Georgia wanted peace so that the Yankees wouldn't come. In Charleston, Illinois the people wanted peace and attacked the Federal soldiers. Five men died and 20 were wounded before more troops arrived on the 28th to put down the revolt.

Through the rest of the month there was skirmishing as Forrest tore through western Tennessee and Kentucky. There was skirmishing as Banks tore through Louisiana.

April 1st was another Day of Prayer for the Confederacy. It didn't appear that God was answering those prayers.

Grant was making his plans and moving his men. On the 4th, he moved Phil Sheridan from the west to head his cavalry in Virginia.

Lincoln was struggling with people, government and himself over the "nigger problem." Lincoln always believed them to be an "inferior" race. He thought this was a "white man's country" and wished to ship all Negroes elsewhere. He wrote, "I am naturally anti-slavery." He felt that slavery was "wrong." However, he did not believe that the Presidency did confer "...upon me an unrestricted right to act officially upon this ... feeling." For political reasons he now was letting some "intelligent" Negroes vote in a Southern state. The right to vote had always been a white man's right until now.

On the 5th, Banks fought and won a skirmish at Natchitoches but the Red River Campaign was just not going as planned. The Rebels wouldn't come out and fight a pitched battle. Always they skirmished and fell back. This Red River kept going and going and the water level was dropping.

General Lee had been studying Grant, the U. S. Congress and Meade. Spring was in the air and Lee knew that his section of Virginia had been too quiet too long. He recalled Longstreet from his winter quarters in East Tennessee on the 7th.

The Red River was so low that Yankee gunboats had a hard time maneuvering but the average Federal soldier didn't know this. The Yankee generals didn't know why the water level was falling but it was all part of the battle plan. Southerners had diverted a major stream up river and its water was no longer helping Yankee boats flow. As the land army marched, it always did so with cannons from the gunboats near by. Banks had Shreveport, in his sights and the Confederates were still falling back. Confederate General Richard Taylor had been falling back and watching. Near Mansfield, the road the Union Army was using was too far from the river for the cannons on those gunboats to protect them. On the 8th, with a Rebel yell, those retreating Rebels, attacked. In a "full scale shooting match," Confederates smashed into the strung out Union line of march. They captured a number of cannon and drove the Yankees in "confusion." Soon panic, the most contagious of all battlefield diseases, gripped the Federals. They broke and ran. Some call it the Battle of Sabine Crossroads but what ever name is used; it was a big Yankee defeat! The Union Army didn't quit running until they reached Pleasant Grove. Union losses were 2,235. Southern losses were approximately 1,000.

While the Federals were losing on the field, the U. S. Senate passed a bill designed to hurt the South financially by granting freedom to all slaves. This bill would one day become the 13th Amendment to the U. S. Constitution.

Apparently Taylor didn't know how close the commander of the Trans-Mississippi, Kirby Smith was. Taylor knew he had given those Yankees a bad licking the day before and he wished to finish them off this day. It was late in the afternoon when the battle got fully underway. Although Banks was expecting the attack, he couldn't stop it. The Confederates drove hard into the Union line. At first it looked like the day would go to the South but a Union counterattack came. Banks retook most of the lost ground. The armies stood near the same positions they had that morning but 150 dead Yankees and an unknown number of Confederates didn't know it. It was very late that night when Kirby Smith arrived.

The *U. S. S. Minnesota* saw a new weapon of war bearing down on her in March of '62; the *C. S. S. Virginia* darn near sunk her at Norfolk. Again she saw a new weapon of war bearing down on her at Norfolk on April 9th, '64; the *C. S. S. Squib* put a torpedo into her side, darn near sinking her again.

The grand plan for Union subjugation of the South called for blockading the South, cutting the country in two via the Mississippi and taking the capital at

Richmond. By '64 the blockade was tight and getting tighter. Grant had helped take the Big River away from the Confederacy; now he was going to take the capital! Grant knew and used the "total warfare" concept better than any other Federal general. He made war on the Confederate army, people, government and land. He used the telegraph to coordinate attacks over vast territories. Many of his tactics foreshadowed a coming conflict, the Great War, or W. W. I. In this conflict, men, weapons, tanks and equipment were thrown wholesale against the enemy. By pure numbers the enemy would be worn down and defeated. Soldier's lives were little more valuable than the guns they carried.

On paper, Grant had to take Richmond. With overwhelming numbers and material he would strike across the entire state at once. There could be no shifting of Confederate troops to meet an attack in one sector because he would attack all sectors at once. Ben Butler was to move on Richmond from the east. Grant was basically going to take over Meade's Army of the Potomac and strike Lee head on at the Rapidan and push him toward Richmond. Fritz Sigel would move south through the Shenandoah Valley and toward the railroad at Lynchburg. George Crook would move from Beckley, (W) Virginia toward the big railroad bridge at Central Depot (Radford). William Averell's cavalry would strike the South's last source of salt, at Saltville or the South's only source of lead at Austinville. In each area attacked, the Union had far more troops and far more equipment. Grant was making his plans and collecting troops and supplies. Grant had over 120,000 men compared to Lee's less than 65,000. Grant knew he could get more; Lee knew he couldn't. The date of the invasion was not set.

By the 10th, Banks knew he was whipped and started to move back down the Red River. Taylor's Boys weren't just going to let the Yankees sail away. They suddenly brought cannon to the shore and shelled those gunboats. Small arms fire struck the fleet and the army, as they retreated. By the 10th, the Yankees from Little Rock knew they were whipped and they started back. The Trans-Mississippi was not going to be cut in two.

Forrest's little band of cavalry had been destroying Union communications, supply depots and railroads while sending Yankees to the after life, as he swept across Kentucky and Tennessee. On the 12th, his force of 1,500 came to Fort Pillow, Tennessee. Forrest told the Federal commander to surrender because he was going to be beaten anyway. Maj. William Bradford decided to be a hero and with his 557 men hold the fort; there were 262 Negro troops in this number. The number of Negro soldiers Forrest commanded exceeded 50. Bradford didn't listen; 231 of his men died, 100 were wounded and 226 were made prisoners. Forrest only lost 14 killed and 86 wounded. There was a large number of dead compared to the wounded and this is where the controversy comes from. Yankee sources are very suspect and only testified to what happened much later. The Yankees claim that a large number of Negro and white troops were "massacred." Southern accounts confirm that lots of men died and a good number were prisoners. In the heat of battle, the Yankees that surrendered were told to go to a particular area and wait for the battle to end. They were loosely guarded. A lot of Negroes were not highly motivated to fight for their new masters and they surrendered en mass. Some prisoners, who had surrendered, still had pistols on them. Using other prisoners as shields they began to fire on the Confederates. Confederates returned the fire and many died. Yes, some innocent prisoners died but it was because their fellow prisoners violated the conduct of surrendered soldiers. It was these few that were responsible for the large number of deaths and the "Massacre at Fort Pillow." Yankees have used this propaganda effectively even to this day. They don't seem to remember the horrible things they did against the South and the Indians.

On the 13[th,] Forrest struck at Columbus and on the 14[th,] at Paducah.

On the 15[th,] the *U. S. S. Eastport* struck a Confederate mine in the Red River. At first her crew tried to save her but they had to give up. It was they that sunk their own gunboat.

Grant's total war cost many Yankee lives. On the 17th, he stopped prisoner exchanges. He knew it was harder on the South to feed the prisoners than on the North. Many a Yankee lad died as the results of starvation because the South had nothing to feed them. The Yankees just delibcratcly kept starving Southern prisoners, even though they had plenty with which to feed them.

In an effort to help Banks, a large number of wagons were sent toward him by the Yankees. Many of the wagons were empty at first and filled by stealing from the Southern farmers. Gen. John Marmaduke didn't like them stealing from the farmers and he didn't want to help Banks. At Poison Springs on the 18th, Marmaduke relieved the Yankees of their stolen cargo. It was a heavy engagement and lots of men fell but when the smoke cleared away, 198 wagons were driven by Confederate soldiers.

In command changes, Sam Jones was sent from Southwest Virginia to replace Beauregard at Charleston. Beauregard was assigned defense along the southeastern part of Virginia and North Carolina.

Southern land troops at Plymouth, North Carolina got tired of watching the action on the water so they built and manned their own ram, the *Albemarle*. On the 19th, these landlocked sailors sunk the *Smithfield* and damaged other Union vessels. This weakened the hold the Federals had on Plymouth and other Confederate troops moved toward the town. On the 20[th,] the town, many supplies and 2,800 prisoners fell into Southern hands!

To the west, Banks continued to withdraw down the Red River Valley heading toward Alexandria.

On the 22[nd,] the U. S. Congress added the motto, "In God we Trust" to Yankee coinage. On this date, President Davis responded to Polk's request for clarification of the captured Negro soldier question. Davis was not changing the policy despite the cruel torture Southern prisoners of war were receiving because of the South's stand. Davis probably thought the treatment wouldn't improve even if he changed his policy. The policy stood, "captured slaves" in Union uniforms were still slaves and must be returned to their rightful owners.

On the 23[rd,] Confederates continued to pound the retreating Banks; this time at Cane River Crossing.

After Plymouth fell, the Yankees had to abandon Washington, North Carolina on the 26th. Having whipped Banks' land army at Cane River Crossing, on this date, Confederates went after the gunboats and a number were damaged.

On the 28[th,] President Davis officially recognized that he was no long the President of the whole country. He made Kirby Smith, the "President" of the department of the Trans-Mississippi; "full authority has been given you to administer...."

On the last day of the month, five year old Joe Davis was playing at the White House when he fell to his death. Now both first families of both countries had lost a son while the father was in office. President Davis prayed, "Not my will but your will be done."

Despite his grief, President Davis addressed Congress on May 2nd. He condemned Yankee "barbarism." "...(their) Plunder and devastation of the property of noncombatants, destruction of private dwellings, and even of edifices devoted to the worship of God; expeditions organized for the sole purpose of sacking cities, consigning them to the flames, killing the unarmed inhabitants, and inflicting horrible outrages on women and children."

On the 3rd, Federal troops attacked the Indians at Cedar Bluffs, Colorado. And Lincoln discussed how best to use the reports of "alleged atrocities committed by Confederates (at)...Fort Pillow."

William Mahone

CHAPTER 15   MAY 4 - MAY 21, 1864

The first part of May, General Lee looked through his telescope at the massive army that lay across the Rapidan east of Orange Courthouse. The genius, Lee, studied the army and Grant's options then he raised his hand and pointed toward the east, "Grant will cross by one of those fords," he said.   Lee knew Grant was headed toward the Wilderness before the first Union boot turned in that direction. After passing through the tangled undergrowth, Grant's Army would be south of Fredericksburg, north of Spotsylvania Courthouse and on open ground.   Here Grant's numbers would simply destroy the Army of Northern Virginia!

Lee was also aware of Butler on the Peninsula; Beauregard was sent to deal with him.   Lee knew of Sigel in the Valley; Breckinridge, from the Department of Southwest Virginia, was sent to deal with him. Breckinridge moved to Lexington and set up headquarters at "Stonewall's" old school, VMI. Most of the rest of the troops from Southwest Virginia were to follow. Lee could read Grant's mind and plans almost exactly but Lee missed Grant's attack on Southwest Virginia, itself.   Breckinridge sent a telegraph to Lee saying he felt sure there would be an attack on the Department. Lee then telegraphed Morgan at Knoxville for him to move his command to defend the area.

On the 4th, Grant's Army started crossing the Rapidan exactly where Lee said he would. Grant knew that Lee would not attack in the tangle of the Wilderness. Because of the dense growth, artillery and cavalry would be useless. Grant pushed his men over those new pontoon bridges; he must get through the Wilderness so he could "crush Bobby Lee."

As soon as Grant committed; Lee committed. Lee ordered his army to converge on the Wilderness!

By late night of the 4th, Lee received news from JEB; the Union Army had stopped moving and was camping for the night. Lee decided to wake them with an alarm at dawn. Ewell and Hill would strike the head of the Yankee column at "first light" and when Longstreet came up his men would attack the exposed flank. While Southern feet rushed toward him, Grant slept peacefully.

On the early morning of the 5th, Federal pickets reported Confederates to their front. Meade thought it was a small band of Rebels and sent a division to clear them out. When the Yankees advanced they "were rocked by a cyclone of fire." It was Ewell's wake-up call and it put a bunch of Yankees asleep, permanently. The surprised Federals broke and ran for their lives. The Confederate attack was halted by a brave Union counter-attack. More men rushed toward the sound of battle from both sides. Charge and countercharge left the lines about where they were. The Union Army was not moving. Ewell was doing his job.

A. P. Hill was trying but he didn't get on the scene in force until noon. By this time, Yankees were there at the intersection where Hill was to attack at "first light." The Yankees were there, in force, and Hill's attack was sent reeling backwards. Meade saw an opportunity and called for more troops to smash Hill. At 4 P. M. the big assault was made against the weakened Hill. The big assault didn't last long or go very far. Highly outnumbered Rebels were dug in on a slight hill and they pinned the whole Union attacking force down.

If there was a "soldier's battle" during the war, this was it. The undergrowth was dense; it hadn't rained much and the brush caught fire; the air filled with smoke; each time a weapon discharged more smoke filled the area. Commanders, on both sides, gave orders and watched their men disappear. Soon no one knew where any one was. No one knew if there was a front line and if there were, where it was. Small groups and sometimes individual soldiers shot, stabbed, clubbed and gouged at the enemy wherever they found them.

The Union attacks died down, darkness came but Longstreet didn't!

In the darkness, Lee received reports from Hill. He had stopped the Northerners that day but his units were cut-up and scattered badly. If the Federals attacked at dawn, as it was believed they would, his force would be destroyed. Now, Lee knew that everything depended on Longstreet. If he wasn't there by dawn, Grant would roll over Hill.

At 5 A. M. on the 6th, the expected Yankee attack came. It had enough men and enough firepower to do what was expected. Hill's line collapsed. A desperate Lee got all the cannons he could find and formed a line. It was load, ram and fire! The Union attack was halted but Lee knew it was only temporary and so did the Yanks.

As the Federals renewed the attack, Lee saw troops coming from the rear. He asked whose troops they were? It was the "Texas Brigade!" Longstreet was here; the army was saved! At this point, one of the most compelling events of the war occurred. It showed how much men could love their leader. Lee, on Traveler, was going to lead the Texas Boys into battle. Battle means death. The Texas Boys surrounded Lee and Traveler, and sat down on the ground. They told Lee that if he was going to the front, where he might get killed, they weren't. Only when Lee moved back to protect his life, did they willingly move forward, perhaps, to give their lives!

Because of the undergrowth and the Rebels, the Federal attack fizzled. About this time, Lee received word from his engineer that there was an unfinished railroad bed that ran along the Yankees' flank. Lee sent several brigades down the track to hit the North's exposed side.

Things were definitely swinging to the Confederate side. The smaller army was beating the heck out of the bigger army but then disaster in the form of one minie-ball struck the South. Smoke, undergrowth, lost men, lost commanders, lost commands all played a part. "Old Pete" Longstreet, Lee's "War Horse," was shot by accident by his own men. About one year before, "Stonewall" had fallen under similar circumstances. The Southern soldier knew all too well what the loss of Jackson had meant; now Longstreet was downed too! As the news spread, the Southern Army's spirit seemed to sink. The attacks lost their fury. At 5 P. M. the last major assault was made on the Union. Part of Longstreet's command drove two Union Divisions in confusion. One of Grant's officers told him that Union losses were very great; he advised Grant to "retreat." Grant would have none of it; a soldier's life meant very little to the Army Commander. Grant spoke to a newspaper reporter who was headed back to Washington to file his story, "If you see the President, tell him, from me, that whatever happens, there will be no turning back." Lee had lost about 7,500 men. Everything in Lee's Army was falling apart. No one really knew how many men the army had and no one really knew how many they had lost. As the Southern Army looked worse and worse; the Northern Army looked better and better. The Yankees knew that exactly 17,666 of their own had fallen.

While Lee and Grant were slugging it out in the Wilderness, the other parts of Grant's plans were taking place. George Crook was making his way from Beckley toward the "long bridge" at Central Depot and William Averell was making his way toward the big salt works at Saltville. Averell was moving his command of 2,500 cavalry and mounted infantry when he took some Confederates prisoner north of Jeffersonville (Tazewell). He questioned the Rebels and what he heard "scared his pants off." John Morgan was not in Tennessee where he was supposed to be. Morgan and his "terrible men" were in the trenches at Saltville; they were backed by artillery and just waiting for Averell! Averell then decided to attack another juicy target, the lead mines at Austinville. The South was well aware that the mines might be a target also but there were no regular troops that could be sent. The home guard from Wytheville was sent with orders to "fight to the last (man)" to save those mines!

When Averell turned east at Jeffersonville, Southern scouts rode to Morgan with the news. Averell was not coming to Saltville; he was after the mines! Morgan immediately loaded all the men he could, 500 troops, on and in a train and sent them to Dublin so that they might help defend the long bridge. He telegraphed Dublin to tell them the men were on their way and that he was moving the rest of his command to Wytheville to intercept Averell.

Crook had been pushing his columns along. His front was mildly bothered by Confederate cavalry under General Albert Jenkins. Crook was slowed more by heavy rains and wet snow than pesky Rebels. Everything seemed to be going his way; he even received intelligence that McCausland's command, the last Confederates in the area, had moved his men toward the Shenandoah Valley.

McCausland had indeed received orders to move and was entraining his men at Dublin when he decided to disobey orders and protect the long bridge. Col. John McCausland moved his men north out of Dublin to Cloyd's Mountain a few miles from Dublin; here he would fight "the battle for the bridge." McCausland placed his artillery near the crest of the mountain. There was a clear field of fire extending down the mountain for half a mile. He placed his infantry, including the home guard, in breastworks in front of the artillery. Every step the Yankees made up the Dublin-Pearisburg Pike (Today, Rt. 100) would cost them dearly.

Early on the morning of the 9th of May, Jenkins cavalry fell back on McCausland's line. Jenkins was older and from the Napoleon era. He would fight this battle the way Napoleon would but Napoleon had no rifled muskets, the war game had changed. Jenkins ordered McCausland to move his guns and men down the mountain.   McCausland objected strongly but Jenkins was a general; the line was moved. The South had 10 guns and 2,400 men, many of this number were untrained home guard. Morgan's 500 were still on the way.

Both McCausland's and Jenkins' lines were set to cover the pike. As Crook approached the mountain, he looked through his field glasses and said, "The enemy is in force and in a strong position. He may whip us, but I guess not."   Crook knew the Rebel force was small. Crook had well over 6,000 men and 12 pieces of artillery. A runaway slave, who knew the area well, was brought to Crook.   The slave agreed to direct the Yankees up a ravine out of sight of the Rebels.

While one brigade was following a slave, Crook opened the battle on the far right flank on the Southern line away from the road. Although the first advances were checked by withering fire, Jenkins knew his men were out of position so he started to shift men and artillery to the right.

Crook saw the movement and ordered an attack on the Confederate left. Jenkins ordered his last reserves to the left and the Union advance was halted as Rebels inflicted heavy casualties.

Meanwhile the first attacking brigade was taking a beating. The flag of the 14th Pennsylvania had 17 holes in it and there were also holes in four of the five flag bearers. Jenkins ordered more artillery to be brought to bear on that brigade.

Both lines broke at about the same time. The Union brigade, led by a slave, popped up not 20 yards in front of the home guard. The guard panicked and ran. Then a regular army regiment also fell back in confusion because of the sudden Federal attack! The Confederate left was broken.

As the Confederates ran on the left, the Yankees ran from the center. Jenkins seemed unaware of what was happening to his left. When he saw the center give way, he thought the whole Union Army was running. He ordered a general attack. Southerners left their protection and pursued the fleeing Yankees. As the Yankees ran, they passed through the line of their reserve force which was laying flat on the ground along a ridge line. As the attacking Rebels came in range the reserve rose and fired. Southerners fell by the dozen and they started to run back. Jenkins, seeing the panic at his front, pulled his sword and charged in to try to put new life in the charge. Jenkins fell wounded; the charge stopped. Then the Yankees started attacking. By the time McCausland got the word that he was now in command, it was too late. The Confederate left and center were collapsing. McCausland ordered a retreat. The panic was now general in the Confederate Army. Their artillery fell into Union hands and men ran for their lives! It was then that Morgan's 500 showed up.

They formed a defensive line and prevented total disaster.

The Yankees lost more men, 688 to the South's 535 but they owned the field and most of the field artillery. Crook pressed toward Military Headquarters, at Dublin. McCausland moved his army toward the only safety, New River. The army had to be moved so fast that supplies and ammunition were left at Dublin. The Southern Army crossed to the south side of the stream in the night. The South had taken a thorough beating and had almost no ammunition. When Crook moved his forces to the north side of the river in the morning, the Confederates had to burn two crucial bridges. When the Ingles Ferry Bridge was burned, it broke over land transportation over the Rock Road (Rt. 11). A ferry was used until the 1930's when another bridge was built down stream. When the "long bridge" went down, it broke the Virginia-Tennessee Railroad for over two months. Slave labor was used to repair the only rail link between Richmond and Knoxville.

Grant had ordered Crook to destroy that bridge and then move along the railroad, "destroying as you go, to Lynchburg." It would seem that Grant's plan was working but Crook discovered two things at Military Headquarters at Dublin. The first thing he found out was that Morgan wasn't in Tennessee; Morgan was on his doorstep. No Yankee wanted to tangle with the "Devil, himself." The second thing he found was a telegram from Richmond. The telegram said that Lee had beaten Grant and that Grant was retreating. It was true that Lee had beaten Grant at the Wilderness; it was not true that Grant was retreating but the telegraph operator did not know that. Crook believed that Grant was retreating. That meant that Morgan was on him now and that Lee could be soon. After a great victory Crook had to retreat!

Averell sent Crook a messenger stating that he wasn't going to Saltville; he was off to the lead mines, via Wytheville. Crook either didn't send Averell a messenger saying he was headed north or the message did not arrive.

After learning that Morgan was at Saltville, Averell took 12 hours to get his command started. Those hours were a gift to the South. Morgan hadn't waited but had started his command toward Wytheville. Averell took a longer route to Wytheville so that his horses wouldn't have crossed as many high mountains. As Averell moved toward Wytheville, his 2,500 men pushed two undermanned Confederate cavalry units in front of them. At about 4 P. M. on the 10th, the two regiments quit falling back and formed a defensive line along a ridge on the Raleigh-Grayson Pike (Cove Rd. Rt. 603 and Rt. 600). Averell wasn't too concerned, it would take a little time but these few men weren't going to stop him. Because of the very hilly terrain, Averell couldn't see that Morgan's Boys were moving in behind those two regiments.

Averell attacked those "two regiments" and was met by a "withering fire" from the Rebels. Averell now knew that he was facing reinforced Rebels; he didn't know it was Morgan. Because of the increased fire, Averell thought he was outnumbered but few of Morgan's men were there at this time. Averell's attacks were turned back and he received word that he was facing Morgan!

Some said that Morgan was, "hungry for revenge for the indignities he had suffered in the Ohio Penitentiary." Morgan said that he was attacking 2,500 with only 750 of his men. "My men fought magnificently driving them from hill to hill. It was certainly the greatest sight I ever witnessed to see a handful of men driving such masses before them...our boys gave them no time to form...this rattled (Averell)."

Averell was being pushed back but he hadn't lost. Averell tried to sneak a part of a regiment around Morgan to surprise him from the rear but Confederates on the hills saw the movement. They attacked the sneaking Yankees. It was Yankees who were surprised and cut-up.

When Averell learned that the sneak attack had been foiled, he could only think of running. He ran to where Crook should be, the Dublin-Central Depot area. Here he learned that Crook was retreating north. He went north and Colonel McCausland followed both of them north.

Once back to safety Averell wrote his report on the Battle of the Cove near Wytheville. This time he won! When his subordinates learned that Averell had written high command a "fairy tale," they tried to set the record straight without calling the boss a big liar. One wrote, "My thanks to the 2nd (West) Virginia Cavalry...while under a galling fire...preserved the rank unbroken... (and) saving the left...." Another wrote, "the 2nd Brigade gave way in some confusion... 34th Ohio...held the enemy...gave time for the broken column to be reformed...thus saving...a shameful rout."

Grant's plan was not working in the Department of Southwest Virginia.

Grant lost the Battle of the Wilderness. Everybody knew that he was supposed to retreat now; just like all the other defeated generals that Lee defeated before him. With Grant, there was "no turning back." Most Southerners were surprised to learn that Grant was still wanting to fight the Great General.

Lee was a master of reading his opponent's mind. Lee thought that Grant may try to move between him and Richmond, thus forcing Lee to fight on a field of Grant's choice or losing Richmond. Before Grant started his move, Lee had a rough road made through the dense forest to another road leading to Spotsylvania Courthouse. Before the first Yankee moved, Lee ordered Maj. Gen. Richard Anderson, who had taken over Longstreet's Corps, to move toward Spotsylvania. Lee also had Stuart's Cavalry positioned to intercept Grant.

At midnight of the 7th, Grant started to sneak around Lee. Early in the morning, Meade, who was leading the advance infantry, came to a complete halt because the road was blocked. What blocked the road was Union cavalry! Stuart had stopped Sheridan and Sheridan had stopped Meade.

Meade ordered the cavalry out of the way and attacked Stuart with infantry. Slowly Stuart fell back toward Spotsylvania. He had to slow the Yankees so that Anderson could be ready to receive.

Just outside of town, Stuart made a stand at Laurel Hill. As Meade's infantry approached one way, Anderson's infantry approached from the other. Meade ordered one of his regiments to clear those pesky Rebel cavalrymen off that hill. When the Yanks attacked, they were cut to pieces by Confederate infantry. Meade still thought he was facing a small group of men and sent more troops to attack. More troops fell. He wasn't facing a small infantry group and Hill and Ewell were marching to join the battle.

As the sun set on the 8th, 17,000 Rebels lay in front of Meade. Grant had arrived. What great plans Grant had made to mislead and cut Lee off. Now, Lee's forces lay right where Grant had intended to march as if to say, "What took you so long?" Grant was very upset.

The Rebels expected the Yankees to attack on the morning of the 9th so they worked feverishly on their breast works. No attack came. Grant was exploring Lee's line. One of Grant's best commanders was also looking things over. Gen. John Sedgwick didn't know that a Rebel sharpshooter was looking him over. Sedgwick would never bother any Rebel again!

Grant decided to outsmart Lee again. This time he sent Hancock's Corps to ford the Po River and strike Lee's flank before Lee knew what had hit him. Hancock didn't move as fast as he should have and darkness stopped his march. On the morning of the 10th, he reported back to Grant that Lee's boys blocked his way. Again, Grant knew he had been out generaled.

Grant recalled Hancock to reinforce the center. If Grant couldn't out general Lee; he would out number him. Massive attacks against Lee's line were launched at 4 and 7 P. M. Massive numbers of Union casualties began to stack up before the Confederate line.

To the east, Meade launched an attack. At first, "numbers prevailed" and the Southerners were driven from their breast works and the line almost broke. At the last minute Ewell's men counterattacked and the Federals were pushed out of the Confederate line. Many a lively Yank in the morning lay dead or wounded by night. The Yankees had taken heavy losses and gained nothing. Every Northerner who wasn't shot or dead, was disappointed, except Grant. Meade's attack had given him hope. Maybe by numbers alone, Lee's trenches could be taken? Grant decided to attack in force at dawn.

During the night, there was a heavy, very damp fog. At dawn, 20,000 Yankees attacked through that heavy fog. In this one attack, Grant advanced with almost half the number of troops Lee had in his whole army. Approximately half of the Confederate rifles wouldn't fire because the powder was wet from that damp fog. Yankees swarmed over the breast works. Guns that wouldn't shoot were used as clubs. The numbers were prevailing. The line was breaking. Grant was winning. A desperate Lee poured more and more men into the "Mule Shoe or Bloody Angle." The "Stonewall" Brigade disappeared that day! Grant committed more men to the slaughter. By afternoon the rain was pouring but the killing didn't stop! "Men stood on bodies and fired blindly at the enemy just a few yards away. Wounded men suffocated in the mud, and corpses filled the trenches." Blood was spilled at Bloody Angle until midnight. Grant now faced about 10,000 less Confederates but there were 11,000 less Yanks for him to attack with.

Grant's plans called for attacking at any point and every point. While Grant had Lee pinned down, Grant ordered his cavalry, under Phillip Sheridan, to attack

Richmond, itself. By the 11^{th,} his force was but six miles from the city. Outnumbered, Stuart was determined to stop him. It was a Rebel victory at the Battle of Yellow Tavern but it was also a great loss. Stuart fell from his horse mortally wounded. Richmond was saved but the brilliant, fearless JEB Stuart, with the plumb in his hat, rode into history. When Lee received news of his death, he was greatly distressed and lamented, that Stuart had "never brought him bad information." Lee was losing men and leaders he could not replace.

Back at Spotsylvania for the next few days, Grant tried to out general and out maneuver Lee. By the 18^{th,} Grant was sure he had out foxed "Bobby Lee." He sent Hancock's entire corps to overrun a weak section of Lee's line. It wasn't weak. Lee was just waiting. Rebel artillery blew Hancock's Corps apart. In minutes, Lee faced 2,000 less Yankee invaders. Again, Lee's men commanded their commander to the rear! They believed that Lee was moving too close to danger.

While Grant was being out generaled in the Wilderness, another part of his plan was being carried out in the Shenandoah Valley. General Fritz Sigel left Winchester with over 8,000 infantry, 2,500 cavalry and three or four field-batteries and moved south, up the valley.

Opposing him was the commander of the Shenandoah Valley Military District, Gen. John Imboden. Imboden had less than 3,000 men and 6 guns scattered throughout the area. Many of these men were untrained home guard units, among his troops was the Corps of Cadets from Virginia Military Institute (VMI). Imboden was a native of Staunton and his knowledge of the area was a valuable military asset.

Imboden was waiting for Breckinridge to come from the Department of Southwest Virginia with 2,500 men. Imboden learned that Sigel had detached cavalry from the main body, so he attacked that force on the 8th killing or capturing 500 men. This slowed Sigel's advance.

On the 12^{th,} Imboden received word that Breckinridge's trains had arrived at Staunton. Breckinridge was to move toward New Market where Imboden was. On the 14^{th,} the two commanders met about 10 miles south of New Market. Because Breckinridge's commission was older than Imboden's, Breckinridge became the commander. Because Imboden knew that area well he recommended that they combine forces and fight Sigel at New Market. While conferring, word reached them that Sigel was moving on New Market. Breckinridge's force had not reached the area yet so he ordered Imboden to stop Sigel. Breckinridge said he must "hold Staunton at all cost!" Staunton was a vital rail and land link with a big depot. All Confederate operations going north, used Staunton as a supply center.

When Imboden reached New Market, he was not greatly alarmed. His artillery and infantry were in a position to check the Union cavalry advance. Sigel wasn't moving in haste. A runaway slave had seen Breckinridge's columns south of New Market and told Sigel that vast numbers of Confederates were moving on him. The slave didn't know how to judge an army's size. It wasn't massive numbers; it was Imboden's small force. Sigel didn't want to get into a general engagement without knowing more about who he was fighting.

At dawn of the 15th, Breckinridge arrived at New Market. The tired 3,000 troops of Breckinridge plus the 1,500 of Imboden's had brought the total to about 4,500. Included in that number were 225 VMI cadets. Breckinridge also brought 8 more cannon. Breckinridge liked the ground Imboden had chosen. "We can attack and whip them here, and I'll do it," said Breckinridge. Breckinridge may have liked the ground but homeowners in New Market would not have agreed. The opposing armies were at opposite ends of town. When the artillery, of both sides, fired, it passed over the community of about 1,000 people.

Breckinridge moved his infantry through the town. Imboden moved on the flank. "Every moment the conflict became more desperate." Because of the woods, the Yankees didn't see Imboden's cavalry. Six Southern guns were moved close to the Union cavalry. When the Yankee cavalry came under fire from the Confederate guns, they fell back. When they fell back, they left a

Union battery without cover. Breckinridge advanced toward that battery. When Sigel saw that his flank had fallen back and the guns were exposed, Sigel ordered his army to fall back about a half a mile. Thus, New Market was now in Confederate hands.

Shortly after noon, the armies were in new lines of battle but it was the smaller Southern Army that was pushing the Federals back. The Yankees' had a six gun battery near the center of the line and it was inflicting many casualties on the South. Breckinridge decided to either capture or drive that battery back. "Its position was directly in front of Smith's 62d regiment... and the Cadet Corps and it fell to their lot to silence it by a charge in the very face of its terrible guns."

The youngsters from the Corps moved more rapidly than did the veterans from the 62nd Virginia Infantry The Corps, in line of battle, took a beating waiting for the 62nd but the brave school boys held their ground. Despite the incoming fire, the boys got "a slight breathing spell before making the deadly run necessary to reach the hostile battery...the order was given to charge at 'double-quick.' The work was then soon done. The guns were captured and also most of the gunners, who stood to them 'till overpowered... A wild yell went up when a cadet mounted a caisson and waved the Institute flag in triumph over it. The battery was taken, but at a fearful cost... the ground was... strewn with their dead and wounded. The cadets lost 8 killed and 46 wounded, out of 225. The 62nd took 241 casualties that day, most at the 'mouth of those cannons.'"

When that battery was taken, there was a general attack made along the entire line. Some say that Sigel got so excited that he started yelling orders in his native tongue, German. Many of his troops knew that language but many could not understand what their commander was jabbering about. The Union veterans fell back in disarray. There wasn't much of an organized attack or an organized retreat. Confederates pushed the Federals back until about 5 P. M. when Sigel placed his cannon on Rude's Hill a few miles north of New Market. The Southern Army was almost out of ammunition. When Breckinridge saw the great defensive position Sigel was in; he halted the attack. The Confederates got re-supplied and the Union artillery played upon their position. With daylight waning, Breckinridge ordered an advance. That was all it took. The bigger, veteran army took to its heels and ran for its life. Sigel's boys had been routed! Darkness and a burned bridge was all that saved them.

John Breckinridge had many titles by his name during his life time. Now, he added one more, Commander of the Shenandoah Valley Military District but that title only lasted a few hours. As soon as Lee heard of the victory, he ordered Breckinridge to join his Army of Northern Virginia. With the threat gone from Southwest Virginia and the Shenandoah, Lee could shift troops. That was the one thing that Grant's plan was going to prevent. Grant's plan was falling to pieces!

Benjamin Butler started his expected move on Richmond from the east. Butler liked to terrify unarmed citizens and cruelties were great at New Orleans. P. G. T. Beauregard was a French-Cajun who had family in New Orleans. He had wanted to meet the "Beast" for sometime. As Butler made his big move on Richmond, Beauregard got his wish. Beauregard threw his army at Butler with great fury at the Battle of Drewry's Bluff. Butler's Army reeled from the attack and retreated. Butler left over 4,000 casualties; these were not unarmed civilians he now was facing. Beauregard constructed earth works and just dared Butler to attack. Butler had, had enough. Beauregard had brilliantly taken Butler's Army out of play! Butler remained sealed up in the Bermuda Hundred "in a bottle strongly corked." This allowed Beauregard to send 6,000 troops to reinforce Lee. Nothing Grant had planned was working out.

On the 19th, it was Lee's turn. He thought that Grant's right may be weak so he sent Ewell to explore that possibility. General Ewell smoked cigars, cursed and rode a carriage toward battle. He had a leg amputated, thanks to some damn Yankee. When near battle, his men would strap him on his horse. Ewell's attack wasn't to be an all out attack, just a probing one. It was late in the evening when Ewell struck the Federal line. Lee's suspicions were correct. The area where

Ewell attacked was defended by "green troops." These boys had been setting in the fortification around Washington and had not seen battle. At first, Ewell's veterans pushed the Yankees back but two battle-tested Union Corps came rushing to stop the rout. The battle only lasted about two hours. Ewell lost about 900 men and one particular horse, Ewell's. When the animal fell, so did the general. Lee was informed that Ewell would be laid up for sometime.

The evening fighting had gone Grant's way but he was worried. The Great General had found a weak spot, would he find another? Grant knew that though Lee faced overwhelming forces; he would take the offensive. Grant decided he had lost too many days and too many men at Spotsylvania; the next battle may not go Lee's way.

Grant had his army do some fancy marching to fool "Bobby Lee." When Grant was sure that he had done so, he moved the army again to get between Lee and Richmond.

When Grant started to cross the North Anna River, there set the Army of Northern Virginia! Grant tried two strong assaults at two different fords. The results were the same; many dead Yankees and his army was still on the north side of the river.

Despite his many losses, Grant bragged to the newspaper reporters that "He had whipped Lee." Rumors of his drinking surfaced again. During this time

Grant was heard saying, "I can lose seven men and Lee lose one man and I win, because I can replace my seven and Lee can't replace his one." At the same time, it was noted that many in Grant's Army would be leaving when their enlistment time was up. Their time would be up within the next month. Re-enlistment bonuses had been doubled to try and keep them.

There Grant sat on the north side of the North Anna. He had been outgeneraled and outfought every step of the way. He had used men's lives as if they were only bullets. In 21 days, he had taken over 37,000 casualties. That is a staggering 30% casualty rate! But with Grant, there "would be no turning back."

When the armies stopped to breathe on the 27th, Grant could see how his grand plans had gone. Butler was "in a bottle." Sigel had been totally routed. Averell had destroyed neither the salt works nor the lead mines. Only Crook had achieved his goal but Grant didn't want to talk about that because he, himself, had failed so miserably. It was Grant's plan and many thousands of brave sons of the North were dead, wounded, or missing. So whose fault was it? Grant, who was the biggest failure of all, knew who the person was who wouldn't be blamed. That person was Grant. In his official report, Grant blamed his entire failure on Sigel. Grant was judge, jury, and he became the executioner also; Sigel was fired!

(Other events occurring during this period)

May 4th on the Red River, the Confederates captured a U. S. steamer and destroyed two more. The water level was so low that the boats became "fish trapped in a bowl."

In Albemarle Sound, on the 5^{th,} the soldiers, turned sailors, of the *C. S. S. Albemarle* took on the Union squadron. They didn't win but they disabled the *U. S. S. Sassacus.* Confederates had hoped to take New Berne but that didn't happen today. On the Red River, Confederate artillery sunk two more Yankee vessels!

On the 7^{th,} Sherman officially began his march on Atlanta. Sherman's Army numbered about 100,000 well supplied men. He was opposed by Joseph "Uncle Joe" Johnston with less than 60,000 ill-fed men. Sherman wanted to take Johnston on in an open field battle. Sherman knew his numbers would simply destroy Johnston's Army of the Tennessee. Johnston wanted to slow Sherman, inflict casualties and lengthen his supply lines. They met at Tunnel Hill, Georgia. Sherman tried Johnston's line and found it too strong. Sherman decided to move via the Snake River to Johnston's rear and stop him from retreating.

Also on this date near Cape Fear River on the coast of North Carolina, the *C. S. S. Raleigh* took on six Yankee ships. There was much damage to some of the Yankee ships as well as to the *Raleigh*. The *Raleigh* ran aground and had to be destroyed.

While Union troops skirmished with Johnston's front, other Yankees attempted to get behind him on the 9th. Confederates stopped the Yankees at the rear in heavy skirmishing. Sherman was very upset at the commander on the scene.

Also today, Yankees worked frantically to build dams on the Red River so that the trapped Federal gunboats could escape down the river. The thieving Yankees didn't get as much Southern cotton as they had expected so they burned Alexandria.

The Federals had not forgotten the pro-Southern Indians; this date they launched raids against them in the Utah, Arizona, and Colorado Territories.

Unlike the unpopular Northern President, this night President Davis was "serenaded." He also said he was happy with Lee's actions at Spotsylvania.

On the 12th, Sherman had succeeded in threatening Johnston's rear. This forced Johnston to abandon Dalton, and fall back on Resaca.

As casualty figures began to come in, some Northern newspapers "accused Grant of butchery."

There was fighting near Resaca, Dalton and Tilton on the 13th, as each army took new positions.

Hood's Texans had reinforced Johnston. Near Resaca on the 15th, Hood took on Hooker and gave him a sound thrashing. Sherman realized that Johnston's line was too strong for a direct attack so he started another flanking movement. Johnston knew he had to retreat so Resaca was abandoned. Johnston fell back toward Adairsville.

By this date, President Davis had heard what Lee's soldiers had done, so he asked Lee not to endanger himself, "The country could not bear the loss of you...."

On the 17th, Sherman tried a double envelopment of Johnston's Army. At Adairsville, Sherman sent troops around both flanks to catch Johnston in a box. Johnston was not boxed in but continued his retreat toward Cassville, and Kingston.

John Imboden

William "Grumble" Jones

It effects us until this date and it passed Union Congress on the 17th; the postal money order system.

Sherman was determined to give Johnston no rest. Fighting broke out in the Cassville-Kingston area on the 18th. While the fighting was going on, Johnston heard from the President. Davis was upset that more land was falling into Yankee hands. Johnston didn't think Davis understood the situation his army was in; Davis didn't think that Johnston was paying attention to what his President was saying!

Both the *New York World* and *Journal of Commerce* published articles that said Union boys were dieing so fast that Lincoln wanted to draft another

300,000 men. This was done in the city of the massive draft riots! Lincoln moved quickly to close the papers and arrested the editors. How dare those newspapers print the truth! What makes them think that there is Freedom of the Press?

Johnston was always watching for any weak point in Sherman's Army so he could attack. On the 19[th,] he saw one and ordered Hood to attack. Johnston was amazed; instead of attacking, Hood retreated! Hood had gotten false information that there were Yankees on his side and at his rear. This forced Johnston to retreat the army over the Etowah River. Sherman, of course, wished to catch Johnston before he could cross. There was much arguing among the Confederate commanders.

By the 21[st,] Banks who had lost on the Red River was ordered to Vicksburg. This would place him in a position to aid Sherman.

This day, Grant relieved Maj. Gen. Franz Sigel and replaced him with Maj. Gen. David Hunter. Hunter was one of the first to disobey his Commander-in-Chief and issue an Emancipation Proclamation. He was now out of the "dog house" and back in command. When Hunter relieved Sigel, he didn't allow the former general to review and address his troops, as was normally done. Hunter literally sent Sigel packing in the night. Sigel didn't like being the scapegoat and didn't like his replacement. Hunter could not understand the German words Sigel used when parting.

On the 23rd, Johnston was in a good defensive position at Allatoona Pass, on the Etowah River. He was trying to find out what Sherman's next move would be. Atlanta was Johnston's supply base and it was a little over 25 miles away. Sherman's base was many miles away. Johnston had a very favorable kill ratio and knew if he were going to stop Sherman, it would happen in the next 25 miles.

All across the South hunger stalked the land. The price of food was higher than most people could afford. The army couldn't feed its own either. Disease rates increased. Lonely, hungry wives, widows and orphans often begged their men to desert. Many did. Every night the South took casualties without the Yankees even firing a single bullet.

Because of Crook's victory and the destruction of the long bridge at Central Depot major problems were occurring. There was no bridge over the New River. Trains used to pass over the river in minutes. Now, it took two trains an entire day to cross. The contents of each train was off-loaded and ferried over the river and then reloaded. It was a major military and economic head-ache. Workers, including slaves, labored hard to repair the bridge but it would take about two months to complete.

CHAPTER 16   MAY 24 - JUNE 21 1864

Grant started moving part of his force across the North Anna. In Georgia, Wheeler's Southern cavalry took some of Sherman's supply wagon train. Johnston knew that Sherman's supply was stretched by every move. The main part of Sherman's Army moved toward Dallas; this made Johnston shift his men toward New Hope Church. And on the Mississippi, Col. Colton Greene's men captured two Federal vessels. The next day, the 25th, he captured another and damaged several.

General Lee was very sick on the 25th; many believe it was another heart attack. Lee knew that part of Grant's Army was south of the North Anna. Grant had made another mistake and Lee's Army was in a great position to destroy that part of the Federal Army. From his sick bed, Lee, almost delirious, ordered an attack. The order was given but the attack did not happen. When Grant's men ran into Lee's strong position, they were repulsed and about 425 dead and wounded Yankees did not re-cross the river. Grant now knew that he had been out generaled again and felt lucky that his losses weren't even higher. Grant was also very upset that Lee knew where he was going, before Grant, himself, did.

This date, Sherman tried Johnston's new line and found it strong; losing many men. In North Carolina, the Yankees tried to destroy the *Albemarle* and failed. In

South Carolina, the Yankees tried to break the railroad at Charleston and failed.

Again on the 26th, Grant tried to outsmart and out-march Lee. He moved his army east away from the North Anna.

Near Winchester, Hunter had taken command of Sigel's old army, the Army of the Shenandoah and the forces from West Virginia. The West Virginia forces were near Meadow Bluff, (W) Virginia. These were the forces of Crook and Averell. Hunter sent orders that both army groups were to move toward Staunton.

The Shenandoah must be saved and Lynchburg protected. After Breckinridge had moved to Lee's aid, William "Grumble" Jones became Commander of the Department of Southwest Virginia. Jones hadn't even gotten his desk chair warm when he was ordered to take everyman he could lay hold of to the Shenandoah. When he arrived at Staunton, this brigade general became the Commander of the Shenandoah Military District. Again, his commission was older than Imboden's.

In Georgia, Sherman moved his army close to Johnston's and heavy skirmishing occurred. In South Carolina, Confederate gunners ran the *Boston* to ground and she was sunk.

On the 27th, Grant's cavalry took Hanovertown, as Grant tried to out-fox Lee. Lee became aware of Grant's movement and started shifting his army east.

In Georgia, Johnston's favorable kill ratio increased when Sherman tried his new line at New Hope Church. Sherman learned that the line was not weak.

On the 28th, Lee moved his army toward a house with a big grape arbor. It offered cool relief in the hot summer. The locals called it Cold Harbor "Cool Arbor." Most of the Confederate soldiers didn't know where they were and they mispronounced the name. There was no big body of water in the area but the place was renamed that day. It became "Cold Harbor." Lee started constructing his line and waiting for Grant.

Because of the defeat of the day before and believing that not all of Sherman's Army was on line, Johnston ordered a probing attack against Sherman. This time it was the Confederacy that bled under Union guns.

In Missouri, the war was as much about revenge as winning; Confederates sacked Lama.

On the 29th, Confederates captured a very large wagon train near Salem, Arkansas.

Because of the many command changes in the Department of Southwest Virginia, Morgan decided to take matters into his own hands. He believed that Stephen Burbridge, the Military Governor of Kentucky, was assembling a force of over 8,000 to attack Southwest Virginia. Morgan only had 2,100 but they were "terrible men." Morgan decided to attack the Yankees before they attacked him. Morgan always considered himself to be a Kentuckian first and a Confederate second. When his army was a day's march away from the railroad, Morgan sent a courier to inform Richmond that he was gone. High command was not happy that he had gone without permission.

Grant was still grinning on the 31st, that he had out-generaled General Lee, when he ran smack-dab in to Lee's Cold Harbor line. Grant was beside himself with anger. The newspapers had been calling him the "Great Hammer" and Grant believed it. Grant decided that if he couldn't get around Lee, then he would go over top of him!

On June 1st, both armies adjusted their line, shifted troops and sparred at Cold Harbor.

Gen. George Stoneman's cavalry took Allatoona Pass and the railroad line. This would permit Sherman to shift to New Hope and move closer to Atlanta.

Gen. S. D. Sturgis got command of 8,000 of the Union's best cavalrymen and orders to ride Forrest to the ground. On this day, they left Memphis.

In Missouri, it was payback time and the Yankees darn near destroyed New Market.

In the Shenandoah and to the credit of the officers and men of the 1st New York Cavalry, Newtown (Stephens City) was not burned. Hunter had ordered the community burnt to the ground. The privates in the saddles were the first to say that they wouldn't make war on innocent women and children. The officers agreed and they all disobeyed Hunter's burning order.

In Richmond, Davis personally called out the home guard for possible defense of the city.

Grant wanted to attack Lee on the 2nd but it didn't happen. Not all the troops were up and there were ammunition supply problems. The officers thought Grant's attack was not a good idea; the common soldiers thought it was a very bad idea! Even the privates knew that it was nothing but a suicide attack. On this day, army "dog tags" were invented. The soldiers knew that when they came out of those breastworks, their chances of returning whole, were not good. They didn't want their bodies to be unknown and buried in an unknown grave. They began sewing pieces of paper with their name and home town on them into their uniforms. As was common on both sides, the Yankees began to throw playing cards and dice away. Cards and dice were a sign of gambling and sin. They didn't want their loved ones to see sin when their body was delivered home. Letters from home were torn into little pieces. If captured, they didn't want some filthy enemy soldier to read and handle their loved one's words.

In the Shenandoah, Hunter bragged that "the South would never forget the passing of his army because I was going to burn something in every community." The people in the towns in the northern end of the Valley were finding out that it was not an idle boast. Others of

Hunter's forces were working their way toward Staunton. Crook had 9,000 men and Averell 2,500 troopers. Col. McCausland was promoted to Brigadier General. He moved his less than 1,500 men in front of Crook and fought delaying battles at Callaghan and Covington.

Everybody from officer to common soldier knew it was a bad idea but at 4:30 A. M. June 3, approximately 50,000 brave Union soldiers left the safety of their trenches at Cold Harbor. Some historians say the whole battle lasted fifteen minutes; other said it was closer to seven! The air was filled with smoke, lead, and mostly Union blood and body parts. Grant's order had led to the bloodiest fifteen minutes in the history of the Western Hemisphere. Estimates ran from 15,000 to 19,000 casualties were taken. Neither Lincoln nor Grant every wanted the true figures released. Many a brave Yankee lad had not wasted his time sewing.

It was still early in the morning, so Grant ordered another attack. Many brave Federals were dead; those that remained were Damn Yankees but they weren't Damn fools. There was no second attack. There was one other thing that didn't appear and that was a flag of truce. As was customary, in this gentleman's war, the loosing general hoisted a white flag and asked permission to remove the wounded and dead. Grant wasn't much of a field general or a gentleman. His ego had been hurt so many times by General Lee. Now, with most of 20,000 Union bodies lying before Lee's line, Grant refused to accept the fact that he had lost again. Brave Union men writhed, screamed in pain, and begged for water or death in the hot Virginia sun!

In Georgia, Johnston found out that Sherman was able to sidestep him again. Sherman, the crazy man, wasn't going to do what, Grant, the drunk, had done in Virginia and attack Johnston head on. Now it was Johnston who knew he must shift his line to get in front of Sherman again.

By late in the day, the first accounts were coming into the Yankee White House. Knowing that his political fate was tied to the war and therefore, to Grant, President Lincoln remarked for the papers, "My previous high estimate of Gen. Grant has been maintained and heightened by what has occurred in the remarkable campaign he is now conducting...." i.e. "dog tags and the bloodiest 15 minutes."

During the night of the 3^{rd,} Johnston moved his army from New Hope and once again was in front of Sherman by the 4th. This day, the wounded were dieing and crying at Cold Harbor and Morgan was cutting the railroad and moving on Lexington.

Finally on the 5^{th,} Grant raised a white flag. Most of those left on the field were dead. The dead were starting to stink!

The hamlet of Piedmont is a few miles northeast of Staunton. Early that morning the forces of Jones and

Imboden took on Hunter. The field didn't favor the Southern defenders thus Hunter had an advantage at the Battle of Piedmont. Although he had over 11,000 men and much more artillery, it took Hunter all day to beat the 4,000 Rebels. Many defenders were home guard. When the Federal breakthrough occurred, William Jones rushed untrained home guard to try and plug the hole. The hole wasn't plugged but Jones was. He died as a result of his wounds. The Southern Army was routed! There were no major Confederate forces between Hunter and Lynchburg. Without the supplies flowing through Lynchburg, Lee could not hold the capital. It appeared that the South had just lost the war! Hunter's force took between 800 and 1,500 casualties; sources do not agree.

Confederate casualties were high but unknown. What was left of the Southern Army moved toward Waynesboro, to defend the railroad toward Charlottesville.

On the 6th, Hunter's victorious army entered Staunton and an orgy of destruction began. The patients of a Southern military hospital were literally removed from the beds and laid in the street, so that Union wounded could be accommodated. Averell and Crook joined Hunter. The army was renamed the Army of West Virginia and now numbered about 25,000 men and 36 guns. Hunter used "Jessie Scouts." These were lying, sneaking, Yankee spies dressed in Confederacy uniforms.

Grant didn't know of Hunter's victory when, on the 7th, he sent Phil Sheridan's cavalry to reinforce him. The last Yankee had not saddled up, when Lee received the news. The information came from loyal slaves who were working for the invaders and supplying their country with intelligence. Lee ordered his cavalry, now under the command of his nephew Fitzhugh Lee and Wade Hampton, to intercept Sheridan.

On the 8th, Morgan took Mount Sterling and his hometown of Lexington. Morgan was happy that his town was back in the Confederacy, if only for a little while. Lexington now held bad memories for Morgan. He recalled how Federals had abused his wife and family earlier in the war. For Morgan this war was very personal.

Most people believe that Lincoln always ran as a Republican but not so. He was so unpopular that he divided his own party. A great portion of the Republicans, called "Radicals" bitterly opposed Lincoln. They didn't just want to force the South back into the Union; they wanted total subjugation of Southern citizens, "(they) dreamed of dictating to every Southerner his future way of life." With the backing of the Radicals, Gen John Fremont got the Republican Party nomination. When Republican, Lincoln, couldn't get his own party's nomination, he formed another Lincoln-ite party, the National Union Party. The citizens of Baltimore had rioted and stopped Lincoln's

Presidential train in '60. Lincoln chose that city to hold his convention in to make sure those people knew who their conqueror was. Lincoln was "unanimously" supported by his new party. Lincoln dumped his Vice President, Hannibal Hamlin, and chose Andrew Johnson, Military Governor of Tennessee, as his running mate. When the news of Hunter's victory and the death of the South were announced, the hall exploded in wild and joyous shouts! THE WAR IS OVER! It was premature.

On the 9th, Butler tried to take Petersburg but Beauregard was there to see that he didn't.

General Sturgis had been hunting for Forrest since the 1st. He found him on the 10th and wished he hadn't. Forrest was outnumbered and outgunned but not out-fought. At Brice's Crossroads south of Corinth, Forrest's 3,500 cavalrymen attacked Sturgis' 8,000. The battle turned into a retreat; the retreat turn into a panic; the panic turned into a rout! Forrest chased Sturgis most of the way back to Memphis. He took most of Sturgis' artillery, 176 wagons and all their supplies. 2,240 Yankees were killed, wounded, captured or missing. Forrest lost less than 500 men.

This date, the Confederate Congress authorized the drafting of men between 17 and 50. Grant was right; Lee was having trouble replacing his one.

On the 11th, one of the bloodiest cavalry battle ever fought in the Western Hemisphere took place at

Trevilian Station. It was charge and countercharge and brave men and horses died. The battle raged all day. In most quarters the Confederates were pushed back.

The Battle of Lexington took place when Hunter's 25,000 attacked McCausland's 1,500 plus the Corps from VMI. McCausland wasn't fighting to inflict casualties but to buy time. The Corps was allowed to retreat first for safety's sake. The school boys moved to defend the pass at Balcony Falls. McCausland's force then retreated over Valley Pike Road toward Buchanan. Lexington was left to a commander, who knew no mercy. Looting, burning and defiling occurred on a scale even greater than at Staunton. Hunter had VMI burned because of the hatred of Jackson. He would later claim it was burned because the Corps was on line against him. Hunter witnessed and encouraged the desecration of "Stonewall's" grave! Hunter had an innocent civilian executed and a captured soldier shot in the head. Even the slaves, that wouldn't submit willingly to Union sexual desires, were taken. The former Governor of Virginia, John Letcher's, home was burned. Unknown to Hunter, one of his own regiments put a guard around Jackson's house to prevent looting and burning. That is the only reason that Jackson's house can be seen today. Hunter knew that he was low on ammunition for cannon and rifles. He sent a simple order to his supply base at Martinsburg, (W) Virginia to "send ammunition." The ammunition never arrived. Who was the commander of the supply base? Franz

Sigel! He remembered how Hunter had treated him and simply didn't send the powder. Later at an official inquiry, he stated that Hunter, "didn't request a size for the artillery or an amount needed." This passed, even though, Hunter's Army was Sigel's Army and Sigel knew the size and amount needed.

Hunter had now lost six days of marching. The army burned but did not move. This gave Lee something he needed badly, time.

Hunter had sent his cavalry to cut the Orange and Alexandria Railroad between Charlottesville and Lynchburg. This would stop reinforcements from reaching Lynchburg. About midnight there was a small encounter at the Tye River Bridge. The South held the bridge and the railroad line stayed open.

On the 12th, the destruction of Lexington continued and so did the Battle of Trevilian Station. When Sheridan attacked today, he found that the Confederate cavalrymen were now infantry. They had dug breast works and were waiting for 8,000 Yankees to attack their less than 5,000. It didn't take Sheridan long to realize that he wasn't going to join Hunter. Union losses were put at 1,007 to Confederate losses of 612.

As Morgan raided through Kentucky, he used the captured telegraph to confuse and scatter Federal forces. False messages were sent informing Union units that Morgan's forces were seen heading in certain areas or that Morgan had been defeated and was retreating. The false messages kept the Yankees running and away from Morgan. The Yankees found out that he was at Cynthiana and attacked in force. Morgan began his retreat with 2,700 prisoners (more than his entire army), many wagons loaded with Union supplies, and 7,000 horses. Morgan had beaten so many Union units and captured or destroyed so much of their supplies, that they couldn't mount an attack for four months!

In Virginia, Grant began to pull out of Cold Harbor to cross the James River. In Georgia, Sherman tested Johnston's new line. There were skirmishes and pitched battles but Johnston's line did not yield.

By the 13th, Lee knew that Grant was leaving Cold Harbor. Lee guessed that Grant would stay north of the James so Lee began shifting forces toward Malvern Hill. For once Grant was acting differently than Lee anticipated; Grant was going to cross over the James. Part of the troops Lee was shifting left the entire area; they were headed to Lynchburg. The delegates that applauded at Baltimore weren't the only ones who knew the war could soon be over. If Lee held Grant out of Richmond and lost his supply line, it would only be an empty victory. Lynchburg had to be saved! The heaviest section of his army was placed under General Jubal "Old Jube" Early and sent to defend that city.

Hunter had sent Averell's Cavalry to hold the big bridge over the James at Buchanan. As the cavalry approached McCausland fired the bridge. Wind blew the flames into some houses which quickly caught fire. Averell's men helped put out the fire. The next day when Hunter found out what Averell had done; he chewed Averell out properly. "How dare him stop houses from burning; they were there to burn houses!" Buchanan was taken and McCausland fell back over the Peaks of Otter.

By the 15th, Grant was crossing the James in force. Beauregard got reports of the buildup in his area and informed General Lee. Lee still believed that Grant would stay north of the James and did not react.

Hunter started crossing the Peaks of Otter. The Corps of Cadets was ordered to float down the James; Breckinridge was coming by rail; McCausland was retreating from the west; the home guard was called out; the stockade was emptied of Confederate wrong doers; even the hospitals were searched for any one who could hold a gun. They would try to hold Lynchburg but few thought they could defeat Hunter's hordes. Early was on his way from Lee but would he make it in time?

In Washington, the House of Representatives voted against the 13th Amendment, which would have outlawed slavery.

By the 16th, a desperate Beauregard had stripped the defenses that kept Butler "in a bottle" and moved as many men to Petersburg (the back door to Richmond) as he could. The Yankees attacked Petersburg in force and pushed Beauregard's Confederates back but they didn't take the city. Despite Beauregard's reports that the Union Army was there in force, Lee sent no reinforcements to Beauregard. He did however send troops to put Butler back in the bottle.

McCausland skirmished with Hunter. Hunter looted and burned at the town of Liberty (Bedford).

In Georgia, Johnston had to establish yet another line. This one at Mud Creek and Sherman took one more step toward Atlanta.

The unpopular Union President was out campaigning. The only place he was invited to speak was to the Woman's Sanitary Fair. There were some men there but women couldn't vote. Lincoln would have been happy to speak to anybody expect the mirror.

On the 17th, Beauregard's little band did great service for the Confederacy. Ninth Corps threw their full weight against the vastly outnumbered Rebels. The line didn't break and Beauregard counterattacked. Beauregard again informed Lee that he was holding back the whole Damned Yankee Army! Finally Lee believed and started sending troops.

By this date, Early had force marched his army to Charlottesville. He had to wait to almost 8 A. M. for the trains to arrive to take his army to Lynchburg. The question was, "Would he arrive before Hunter took the city and ended the life of the Confederacy?" Hunter should have attacked the city earlier but a burnt bridge and pride stopped him. The bridge took much too long to rebuild (Hunter amused himself by burning some houses in the area). Crook was poised to attack the city but Hunter ordered him not to, until he could join him in the glorious defeat of the Confederacy! Hunter didn't think that Lee would reinforce Lynchburg.

It was 1 P. M. when Early arrived and started de-training the part of the army that he had transported. He talked to other Confederate commanders and tried to get a feel for the lay of the land. At 4 o'clock the tour came to an end. Hunter arrived and gave Crook permission to attack. McCausland's and Imboden's boys fought like tigers to buy Early time. As the cavalry line collapsed, Early's infantry came on the field. Hunter's masses drove Early before him. Despite taking heavy casualties, Early kept Hunter out of Lynchburg that night.

On the 18th, Grant arrived at Petersburg and so did Lee. Grant inspected Lee's lines and decided not to attack. The Battle of Cold Harbor was still fresh in his mind. Lee had stalemated and stopped him again! On paper, Grant couldn't lose. By now, he should be in Richmond but he wasn't fighting paper. Grant had taken more casualties than Lee had men in his army! Grant's offense had met Lee's defense; Grant could move no further. The Siege of Petersburg had begun.

During the night time hours of the 18th and into the early hours of the 19th, Early tried his famous train trick. He sent his empty trains outside of town and then had them returned. When the empty cars arrived, bands played "Dixie" and crowds cheered! Many of Hunter's subordinates believed that Lynchburg was being reinforced. Hunter still believed that Lee could send no one to help but because his junior officers did, Hunter did not launch a big dawn attack. There was attack and counterattack until Hunter captured some prisoners. The prisoners were part of Early's Army. Hunter now knew that everything had changed. Hunter tried a couple more attacks. One of those attacks came very close to taking the city. The Yankees were so close they could see the church steeples but not close enough to take the city. Hunter "…was better at making war on innocent women and children than armed Confederate soldiers." Early had stopped him, so under the cover of darkness, Hunter began to retreat. Lynchburg was saved! The Confederacy was saved! A little over a week ago, applause rang because of Hunter and the soon end of the Confederacy! Now, there was nothing to cheer Lincoln's black heart.

In Georgia, there was more fighting and more flanking; and more of the same. Johnston fell back again, this time toward Marietta and formed the Kennesaw Line. Sherman stepped toward Atlanta. The people of Georgia and the President of the Confederacy were not happy with the way Johnston was losing the campaign.

The short, adventurous life of the *C. S. S. Alabama* came to an end off Cherbourg, France on the 19th. The

Alabama had sunk or captured 65 enemy vessels but the *U. S. S. Kearsarge* had her outgunned and outrun. People on shore and on boats watched the ships slug it out with broadside-after-broadside. They also saw the *Kearsarge* continue to fire even after the *Alabama* lowered her colors. Water-born, Yankee cowards killed surrendering Southerners. A colorful and hate-filled chapter of Confederate Naval history came to an end.

In Georgia, the same pattern was repeated on the 20th. More Confederate homes came into Union lines; more looting and abuse occurred. More fighting as Sherman tested the lines and looked for a way to flank Johnston again; more Confederates demanding action of Johnston.

As Lincoln campaigned, he learned that Vallandigham had come back from exile. No one, even political prisoners, seemed to listen to Lincoln. Lincoln wrote his military governor of Ohio. Lincoln told him to watch Vallandigham and lock anybody up he wanted. Just don't let that man and free speech interfere with the election!

Lincoln had also been reading Grant's dispatches. Grant didn't sound like himself. Was he really starting to care for his men? Was he really going to admit that Lee had him whipped? Would there be no quick victory over Lee? If Grant lost, how could he win the Presidency again? What was Grant thinking? Lincoln decided to go see for himself.

Hunter retreated from Lynchburg during the night. Early started chasing him early in the morning.

On the 21st, forces under Early caught Hunter near Salem. In battles south and then north of the town, Hunter was defeated. Over half of his artillery was taken and he was sent running toward Charleston, (W) Virginia.

Joseph Kershaw

CHAPTER 17 JUNE 22- AUGUST 31, 1864

Grant knew Lincoln was coming so he decided to impress the boss. James Wilson's cavalry boys were sent to disable the South Side Railroad. It wasn't until July 2, that what was left of Wilson's command straggled back into Union lines. The whole raid was a disaster. Whipped at every turn by Fitz Lee's cavalry, Wilson only managed to rip up some track which the South replaced in hours. A lot of dead and captured Yankees paid to disrupt the time schedules on the South Side. Also, to impress the President, Grant sent Second Corps to threaten one of Lee's main supply routs, the Weldon Rail Road. A. P. Hill would have none of it and routed Second Corps. Lincoln received the news of many potential voters dieing and 1,700 made prisoner. Lincoln was not impressed. The only good news came from an attack that Grant did not personally order. Late in the day, news came in about Sheridan's cavalry whipping the other part of Lee's cavalry, under Wade Hampton, north of the James. Sheridan had captured 900 wagons; this would affect Lee's ability to move his army. Grant was still trying to think of ways to make the boss happy. Late that evening, Grant, Lincoln and party steamed off to visit Butler. It was hoped that Butler would tell the President of torturing some innocent civilians and that would raise Lincoln's spirits.

Also on this date, Morgan returned and assumed the command of the Department of Southwest Virginia and East Tennessee. And in Georgia, Hood, under Johnston, attacked Sherman at Zion Church and lost.

Before Early left Richmond, Lee suggested that once Hunter was defeated, Early move on Washington. It was hoped that this would take pressure off Richmond. On the 23^{rd,} Early started toward that city.

Grant's boys had done it before in the west, now on the 25^{th,} they started digging a tunnel under the Confederate lines at Petersburg.

The "crazy man," Sherman had been reading about what the "drunk," Grant had been doing and decided to try it. Grant hadn't been able to outgeneral or outfight Lee so he had tried to go over him at Cold Harbor. The same thing was happening with Sherman and Johnston in the west. Sherman tried to do the same thing near Marietta on the Kennesaw Line. Brave Yankees rushed "pell-mell" to their deaths before Johnston's entrenched Confederates. Sherman lost over 2,000 men to less than 500 for the South. This increased Johnston's favorable kill ratio.

On the 28^{th,} Early was at the blackened town of Staunton as he moved toward Washington. By the 30^{th,} he was in New Market. On this date in Washington, Lincoln wrote to Secretary of the Treasury, Salmon Chase, "You and I have reached a point of mutual embarrassment in our official relation...." Why was

Lincoln "embarrassed?" He had learned that Chase wanted his job and was secretly working with Radical Republicans to get that party's nomination. Lincoln's first thought was to treat Chase like he did anyone else who opposed him and jail him. Because of the negative publicity, Lincoln decided to fire him instead.

As June closed and July opened, President Lincoln was under considerable political pressure. There was little happiness at the White House. Lincoln had fired Chase; been unable to get the Republican nomination; McClellan was moving toward nomination by the Democrats as a Peace Candidate; Congress was pushing for a punishment policy against the South, and in spite of his cover-up, the people were learning about the tremendous casualties Grant had taken. Now, Lincoln learned that Early was on his way to pay him a visit. "What next," thought Lincoln?

Early was at Winchester by the 2nd. In Georgia, Sherman had been unable to outfight Johnston so he outflanked him which caused Johnston to fall back on a prepared line. Also on this date, Congress passed a bill to help create the Union Pacific Railroad.

On the 3^{rd,} reports reached Washington that Early had driven Sigel from Winchester and was moving north. Requests were sent to Grant for troops; Lee's strategy was working.

The Yankees had been shelling Charleston and Fort Sumter. This day they landed on Morris Island but they didn't stay long. The Confederates attack, killing and capturing many. By the 5^{th,} the Federal Navy was frantically evacuating troops.

In Georgia, Sherman took Marietta and moved one step closer to the all important City Atlanta; and Early was at Harper's Ferry.

On the 4^{th,} Lincoln vetoed a bill that gave Congress control of bringing the secession states back into the Union. Congress wanted to take the right to vote away from Southern whites, take their slaves (property) and pay them nothing. Lincoln wanted those "Free States" Electoral Votes to help him win reelection. Congress and the President had locked heads!

Sherman had outflanked, not outfought, Johnston, but by numbers alone caused him to make one more step backward toward Atlanta.

On the 5^{th,} Early started crossing the Potomac. In Washington, Lincoln issued a decree to jail anyone who opposed his re-election in Kentucky. If all opposition was in jail, it would increase his chance of carrying that state in the November elections. Also, he received word that two Confederate "emissaries" were in Canada with the power to "negotiate peace." Advisers urged him to send someone to talk to them. This unpopular war was going to cost him the Presidency. A. J. Smith's Cavalry headed toward Northern Mississippi hunting Forrest, this day.

On the 6^{th,} McCausland, under Early, took Hagerstown. He threatened to burn the town as payback for what Hunter had done in the Shenandoah. The citizens raised $20,000 and the town was not burned.

Frustrated Yanks sent almost 800 shells flying toward the pile of rubble that once was Fort Sumter on the 7th. Four times the Confederate flag was blown away and four times, brave Confederates put the symbol of defiance back up. Grant and Lee were staring at each other along the trench line at Petersburg.

On the 8^{th,} Sherman outflanked Johnston again and moved one step closer to Atlanta.

On the 9^{th,} Federal forces under Gen. Lew Wallace drew a defensive line along the Monocacy River south of Frederick to stop Early. Early attacked Wallace's 6, 000 with almost 10,000 mean Confederates. It took much of the day for Early to rout Wallace inflicting about 2,000 casualties. Southern loses were about 700. When the Union Army ran, there were 1,200 men that couldn't be found. Wallace was thoroughly beaten! As the word of the defeat spread, Washington was near panic. Lincoln worried that Early may act like a Yankee and either "Baltimore or Washington will be sacked." Later Wallace would prove that "the pen is mightier than his sword." He won glory not on the battlefield but by writing *Ben Hur*. Later that day more bad news for the Yankees reached the capital. The *C. S. S. Florida* had taken four Union vessels only 35 miles off the Maryland coast.

Lew Wallace

Johnston fell back over the Chattahoochee River; Atlanta was threatened. President Davis sent Bragg to consult with Johnston. The President wanted to know what Johnston was going to do to save Atlanta. When was Johnston going to fight?

On the 11th, Early was at Silver Spring and looking for a way to attack the city. President and Mrs. Lincoln rode to the line at Fort Stevens. They wanted to see men die in this war; after all Lincoln had caused it. While there, some of Early's men obliged the President. Soldiers shouted to the President to take cover; he did.

By the 12th, Early had decided that he couldn't take the city but he would pretend that he was and "scare the Hell out of them!" All the noise brought the President back to Fort Stevens. Again, Lincoln exposed himself to incoming fire until a certain private yelled at him, "Get down, you fool!" Lincoln knew who the fool was; he had been called one often enough. The private would "yell" at other future presidents. He became Chief Justice of the Supreme Court, Oliver Wendell Holmes.

At the Confederate capital, President Davis wrote to Lee on the line: "Johnston has failed... (fearful that he)...will abandon Atlanta...necessary to relieve him at once...What think you of Hood?"

By the 13th, Early was in full retreat. He was leaving Washington before the Federals could attack him.

Smith had been hunting Forrest but when he found him on the 14th, it was the Yankees who fell back to a defensive position. The fact that Smith greatly outnumbered him and held a good defensive position didn't stop Forrest from attacking. The battle raged most of the day. Forrest lost a lot of men, over 1,300 but he kept pounding Smith. Although a Union victory, Smith and his men had the fear of Forrest put in them. It was they that started retreating. Also, on this day, a retreating Early crossed back into the safety of "Old Virginia."

Lincoln took his advisers' advice and sent a man to New York City on the 16th to meet with those involved in starting peace talks. It was unofficial contact.

An anxious Davis wired Johnston, "What do you plan to do to stop Sherman before he takes Atlanta?" Johnston did wire back but didn't give the President a direct answer. This only upset Davis further. While the two were writing each other, Sherman crossed the Chattahoochee north of Atlanta and moved toward Decatur on the east.

On the 17th Sherman's Yankees continued to cross the river and the President wired Johnston again. Davis basically wrote, "You're fired! Hood is now in command." The Army of Tennessee loved their commander; he would not needlessly sacrifice their lives; he had a very favorable kill ratio; the men did not want Johnston to go. However, the worried people of Atlanta were happy to see him go; "now they had someone who would fight the army!" Sherman was glad to see him go "now they had someone who fights the army!"

Lincoln had been reading the newspapers and worrying about his re-election. Grant hadn't made any suicide charges lately but he might. Lincoln wrote to him don't do anything that would cause "...great loss of life."

John Pemberton

James Pettigrew

Grant had bragged that he could replace his men he had killed and on the 18th, Lincoln called for 500,000 more "volunteers" to replace those Grant had lost. Also on this date, Lincoln received word that the "peace feelers" weren't going anywhere. Why? Those Rebels were still demanding that they continue to live in their own country. They weren't willing to surrender to the Yankee aggressors.

John Bell Hood was a fearless fighter and had given both an arm and a leg for the Cause. He had to take much medicine for his pain; the medicine contained opium (dope). Many thought the dope stopped Hood from thinking clearly. On the 19th, he made plans to attack, in force, against Sherman's forces. He was hoping to catch Sherman with his forces divided.

On the 20th, Hood struck Sherman at the Battle of Peachtree Creek. George Thomas, the Rock of Chickamauga, was somewhat separated when Hood ordered the attack but it was three hours before the attack came. This gave Thomas time to prepare. "The fierce Southern assaults failed." Thomas could now also be called the "Rock of Atlanta." This action made the Yankees smile and his parents weep. The Yankees lost about 1,800 men but held their ground. The South lost almost 5,000 men; Johnston's favorable kill ratio was gone and Atlanta was in even greater danger. Hood blamed the failure on General Hardee. If the battle had been won, would Hood have given credit to Hardee for winning the battle?

In the Shenandoah Valley, Federal forces continued to push Early south.

On the 21st, Sherman ordered his men to attack Hood. Hood's men, under Patrick Cleburne, put up a stubborn and determined defense but there were simply too many Yankees to stop. When day was done, the Yankees could see Atlanta from the top of Ball Hill. Standing in the same position, the next day the Yankees viewed Atlanta from Leggett's Hill. They had renamed the hill for the Federal General who took it, Francis Leggett.

Hood decided to strike again on the 22nd. According to Hood, Hardee had messed everything up at the Battle at Peachtree Creek. That should mean that he had little confidence that Hardee could win another battle but it was Hardee who was to lead the next attack.

It was hot the night of the 21st as Southern columns force marched. By daylight, they were in position to strike Sherman between Decatur and Atlanta but they were dog-tired. Hood thought he had found a weak spot in Sherman's line to attack. It was by accident, not intent, that while the Southern boys marched that night, two fresh Union divisions camped in that weak spot. When dawn came, the Southern attack was spirited and hard but it was countered. Maj. Gen. W. H. T. Walker was killed as was Union Maj. Gen. James McPherson.

Union losses numbered about 3,700 while almost 10,000 Confederate soldiers did not answer the roll call that night. Hood now moved to the defensive and the Siege of Atlanta began. Now four great armies stared across siege lines at two great Southern cities; Lee vs. Grant at Richmond and Hood vs. Sherman at Atlanta.

In the Shenandoah Valley, the Yankees had been pushing Early south but on the 24th, he moved north. Moving over Valley Pike (Rt. 11), Early's whole force met George Crooks Federals at Kernstown. Crook was an able commander and gave Early a good fight until Confederates punched a hole in the center of his line. Crook's Army was forced to retreat toward Winchester; it was nearly routed.

The next day, Crook tried to make a stand at Bunker Hill just north of Winchester but Early smashed this line also. Also on the 25th, Lincoln wrote about the upcoming election. He basically said that unless he was elected, his war to subjugate the South would not be continued. If the Peace candidate won, "...disunion certainly following the success of the later."

On the 26th, Early destroyed the Baltimore and Ohio Railroad at Martinsburg.

On the 27th, Sherman started investing Atlanta and trying to cut rail service to the city. On the 28th, Hood tried to stop Sherman's advance on the railroad running south of the city. Although it was Thursday, both armies went to church. The blood-bought Ezra Church was the scene of bloody-battle. It took all afternoon for 500 Yankees to go down in blood and over 5,000 Confederates to do the same. One writer understated the obvious: "Hood's policy of attack proved even less successful than Johnston's policy of withdrawal and preservation of his army."

On the 29[th,] Early was back across the Potomac and he sent his cavalry under John McCausland forward. Near Petersburg, the Union tunnel under Confederate lines was reaching completion. Slaves who moved in and out of Union lines had warned the Southerners that the Yankees were digging a tunnel. Southern soldiers had placed their heads on the ground to try and hear the Yankee miners. Test holes had been dug but no tunnel was located.

At 4:30 in the morning of the 30[th,] "Probably the most terrific explosion ever known in this country" went off at Petersburg. In trenches where about 300 Confederates were stationed, there was now a hole 170 feet long, 80 feet wide and 30 feet deep. Confederates who one minute stood on the solid ground, the next were "...literally hurled a hundred feet in the air." Grant believed that the surprise of the big explosion and the big hole in Lee's line should open the way for a big Union victory. 15,000 Yankees attacked where the big crater now was. As was Union practice, they used Negro troops as shock troops. The speed of Rebel recovery was astounding. Gen. John Mahone sent Confederate troops to plug the hole. Southern mortars were very effective against the attacking black and white Federals. Some Southerners yelled, "take the whites; kill the niggers!" Many Yankees attacked through the crater and Southern rifles cut them down. It was noted that many white soldiers seemed to turn black as they fell in the crater. There wasn't enough oxygen and many Yanks died of suffocation not Southern shots. When it was over, Grant's great crater that was to break Lee's lines became a great Union grave. Southern losses were put at about 1,500 while the North lost over 4,000!

On this same day, McCausland's Cavalry rode into Chambersburg, Pennsylvania. Following Early's orders, McCausland informed the people that he was in their town to repay the North for what Hunter had done in the South. Unless $100,000 in gold or $500,000 in Green Backs was raised, their town would be razed. The money was not paid and Hunter caused yet another city to be burned. This time it was the Southern Army did the burning. This time no women were raped and no innocent civilian executed. McCausland had done what many other Yankees had done but the Yankees won the war so McCausland became a marked, hated, vilified man until his death.

By August 1st, Grant had had enough of Early making fools of the Yankee Army in the Valley, so he placed Sheridan in command. Sheridan was told to lay waste to the beautiful Shenandoah so that it would be of no use to the Confederacy.

On the 3rd, an expected but unwanted blow struck the Confederacy. The Yankees were making their move on one of the two last remaining deep water ports the South still had. On this date, Federal forces landed on Dauphin Island to attack Fort Gaines at the entrance to Mobile Bay, Alabama. On the 5th, Admiral David Farragut's fleet of four ironclad monitors and fourteen wooden vessels started the dangerous approach to Mobile Bay. Fort Gaines and Fort Morgan started throwing shells at his fleet at 5:30 A. M. Not only were there forts to stop the Federal fleet, there was a long narrow channel the ships must move through in order to reach the bay. The channel had mines (torpedoes) along its sides. At the end of the channel sat the Confederate Navy. This "navy" only had four ships. Three were small vessels but the *C. S. S. Tennessee* "was the most powerful (not the swiftest) ironclad afloat." The *U. S. S. Tecumseh* was about to clear the channel and head toward the *Tennessee* when it struck one or more torpedoes and in seconds disappeared under the water. This forced Farragut's ship the *Hartford* to take the lead. The fearless leader shouted his most memorable words, "Damn the torpedoes, full speed ahead!" If the Yankees had lost this battle, those words also would have been lost.

Three Yankee rams struck the *Tennessee* while Union monitors poured shell-after-shell into her. At 10 A. M. an admiral with a broken leg, Franklin Buchanan, surrendered the *Tennessee*. One of the other Confederate ships was sunk and another surrendered before it was sunk. The Battle of Mobile Bay was over. The forts and city were still in Confederate hands but the bay had been closed to outgoing traffic. The South now had only one deep water port left, Wilmington, North Carolina.

At Petersburg on this day, Confederates got a little revenge by exploding a mine of their own right in the faces of the 18th Corps.

As the mine exploded in Petersburg, Congress exploded right in Lincoln's face. Congress was mad because the President wanted to have the lead in the post-war administration of the South. The Congressmen accused him of being a "dictator." (Lincoln showed Hooker who was the real dictator.) They said Lincoln was making laws (a function of Congress) not just enforcing them. They said "it is the right and duty to check the encroachments of the Executive on the authority of Congress...."

On the 6[th,] the Union was tightening their grip on Mobile Bay by shelling and then taking Fort Powell. At the other deep water port, the *C. S. S. Chickasaw* sailed forth and captured or sunk more than thirty Union ships on her maiden voyage. On the 7th at Mobile Bay, Fort Gaines fell.

Confederate secret agents did a great job on the 9th and almost killed Grant as an extra. City Point (Hopewell) was the main exchange point for prisoners, which was until Grant took over. He stopped the prisoner exchange because it hurt the South more to keep those prisoners. So Grant willfully forced men to die that could have been exchanged. Grant may have been in City Point related to those exchanges when a terrific explosion went off. Confederate agents took a bomb aboard a transport. When the bomb exploded the cargo also exploded, 43 were killed and 126 wounded. Grant was covered by dust but not blood, so he was not numbered among the casualties.

To take the pressure off Atlanta, Joseph Wheeler started a raid into northern Georgia and east Tennessee on the 10th. They did considerable damage and returned on September 9th.

Sheridan advanced with numbers and materials that far surpassed anything the Confederacy could offer Early. On the 11th, Early was forced out of Winchester and fell back on Cedar Creek.

The 12th was not a good day for Lincoln. By now, Congress had said the illegal "Free States," like Louisiana, Tennessee and Arkansas, couldn't vote in the election. And Poor little Dishonest Abe had worked so hard to make sure that only Lincolnites could vote, too.

He heard rumors that his "drunken" general, Grant was going to run against him for President. He had been hearing from so many who opposed him, he may have wondered if anyone out there supported him? One of the biggest of the party bosses, Thurlow Weed, told the President, you "are in danger of being defeated in the election."

The 13th held no good news for Lincoln either. Today in Shawneetown, Illinois there were pro-Southern riots. The Union army had to fight the Union people.

Sheridan's hordes had made contact with Early's fighters at Cedar Creek on the 11th. Early had skirmished sharply with Yankees and made a big show. That was enough for Sheridan. On the night of the 15[th,] he began to withdraw toward Winchester.

Grant's hole in the ground had come to nothing but more Northern casualties. On the 18[th,] he started a move toward the vital Weldon Railroad. It cost Grant about 900 men but his army occupied almost a mile of the tracks.

As Grant's men moved on the ground, Grant wouldn't be moved by humanity. Confederate Commissioners formally petitioned Grant to start the exchange program again. This would keep many Yankees from suffering and dieing in Confederate prisons. Grant's answer, "No!" Let them die because it was harder on the Confederacy to maintain their prisoners.

Lee launched an attack on the 19th to get the Weldon back. A. P. Hill fought his men hard and many fell; the Yankees pushed back in some areas but at day's end the Yankees still controlled the railroad. Confederate casualties were high but unknown; everything was breaking down in the Southern Armies. The Federals lost about 2,500 men.

Lee launched another attack on the Weldon on the 21st. More men died on both sides but the results were the same. Lee realized that he didn't have enough men to retake the railroad and one more vital supply link was lost.

A. J. Smith had been sent to destroy Forrest but Forrest sent him running. Now, Forrest went after Sherman's supply line. In a daring, gallant attack, Forrest retook Memphis. For a few brief hours the city was part of the Confederacy again! Forrest took or destroyed massive amounts of supplies, took prisoners (two Union generals barely escaped) and secured many horses. The Yankees were "demoralized and embarrassed." "Could nothing be done about Forrest?" cried the newspapers.

On the 23^{rd,} Fort Morgan at Mobile Bay fell. The bay was closed to Confederate shipping and the city was now open to attack. Almost everyday, there was a new nail in the Confederate coffin but the man who started the war was not celebrating. In Washington, Lincoln informed his Cabinet of what everyone was saying anyway, "...it seems exceedingly probable that this Administration will not be re-elected." Everyone had been telling him that his war to subjugate the South was wrong and cost too many lives; it was time to stop the "effusion of blood." Lincoln admitted that the general who was now the peace candidate, McClellan, was likely to win.

Later on that same day, a desperate President wrote to an editor who had contacts in the South, Henry Raymond. He wanted Henry to set up a conference with President Davis to discuss "Peace." "War President Lincoln" now wanted to change horses and become "Peace President Lincoln." The office of President was more important to Lincoln than his word or the mountain of blue clad bodies he had, had killed in battle. It was Lincoln's official policy that the states were in "rebellion" against the central government; that no Confederacy existed. If there were no Confederacy, who was Lincoln willing to talk "peace" with? He postured by demanding the South re-enter the Union but everyone believed that this statement was no more truthful than any other statement he made. The truth was that Lincoln didn't really want "peace;" he just wanted to claim to be the "Peace Candidate," to fool the people. "You can fool all the people...."

On the 25th, there was a clash near Ream's Station on the Petersburg Line but Richmond remained safe. In Georgia, Sherman continued the southern movement but

Atlanta remained safe. By the 27th, Sherman was threatening the Montgomery and Atlanta Railroad. Also, this day, Sheridan quit retreating and advanced on Charles Town, (W) Virginia. The Yankees in Charleston, South Carolina had heard about Grant's big explosion at Petersburg so they tried the same thing. They couldn't dig a tunnel so they floated a raft filled with explosives toward Fort Sumter. It blew a big hole, in the water, and nothing more.

Although it had been quite in the Trans-Mississippi, the war was not over, over there. On the 29th, General Sterling Price moved toward Missouri, which he hoped to free.

In Chicago, Democrats opened their convention with speeches that blasted President Lincoln: "Four years of misrule by a sectional, fanatical and corrupt party, have brought our country to the verge of ruin."

On the 30th, Sherman took the Montgomery and Atlanta Railroad. This left only the Macon Line to supply the city. In the east, the evil and ineffective David Hunter was replaced by George Crook.

In Chicago, former general, George McClellan became the Democratic candidate for president. McClellan said he wanted to restore the Union but when he said, "restore the Union" it didn't mean the same thing that Lincoln did. McClellan wanted the Union to function as the founders had wanted. He said, "...peace may be restored on the basis of the Federal Union of the

States." That is, the states had every right to secede and that was permitted by the Constitution. McClellan also said that he would follow the Constitution, unlike Lincoln. He pointed out the truth, that Lincoln was a "...administrative usurpation of extraordinary and dangerous powers not granted by the constitution." He went on to list some of the unlawful acts of the Lincoln Administration. For example he spoke of the "arbitrary arrests, subversion of civil by military law, test oaths..." and so on. McClellan was a breath of flesh air to a country sick of Lincoln and sick of Lincoln's war.

On the 31st, Hood attacked Sherman. The Yankees lost 170 men, the South lost 1,700 men and Atlanta was still besieged. The soldiers of the Confederate Army of the Tennessee knew they didn't want to see "Uncle Joe," Joseph E. Johnston, replaced by Hood. Now the people of Atlanta were wondering if replacing Hood was a good idea?

CHAPTER 18 SEPTEMBER 1 - NOVEMBER 8, 1864

Lincoln's one consuming thought was trying to win the election. The nation, the lives of the soldiers, truth, fair-play, everything came second to his campaign. Lincoln's eyes were welded on Atlanta. If Atlanta fell, he could offer concrete proof that the Union was winning the war and thereby he may win the election.

Sherman was doing his best to help the boss. He sent Howard's entire army well south of the city to attack Hood's last railroad into Atlanta. Howard struck the Macon and Western at Jonesboro. Hood had sent his cavalry, under Wheeler, to attack Sherman's supply line. Without his eyes, Hood was unsure of Sherman's intentions and the strength of Howard's Army. He sent Hardee's and Lee's Corps to check things out. When Hardee realized the threat to the railroad, he attacked but Federal troop strength overwhelmed him. By the 1st, Jonesboro was in Union hands; the railroad cut; the fate of Atlanta sealed!

When the news of what happened that night and the next morning was relayed through the South, a great "wail" was heard! When the news of what happened that night and the next morning was relayed through the North, a great "hooray" was heard! After destroying supplies that might be useful to the conquerors, Hood had evacuated Atlanta! Sherman wired Lincoln at Washington, "So Atlanta is ours, and fairly taken."

David Hunter

Joseph Hooker

When Lincoln received the news, he talked to politicians and party bosses, "to get a feel of the nation in respect to the coming election." Lincoln knew that the clouds over his campaign were lifting.

In Virginia, Lee wrote President Davis, "Our ranks are constantly diminishing by battle and disease, and few recruits are received; the consequences are inevitable...." Lee formally suggested that Negroes be enlisted in Confederate service. There were many Negroes already serving their country, now Lee wished to open the ranks to slaves in general.

On the 3rd at Atlanta, Sherman was "beginning his personal rule over the Confederate citizenry." Sherman would provide evidence that the Union could produce war criminals that could rival, Attila the Hun and Genghis Khan. In Washington, Lincoln declared that the 5th was to be celebrated as a holiday for the victories in Atlanta and Mobile. Such public rallies were, in his eyes, re-election Lincoln rallies.

By the 4^{th,} John Hunt Morgan and his "Terrible Men" had left the Department of Southwest Virginia and were moving toward a raid on Knoxville. The command halted for the night in Greeneville, Tennessee. Morgan didn't know that the house he stayed in was owned by a Northern soldier. That night the wife of the Federal soldier, Mrs. C. D. Williams, rode north and told a Yankee garrison where Morgan was and that one road into town had no guard. By dawn 2,000 Union troopers had the house surrounded. After going to the Ohio pen, Morgan vowed he would not be taken alive again. He wasn't; he was shot and killed by a private. The hate-filled Yankees threw a rope about his corpse and dragged him through the muddy streets of Greeneville. Some of Morgan's men came under a flag of truce and recovered his body. He was buried first at Abingdon, Virginia but at this late stage of the war he was too important to just let die. His remains were transported to Richmond and given a state funeral. After the war, he went back to his beloved "blue grass" country and was buried at Lexington, Kentucky.

The worst war criminal in the history of this continent, Sherman, wrote, "I have deemed it to the interest of United States that the citizens now residing in Atlanta should (be) remove(d)..." on the 7th. About 1,600 citizens were forced from their homes. Many were old, frail, sick; some young and taking suck; some blind, some crippled. Some were bodily dragged from the houses and thrown in the streets but all, both white and black, were driven from their homes. What they could carry, was all they had. Most had no food or shelter. Southerners were shocked by the "barbarity and cruelty" but this greatest of all war criminals was just getting started!

Yankee cruelty knows no limits. On this date, 600 Confederate officers arrived at Morris Island, South Carolina. They were captured and held at Fort Delaware before being sent south. Federal guns from Morris Island had been pounding Fort Sumter and guns from Fort Sumter had been pounding Morris Island. To stop those Rebel guns, the 600 were placed in pen next to the Yankee fort. The Federals, who often screamed about the way the South treated Union prisoners, used them as a human shield. It was believed that the Confederates wouldn't shoot their own. Twenty-one died from the time they left Fort Delaware until they returned in October. Not one officer raised his hand and said, "I want out; I'll take the pledge." Confederate gunners were so accurate, that they fired over the captured officer's heads, not one died of Rebel shell. History remembers them, deservedly, as the "Immortal 600." The twenty-one who died? The Yankees starved them to death!

Lincoln wasn't the only candidate who was "feeling" the country. McClellan was running as a "Peace Candidate" but with the fall of Atlanta, he decided that he had better change, somewhat. On the 8th, he said he wasn't in full agreement with his party's platform but now didn't favor the division of the Union.

The Cherokee Nation had been forced to sign a "Peace Treaty" with the United States. Following the United States example, they broke their treaty. Confederate soldiers in war paint did battle against the Damned Yankees in Indian Territory.

The bleeding South was losing men and territory rapidly. Lee didn't think he could hold the capital without additional men. A large corps was pulled from Early and sent to Lee on the 14th. Sheridan didn't know that they were gone and that he had Early vastly outnumbered.

Sherman had many more men than Hood but Sherman had a very long supply line. It was decided to try and starve the Yankees into defeat. To this end on the 16th, the Confederate Legend, General Nathan Forrest started a raid in northern Alabama and middle Tennessee.

Grant couldn't do much against Lee so on the 16th he traveled to Sheridan in the Shenandoah Valley. Sheridan was very surprised when Grant informed him that he vastly outnumbered Early. The two made plans to attack Early as early as possible.

While Grant was away, the Confederate cavalry went into play. In a spectacular, daring raid, Wade Hampton's Troopers became "cow hands" and stole 2,500 head of Union beef. The hungry soldiers and citizens cheered wildly as the cattle entered Richmond!

In the Shenandoah, Early did the unexpected. Sheridan thought Early would fall back and let the Federals have the offensive but on the 17th, Early moved toward Sheridan's supply line, the Baltimore and Ohio Railroad.

John Fremont thought he was running for President against McClellan, with the unpopular Lincoln as just a side show. Now with Atlanta to brag about and all those government sponsored "Victory Rallies," John began to re-think his position. He had entered the race thinking that Lincoln had no chance. Now he believed that Lincoln could win. If he stayed in the race, he may split the pro-Union vote and let McClellan win. Therefore, he withdrew from the race. Now, Lincoln had the backing of the Republicans too.

On the 18th, Early was at Martinsburg on the B. & O. Railroad, again, Sheridan seemed to be the last one to know anything. When he learned that Early was at Martinsburg, Sheridan decided to attack toward Winchester and attack Early's Army piece meal.

Winchester had changed hands so many times during the war that people lost count. On the 19th, it changed again. When Sheridan's almost 50,000 men struck Early's column of less than 12,000, it was called the Third Battle of Winchester. Both sides took about 4,000 casualties but Early was badly beaten and retreated south.

The Confederacy faired better in other parts of the country this day. Sterling Price entered Missouri. Indian-Confederate General Stand Watie and Richard Gano hit a Union supply train in Indian Territory; the Yankees lost over 200 wagons, and many horses and men. In a daring undercover operation, Confederate agents moved to free Southern prisoners held on Johnson's Island in the middle of Lake Erie. Agent, John Beall's plan was to capture the three ships guarding the island and use the ships to transport the prisoners to Canada. The *Philo Parsons* and *Island Queen* were captured but the Federals got word and stopped the attempt on the *Michigan*. With the *Michigan* in place, Beall couldn't take the island. First the *Philo Parsons* was burned and Beall sailed the *Island Queen* to Canada where it too was burned. The Confederate prisoners continued to languish in the brutal hands of their captors.

By the 20[th,] Sheridan's chase of Early was ended at Fisher's Hill. Early knew that he had barely escaped and felt that if Sheridan were any kind of a general, he would have "crushed" him at Winchester.

The Great Forrest crossed the Tennessee River and moved toward Athens and more Union supplies.

Lincoln was more worried about his re-election. He sent members of his cabinet on the campaign trail.

On the 22[nd,] Union atrocities crossed the line again! In the Shenandoah, the Yankees hung two of Mosby's men; "The other four were tied to stakes and mercilessly shot through the skull...." Mosby sent a courier to Sheridan telling him that he didn't want "to execute Union prisoners" but the dead Rebels would be avenged. Soon six captured Yanks left this world. Later Mosby wrote Sheridan again. "Hereafter any prisoners falling into my hands will be treated with the kindness due to their condition, unless some new act of barbarity shall compel me, reluctantly, to adopt a line of policy repugnant to humanity." Mosby let Sheridan know that he could also act like a Yankee. Sheridan didn't wish to face a Confederate commander that was as low down as he was, so the prisoner killing stopped!

General Early held a good defensive position on Fisher's Hill and he was more than willing to do battle with Sheridan. Sheridan drew his forces up in front of Early and Early waited. During the night of the 21st, Sheridan sent George Crook's Division circling around Early's left flank. By dawn, Crook was behind Early. It was afternoon before Crook's men yelled and fell upon Early's rear and left flank. At the same time, Sheridan advanced his superior force directly at Early. The attack was sudden and overwhelming. Early was all but routed. The Confederate losses approached 2,000 irreplaceable men.

When word of Early's defeat reached Lincoln, Lincoln again showed his lack of concern for the soldiers, bleeding and dieing. President Lincoln stated that this victory could only help him in his campaign.

While Early was losing and Lincoln crowing, President Davis tried to turn Sherman's victory into hope for his defeat. In Macon the President addressed a crowd and told them, "Our Cause is not lost. Sherman cannot keep up his long line of communication (supply line) and retreat, sooner or later, he must. Let no one despond."

To help his campaign on the 23^{rd,} Lincoln fired a long time friend and supporter, Blair. Postmaster General Montgomery Blair was not liked by the Radicals but friendship and trust meant nothing to Lincoln.

On the 24^{th,} Forrest defeated the Yankees at Athens, Alabama and Price defeated the Yankees at Fayette, Missouri. In the Shenandoah, Sheridan believed he had pounded Early's Army into impotency. Now another war criminal was born! Sheridan spread his troops across the valley floor and made war on helpless citizens. The smoke rose, the valley burned, the people wept. It was said that after the hell of fire Sheridan unleashed on the people, that a "Crow flying across the valley would find it needful to pack his own rations." The cruelty of Sheridan has never left the valley.

By the 27^{th,} the Federals at St. Louis were getting nervous because Price was coming nearer. At Centralia, Confederates took revenge for Yankee atrocities. "Bloody Bill" Anderson's force, which included the James brothers, took the town. The town was looted and twenty-four Federals executed. When other Yankees attacked, they were cut to pieces and left with 116 less men than they attacked with.

Hood had blamed all his losses, including Atlanta, on Hardee. On the 28^{th,} President Davis gave Hood permission to fire Hardee. The President still liked Hood even if no one else did.

Along the Petersburg line, Grant worried that Lee may send troops to Early and stop the rape of the valley. To prevent this, Grant with his overwhelming numbers attacked Lee in two places on the 29th. He struck Lee north of the James and south of Petersburg. Confederate Fort Harrison became Federal Fort Harrison north of the James. To the south, the Union attack extended their lines toward the vital South Side Railroad.

Early's men showed Sheridan that their spirit was not broken as they fought the enemy at Waynesboro.

On the 30th, it was Lee who renewed the fighting. He wanted Fort Harrison back. Many a good man fell but the Yanks held the fort. South of Petersburg A. P. Hill drove the enemy back at the Battle of Peebles' Farm.

On October 1st, Forrest continued his successful raid on Sherman's supply line by defeating Federals at Athens and Huntsville and then crossing in to Tennessee to strike at Carter's Creek.

Now that Morgan was dead, the Yankees showed a renewed interest in destroying the massive salt works at Saltville. Jacob Ammen's Cavalry of 1,500 men moved from east Tennessee, while the main force of infantry, numbering 5,200 men and artillery moved south out of Pikeville, Kentucky. The "most hated man in Kentucky" General Stephen Burbridge commanded.

Off the coast of North Carolina, near Fort Fisher, Northern warships ran the *Condor* aground. On board the *Condor* was a famous Southern spy, Rose Greenhow. It was she who told Beauregard of the Union advance from Washington to Manassas at the first of the war. Rose was attempting to escape capture by taking a smaller boat to shore. She was carrying $2,000 in gold on her person. The boat overturned in the surf and Rose and the gold went to the bottom. The South had lost another martyr to the Cause.

On the 2^{nd,} Hood went after Sherman's supply line by attacking the Western & Atlantic Railroad.

South of Petersburg, it was Hill who was now driven back. The Union had advanced three miles closer to the South Side Railroad.

After Morgan's death, Breckinridge had been appointed commander of the Department of Southwest Virginia. Breckinridge sent every man he could find to defend Saltville but at the time of the battle, the Confederacy was vastly outnumbered. Burbridge did not use his forces effectively but committed them piecemeal. He used his Negro troops as "cannon fodder" and their casualties far exceeded any other white Union units. The Southern line held and Burbridge retreated during the night leaving his wounded on the field. The following morning, Southern troops took revenge on their former slaves. A massacre of Negro troops took place.

By the 3rd, Hood was setting on top of Sherman's supply line by controlling the Chattanooga-Atlanta Railroad. As expected, Sherman started sending troops from Atlanta to deal with Hood. Hood thought his plan was working but Sherman was out-thinking him. Sherman believed that Hood might strike at Nashville so he sent his best defensive man, George Thomas, to prepare the city for Southern attack.

In the Department of the Trans-Mississippi, Price was operating just west of St. Louis. To the south, President Davis arrived in the capital of South Carolina to "enthusiastic" crowds. In a speech, Davis returned to the theme of Sherman's long supply line, "I see no chance for Sherman to escape from a defeat or a disgraceful retreat."

The Engagement of Allatoona took place on the 5th. Hood's men had been wrecking the railroad and now they were heading for a pass the Yankees were holding at Allatoona. Before Maj. Gen. S. G. French attacked he gave the Union commander, Gen. John Corse, the option of surrender. Corse refused and wired Sherman for reinforcements. The battle started and many men fell defending or attacking that mountain pass. During the battle Sherman wired Corse to hold on that reinforcements were on the way. While fighting was under way, French got word of Sherman's telegraph. Although the South was winning, French decided to retreat. Only later did Corse learn that Sherman was lying and no reinforcements were on their way.

This day, Lincoln sent his Secretary of the Navy to Missouri to campaign for him. In Indiana a prominent peace activist, Lambdin Milligan was jailed. The Northern President's campaign slogan could read, "Vote for Lincoln or go to jail!"

The President, Davis, was upbeat in a speech in Augusta, Georgia. "Never before was I so confident that (we can)...rid the country of its enemy....a free and independent people... must beat Sherman, we must march into Tennessee... we must push the enemy back to the banks of the Ohio."

Gen. George Custer's Cavalry was out burning homes, mills, barns and lives on the 6th, when Early's Cavalry under Thomas Rosser struck. Rosser didn't win but Custer was aware that his inhuman acts would be opposed.

On this date, there were articles in the newspaper in both South and North about the Negroes. The importance of Lee to the Cause was reflected in an article in the Richmond *Enquirer*. The paper endorsed Lee's suggestion to draft Negroes into Confederate service. In the North, newspapers were screaming about the Massacre at Saltville. The papers said that more Negro Union troops were murdered than the total official loss for the whole regiment. Many of the wounded enemy from Saltville, both white and black, were taken to a hospital at nearby Emory and Henry College. Some Southern troops forced their way into the hospital and shot at least two more Negro soldiers in their beds. Partisan Ranger, Champ Ferguson, shot a white officer with the 13th Kentucky Cavalry. Lt. E. C. Smith was one of a group of Yankees who had entered the Ferguson's Kentucky home, raped the wife and daughter and then forced the two women to walk naked through the town. When word reached Champ at the front, he swore he would kill every one of those Damned Yankees who committed that crime. This night one of the criminals was executed. It is uncertain why only one person was held by the Confederacy for the Massacre at Saltville. That person was Champ Ferguson.

On the 7th, Price closed in on the capital of Missouri, Jefferson City. The *C. S. S. Florida* had taken or sunk 37 enemy ships. On this date, the Union fleet spotted the Confederate ship in a Brazilian port and went in after her. Brazil resented the invasion of its territory and fired at the Yankee ships but that didn't stop them from taking the *Florida*. Later Federal Secretary of State, William Seward "condemned it as unauthorized and unlawful."

Rosser and Custer met again at the Battle of Tom's Brook on the 9th. Custer had more and could replace his losses. Rosser ran and could not replace his losses.

Sherman was trying to cover his supply line on the 10th when his men skirmished with Hood's near Rome,

Georgia. Sherman sent gunboats and troop transports up the Tennessee River to rid himself of Forrest. One gunboat was damaged, two transports disabled and the rest of the pack, abandoned their comrades and sailed away. Forrest was showing the Yankees he could lick them on land or water.

By the 11[th,] Price fought skirmishes at Boonville and Brunswick, Missouri. Partisan Rangers fired on the Yankee gunboat, the *Resolute* in Arkansas. Near Fort Donelson, Confederates attacked a Federal "Negro recruiting detachment." That is to say, that white Federals were out stealing slaves. Today's slave was tomorrow's Northern Negro soldier.

Lincoln was up past midnight at the War Department listening to the telegraph click. Not war news, soldier's deaths didn't disturb the President's sleep. He was following politics. There was a Governor's race in Indiana and Congressional races in Pennsylvania and Ohio. Republicans did better than expected. Lincoln felt the elections were positive news for his re-election hopes.

When President Lincoln awoke on the 12[th,] he got more good news. Chief Justice of the Supreme Court, Roger Taney, was dead. He had presided over the Dred Scott Case and had told Lincoln, time-after-time that his actions were unconstitutional. Although Lincoln had ignored Taney, now he wouldn't even have to listen to him any more.

Sterling Price

William Barksdale

When Lincoln awoke on the 13th, he was thinking of the individual soldiers. He issued instructions to the War Department that he wanted as many of them as possible to be given a leave. Was he worried about their welfare? No, he was worried about his welfare! The leave was to be given so that the soldiers could be home in time to vote. The soldiers were also to be instructed as to whom to vote for. Did Lincoln believe in fair play? No, he believed that most soldiers would vote for him, not McClellan? Did Lincoln believe that he should use the power of his office in a fair and democratic way?

This day in Georgia, Hood showed Sherman that he just couldn't protect his entire supply line. After an attack at Resaca failed, Hood destroyed the railroad at Dalton. This day in Virginia, Partisan Ranger, John Mosby, showed Sheridan that he just couldn't protect his entire supply line. Mosby ripped a section of the B. & O. Railroad near Kearneysville and took a Yankee train. Before the train was burned, the supplies were removed. Part of what was removed was Federal payrolls worth, $173,000.

On the 17th, General Lee got some good news for a change. General Longstreet had been wounded at the Wilderness, but now his "War Horse" was back. Longstreet had recovered enough to assume command.

In England, the ladies held a benefit for Confederate soldiers on the 18th. In the Shenandoah

Valley, Early and his map maker looked down on Sheridan's force and plotted strategy.

When Early surveyed the Federals on the 18th, he didn't know that Sheridan had been to a conference in Washington. Sheridan was returning to his army on the 19th. As he returned, Early was making his move in the early morning fog. Early had seen a way to move his army toward the enemy without being seen. At dawn, Early attacked in what is known as the Battle of Cedar Creek. Some Yankees were still asleep but Early woke them up. The fog, the secret move and surprise allowed a Confederate success! The Union camp was over run; many prisoners taken; supplies and artillery were captured. The Union 8th and 19th Corps were smashed! Next Early turned on the 6th Corps. The 6th was driven back but Early's attack lacked the punch because half-starved Johnneys stopped to loot and eat and failed to push the attack. Sheridan rode at break-neck speed from Winchester. He arrived about 10:30 A. M. and began to rally his broken forces. They formed a line and halted Early's advance. By 4:30 P. M. Sheridan had enough of his massive army in line of battle and now it was his turn to attack Early. Southern men fought gallantly but Sheridan had too much. The lines bent and then broke. Dead men, animals, supplies and wagons littered the road all the way back to Fisher's Hill. Early lost about 3,000 men. Southern general, Stephen Ramseur would soon die of his wounds. Early's Army was so badly beaten that it could no longer offer much resistance to Sheridan.

Vermont is a state that was far from the fighting but this date, twenty-five daring Confederates crossed from Canada and brought the war to them. The soldiers took St. Albans with plans to burn the town. The Southern invaders did manage to relieve the town banks of $200,000 before they ran. Most Rebels crossed back into Canada. Later Canadian authorities arrested the leader, Lt. Bennett Young and twelve of his men. They only recovered $75,000 of the confiscated money.

Forrest had just completed one successful raid against Sherman's supply line and on this date he left Corinth, Mississippi to do it again.

In Missouri, Price met strong resistance at Lexington and had to fall back.

President Lincoln had strong indications that the Democrats wanted to stop the war as soon as possible. If McClellan won, there was a plan to immediately take control of the government. Lincoln gave a speech in Washington saying, "I am struggling especially to prevent others from overthrowing it (the government)." By now, McClellan had played the race card. He said that Lincoln was so much for the Negro that Lincoln favored "race mixing." Lincoln was now considered a "nigger lover."

On the 20[th,] Price began withdrawing from Missouri. His invasion had caused a great stir and disruption in Union plans but it had not changed the war in the Trans-Mississippi.

Confederate Indians struck settlements in the Platte Valley in Nebraska Territory.

By the 21^{st,} Price's Confederates forced the Union out of Independence, Missouri after the Battle on the Little Blue. By now the people of both countries, indeed the world, were learning of the terrible atrocities the Union Army was committing. Sherman was reaping havoc on the people of Atlanta and Sheridan, following Grant's orders, was destroying the beautiful Shenandoah. What was Lincoln's reaction to the news? At the White House, he "proposed three cheers for Sheridan, Grant, and all our noble commanders...." Now it was "noble" to burn, loot and rape!

As the Yankees closed more Southern ports, it made blockade running more dangerous. Now, Wilmington and Charleston were the South's last outlets. Federal vessels concentrated on these. It was noted that the amount of goods reaching the Confederacy was decreasing and the cost of those goods was increasing.

In Missouri, Price was aware that the Yankees were closing in on him. By the 22^{nd,} he had devised a daring plan. With limited numbers, he would attack not retreat. Near present day Kansas City. Price sent his wagon supply train south and Jo Shelby and James Pagan to attack Maj. Gen. James Blunt.

Also on this date, Federals skirmished with the Rebel Indians at Midway Station, Nebraska Territory and on the White River in Arkansas. Partisan Rangers attacked a Union troop transport.

On the 23rd, near Kansas City the South attacked the Federals. It was hoped, that victory could be achieved before both parts of the Union Army could come together. At first Confederates drove the enemy from the field and across Brush Creek. The Union counterattacked and for two hours it was a struggle to see who would control the field. The stalemate was broken when the boys in blue found a ravine to move undetected on the Confederate left. As the Confederate left flank was being struck, the other part of the Union Army advanced. The Yankees were able to push Marmaduke back and attack Shelby from the rear. When this happened, Price knew it was over and started a withdrawal from Missouri. Some 20,000 Yankees had engaged 8,000 Rebels in the largest battle in Missouri, the Battle of Westport.

A campaigning Lincoln addressed the 189th New York Volunteers on the 24th. He told them, "(the soldiers) have not only fought right... they have voted right...." Thus, it was President Lincoln, who encouraged soldiers to vote by absentee ballots. He also asked the generals to furlough the men who would "vote right." It was made clear to the soldiers that only pro-

Lincoln men got to go home to vote; another abuse of power.

The Federals followed up their victory at Westport by attacking a retreating Price on the 25th. Two undermanned, Confederate divisions broke and part of the wagon train was lost. Other Confederates rushed to protect the supplies. Even with reinforcements, Price lost over a third of his wagon train as the army retreated southward.

Grant believed he saw a way to out-flank Lee and take the Southside Railroad. On the 27th, he sent 17,000 Blue Bellies to stop those Rebel trains. Wade Hampton's Cavalry backed by Heth's and Mahone's Infantry stopped the Yankees dead at Hatcher's Run. Lee had beaten Grant again! There would be no major fighting until spring; by then Confederate trenches would extend thirty-five miles and be manned by men that were ill-clothed, ill-fed, ill-armed but with a spirit of determination!

During the night of the 27th, it was the Yankees who used a new weapon. A "steam launch" with a torpedo tied to a pole went up the Roanoke River toward Plymouth, North Carolina and the Confederate Man-of-War, the *Albemarle*. It was a daring and successful Northern raid and the *Albemarle* went down.

Also, during the night Partisan Rangers pulled off a daring attack on the *Belle Saint Louis* at Fort Randolph, Tennessee.

By the 28th, both Hood and Forrest were operating against Sherman's supply line. President Davis and all the generals had been saying that Sherman couldn't maintain his supply line and that a Southern victory was soon to come. Sherman knew he couldn't maintain his supply line but he didn't believe a "Southern victory was soon to come." After Sherman had sent Thomas, the Rock of Chickamauga, to defend Nashville, he broke off contact with Hood and returned to Atlanta.

On the 29th, Forrest showed that his men were the equal of any Yankee on land or water. Near Fort Henry, on the Tennessee River Forrest attacked and captured the iron clad *Undine* and the transport the *Mazeppa*. The transport contained 9,000 badly need pairs of shoes.

In other water borne action, the Confederate raider *Olustee* made it past the Union blockade at Wilmington and took six Northern ships in a week.

On Halloween, Union forces gave Plymouth a trick and no treat. After heavy shelling they took this Confederate base on the Roanoke River. The noose grew ever tighter.

By this date, Forrest had captured so many Federal vessels that he started his own "Confederate Navy" on the Tennessee.

The upcoming Presidential elections occupied Lincoln's attention more than did the war. On November 2nd, Forrest's (two vessel) "navy" was attacked by two Union gunboats near Johnsonville on the

Tennessee. The transport was run aground and Forrest's naval strength was cut in half. The next day, Forrest's (one vessel) navy challenged three Federal gunboats but this time it was the Yankees who ran.

When the Yankees chickened out on the 3rd, Forrest decided to have some fun on the 4th. He "...shelled the Federal gunboats, transports, barges, bulging warehouses, open storage, two wagon trains, and the Union soldiers at the supply base of Johnsonville. Sherman wrote, "...that devil Forrest was down about Johnsonville and was making havoc...." After a day of fun, Forrest moved south toward Corinth and Hood.

On the 5th near Charleston, (W) Virginia, Confederates captured two Union transports.

Daring Confederate agents planned to take the city of Chicago and free prisoners held at Camp Douglas. On the 6th before they got the chance to try, they were arrested.

On the 7th, President Davis wired Hood that he desired Hood to march toward the Ohio River. That same day, the President's speech was read to Congress. The President was upbeat. Though Atlanta was lost, Davis said that no one point was critical to the survival of the nation. President Davis said he believed the economy was getting stronger. He asked Congress to buy slaves to work on the defenses of the country. Although he didn't call for Negroes to go directly into Confederate service, he didn't close the door on the idea.

John Hood

Albert Jenkins

He said he would be willing to talk peace with the Yankees but not "our unconditional submission and degradation."

The 8th was Election Day and "Honest" Abe had done everything within his power to make sure it was a "dishonest" election. He had created illegal "Free States" in the South, with only pro-Lincoln votes. However, Congress wouldn't allow the President to use them in his re-election bid. Pro-Lincoln soldiers were furloughed for the expressed duty to return home and vote. Conservative estimates set a figure close to 40,000 as the number of people jailed illegally. These included party opponents, journalists, and people who spoke the truth. There was much opposition to Lincoln in the border state of Kentucky. The Military Governor of the State, Burbridge, had his orders: he was "arresting any man, who he even suspected of not voting for Lincoln." It is assumed that all other government officials were given the same order. Poor George McClellan had no chance to get his message out but the government controlled media repeatedly told the public about recent Union victories, most notably, Atlanta. Peace through conquest was just around the corner. McClellan's position of peace through negotiations was downplayed.

That night, President Lincoln spent time in the War Office listening to the telegraph "tick" and wondering if he had failed to arrest someone, or threaten a newspaper editor, or cancel a military contract with any supplier that didn't donate to his campaign, or if some of those ungrateful soldiers he had furloughed might vote for McClellan?

As the telegraph "ticked," Lincoln felt good about what he had done. Of the 25 states left in the Union, 22 had voted for him. Almost 100% of the boys that got furloughs from the Army of the Potomac voted for the Commander-in-Chief. Apparently, Burbridges' jails in Kentucky weren't big enough because almost 70% of the people voted against Lincoln. When the popular votes were totaled, Lincoln noted that he had 400,000 more votes than McClellan (out of 4,000,000----10%). Lincoln may have wondered if he could have won the election by truly being "Honest, Abe?"

After the Republican candidate, John Fremont, withdrew from the race, Lincoln claimed to be "the Republican candidate." There were only 52 days from the time Fremont gave notice that he would not run and the election. This author found no evidence that the Republican Party formed a committee to decide on a date and place to hold a convention or that Lincoln was nominated by such a convention. The Yankee "glorification of Honest Abe" required that truth be lost, and he did not run as a Republican!

CHAPTER 19 NOVEMBER 9- DECEMBER 31, 1864

While Hood was making plans to move north on the 9th, Sherman was making plans to move east. He organized his Federals to cut loose of any supply base and live off the land. That is to say steal off the people. He told his commanders that few wagons would be used, "The army will forage liberally," horses and mules were to be stolen when possible, and if any person, town or armed group should oppose the theft, then "...enforce devastation more or less relentless." The South would pay for her sin; daring to defy their Northern masters.

In Washington on the 10th, Lincoln was putting his spin on the election. After corrupting the election process, he claimed the election showed just how "free" the country really was. The Freedom of the Press and Freedom of Speech were greatly curtailed. He was right; this crooked election showed just how "un-free" the country really was. He also claimed the election as a mandate to continue the war.

A large number of those who voted for him were enraged by Lincoln's statement. He talked of "peace" and many voters were fooled; "you can fool some of the people..." It was unwise to stand on the courthouse steps and call the President a "Tyrant" and call for his removal by any means necessary but that is what many thought. Within small groups of friends, there was talk of his "removal."

George Thomas

George Stoneman

In the Shenandoah Valley, Early moved toward New Market as if he were threatening Sheridan but Early didn't have an army left that could defeat Sheridan.

On the 11[th,] Sherman was moving away from Atlanta. The first flames, of his march of terror, were starting. Anything the South could use was destroyed: railroads, flour mills, food warehouses, supplies, shops, overland road bridges and even homes. Rails were heated and wrapped about trees; these were "Sherman's Neckties;" the blacked chimneys were, "Sherman's Sentinels." Sherman was preparing to leave Atlanta on the 12th and everything except for houses and churches were burned. The band gleefully played *The Battle Hymn of the Republic.* His cavalry, under Judson Kilpatrick, was already gone. Sherman and 60,000 infantry followed and there were 5,500 men to man the cannons. The Yankee nation thought of "...them as moral, honorable young Americans, ideal products of the world's most enlightened system of government. In fact, they were potentially cruel and heartless pillagers, many of whom awaited only the opportunity to plunder, burn and rape." Sherman told Grant that he would make "Georgia howl!"

Early had little to defend the Valley and on the 13th it got to be even less. Lee ordered some of Early's troops to help defend Richmond. Since Early took command in June, he showed what a fighter he was. His army had marched over 1,600 miles, attacked

Washington and fought over 75 engagements. Now, it could do little against the army that wanted to burn the Valley and commit war crimes against defenseless citizens.

The Yankees attacked Confederate-Indians near Fort Larned, Kansas and chased Partisan Rangers in Pemiscot County, Missouri.

On the 24th, Sherman destroyed the railroad toward Decatur and Stone Mountain. Hood was waiting on Forrest to join him and Thomas began to collect his forces near Nashville to oppose Hood.

In Washington, Lincoln took great pleasure in firing McClellan from the army. Lincoln also received a letter from Maj. Gen. Stephen Hurlbut Lincoln had appointed him "Governor of the Free State of Louisiana." Hurlbut complained that Lincoln had done nothing to help the Negroes. The government had stolen them from their rightful masters and now no one was taking care of them. After Dis-Honest Abe found-out the so-called "free states" wouldn't help him get re-elected, Lincoln had ignored the "free states" and the Negro. Lincoln cared little about the treatment of the Negro, so he also ignored the letter.

On the 16th, the last of Sherman's men left Atlanta; there was now no supply line or communications line left to the North. As the artillery left the city, they unlimbered their guns and shelled the city. The smoke from Atlanta was so thick that it offends the nostrils of History to this day!

Breckinridge had taken the army from Southwest Virginia and moved toward Knoxville. This was to help take pressure off Hood. After an engagement at Strawberry Plains, Breckinridge started back toward the Southwest Virginia-East Tennessee Department. On this date, Forrest joined Hood at Tuscumbia, Alabama.

The Senate of Georgia saw that there was no one to oppose Sherman and that Sherman was determined to destroy their state. So, some suggested that Georgia should make a separate Peace Treaty with Sherman and dropout of the war. On the 17th President Davis wrote to the Georgia Senators that he strongly opposed any separate peace treaty; the idea was dropped. On the 18th, Davis wired Gen. Howell Cobb in Macon to get out every man he could to oppose Sherman. Davis did not call for arming the Negroes. On the 19th, the Governor of Georgia, Joe Brown signed a bill to draft all men from 16 to 55 to fight Sherman but there weren't many left to draft.

On the 21st, Hood started north with his army. He had about 30,000 infantry and Forrest's 8,000 cavalry. When planning took place, it was believed a northward move would force Sherman to abandon Atlanta and follow Hood north but Sherman was already on his way to the sea.

Lincoln wanted everyone in the Union to know of his great compassion so he had the letter he wrote Mrs. Lydia Bixby published in leading Northern newspapers. He told Mrs. Bixby that his heart was broken because she had lost five sons on the field of battle. The letter was a tear jerker. President Lincoln "beat his breast and gushed forth great tears" as he publicly wrote this woman a letter of private consolation. It later turned out that Mrs. Bixby did have five sons in the army. One had returned with an honorable discharge; two had been killed as the President said and two had deserted. As the President wrote, the Union Army was trying to find her two deserter sons so that they could kill them.

By the 22nd, the Georgia legislature had fled and Sherman's forces took over the capital, at Milledgeville. The Damned Yankees, who were destroying the state, now set up a mock session to make fun of the government and people of Georgia; drunken Yankees lit cigars with Georgia dollar bills. The vile looting, burning and "unspeakable dishonor" (raping) continued. Literally hundreds of Georgians were murdered during this march of shame. Union General, Frank Blair placed a 50 cent fine on his soldiers for unnecessary shooting "...in hope of preventing civilian deaths." A church was looted and the pipe organ filled with molasses. The worshippers said, "God will not permit the desecration of His Holy Temple to go unpunished."

On this day, President Davis sent Bragg to Georgia to try and stop Sherman. When Bragg arrived he found that he commanded Beauregard and Hardee. Both men held Bragg in low esteem.

Hood tried to beat the Union army to Columbia, Tennessee. Forrest was there before the Federal Army but Hood's infantry was too far back to support Forrest so the Yankees took Columbia on the 24th.

A lot of planning went into the raid on New York City. Confederate agents crossed from Canada and waited for a windy night. The men rented at least ten hotel rooms in different parts of the city. On the night of the 25th, the ten hotel rooms were set on fire as was the Barnum Museum but nothing happened. In the planning, there was a big failure. The chemical used needed a great deal of air (oxygen) to burn. The agents didn't open the windows so the stuff smoldered and did not burn. The raid was a failure. One Confederate, R. C. Kennedie, was caught and hung.

On the 27th, Joe Wheeler's Southern cavalry stopped Kilpatrick's Boys cold at Waynesborough, Georgia.

Confederate agents planted a bomb on the steamer, the *Greyhound*. The "Beast Butler" was using the steamer as his head quarters. The steamer went to the bottom of the James, unfortunately Butler wasn't with it.

Hood and the Yankees had been facing off at Columbia. The Federal cavalry commander kept bringing the Union generals false reports about the size of Hood's Army. That night the Yankees ran from Columbia, although there were more Blue-Bellies and they had a better defensive position.

Thomas Rosser, in a daring raid from the Shenandoah, struck New Creek (today Keyser, WV) and the B & O Railroad on the 28th. The suddenness of the attack overwhelmed the enemy. Much of the railroad was damaged; supplies and prisoners were taken.

It was an "Affair not a Battle of Spring Hill" in Tennessee on the 29th. It is one of those "might have beens." Hood's army could have easily cut the main retreat route to Nashville for John Schofield and his Federal Army, if Hood had only known how close he was and how few Yankees he opposed. As was, the fleeing Yankees continued north.

The hatred, deprecations and the bloodlust of the Yankees knew no limit. On this date, Col. J. M. Chivington's nine-hundred men surrounded six-hundred Cheyenne and Arapahoe Indians near Denver. The Colonel accused the Indians in involvement in pro-Confederate raids on whites. The Indians denied that they were involved. Col. Chivington gave the out-numbered, out-gunned Indians no warning but just opened fire! Over 600 men, women and children were slaughtered! In his report Chivington wrote, "It may perhaps be unnecessary for me to state that I captured no prisoners." The Yankees even murdered the babies!

The Northern press yelled loud and long when a few Negro troops were massacred but when hundreds of whites and Indians died by Federal murder, few even covered the story in their newspapers.

"The Army of Tennessee died at Franklin on November 30, 1864." Hood was aware of the Union's narrow escape at Spring Hill. He also was determined that the Yankees not be allowed to go to Nashville. Hood was a valiant fighter. He had only one leg and the use of one arm. By separate actions for his country, Hood became half a man. The pain he bore was so intense that he used large quantities of Laudanum (dope).

At a conference at 2:30, Hood ordered an immediate full frontal assault. Generals Forrest, Cheatham and Cleburne joined in a chorus strongly advising against the attack. "Attack and attack now" was the order of the day. Not all the army, including the artillery, was on line when the attack began. These weren't the gay lads of '61; these were the veterans of a hundred battles. The common soldier knew what the generals knew; the attack was "suicidal." Brave Confederates formed shoulder-to-shoulder and attacked along a two and one half mile front. For the next five hours "Men were clubbing, clawing, punching, stabbing, and choking each other." These were the "bloodiest hours of the war." The Union line held. Approximately 7,000 Rebels went down. Fifteen of the twenty-eight

Confederate generals were casualties. Sixty-five officers fell. Some units lost two-thirds of their strength. After the battle, many Confederates kept retreating. The desertion rate was very high. The common soldier knew that dieing in battle was an occupational hazard; they accepted that. Suicide wasn't. They would no longer fight under Hood. Some say that after the battle, Forrest threatened to kill Hood and stated that he would never fight under his command again! The Army of Tennessee died at Franklin on November 30, 1864.

As the Army of the Tennessee was bleeding at Franklin, Yankees moved out from Hilton Head with the aim of cutting the Charleston and Savannah Railroad. However, it was the Georgia home guard that cut the Yankees up at Honey Hill and Southern trains kept on rolling.

Although, the Southern Army had been decimated at Franklin, Union general John Schofield decided to withdraw to Nashville under the cover of darkness. By the 1st of December, his men were linking up with George Thomas in defenses about that city. When Hood realized they were gone, he ordered an all-out pursuit. A bleeding army tried to catch Schofield but failed. After a quick inspection of the Federal defenses, Hood knew he couldn't carry the works. The army couldn't attack; the armies couldn't bypass Thomas and just leave him to threaten the rear; there was no reason to retreat; so the army just sat and shivered in the cold in front of Nashville.

On the 3^{rd,} the Union went after another salt work, this one at Rocky Point, Florida.

At Waynesborough, Georgia on the 4^{th,} the cavalries of Wheeler and Kilpatrick met. After a day of bloody fighting, Confederate Wheeler withdrew.

Salmon Chase was always on Lincoln's case when he was Secretary of the Treasury. Lincoln fired this "pain in the butt," when he found out that Chase was after his job. Chase was out of government but still power hungry and still on Lincoln's case. On the 6^{th,} Lincoln appointed Chase to head the Supreme Court to replace the dead Taney. Chase had crossed Lincoln politically. Lincoln had ignored Taney and now he could do the same with Chase.

After putting Chase in his place, President Lincoln sent a message to his Congress. He basically said that he lied in the campaign when he said he would talk to the South about "Peace." He wrote Congress, "The issue can only be decided by war." When "Honest Abe" realized he had cheated his way to re-election, he claimed the vote was a mandate from the people to continue his war. Now, he told Congress, that it was a mandate to abolish slavery. Lincoln lied so much that words meant nothing. Congress sat there as the message was read, as if they could believe anything the man said.

Offensive military campaigns are almost always fought in the spring and summer because bad weather fights on the side of the defender. Yankee high command recognized that the South had so little to eat, to wear and shelter; that the weather would fight with well clothed and fed Blue-Bellys.

Sherman's Army had been eating Georgia and South Carolina alive. A sixty mile wide path of utter destruction and fire was cut across those states. Rape, pillage, and cold-blooded murder were common! Sherman is America's most monstrous war criminal. When he was questioned by a newspaper man about all the atrocities, Sherman replied, "War is hell." It was "hell" for the citizens, their homes and livestock that got in his way but a picnic for his soldiers. The private's pockets were filled; the officers grew rich by stealing from Southern citizens. At Christmas time in many Northern homes, the "old family silverware" is brought out and polished for the annual dinner. A great deal of the "old family silverware" is really stolen; "old Southern family silverware."

In winter, Sherman was looting the Deep South while other Yankees were gathering supplies and troops to attack Southwest Virginia. The Federals had been wanting to attack the lead and salt resources but had to wait to see if they may be needed against Hood. After Franklin, it was obvious that they wouldn't be needed.

John McCausland

Richard Taylor

General of the Armies, Grant, Secretary of War, Stanton, and the whole Damn-Yankee War-Department had been sending George Thomas telegrams screaming, "Attack Hood, now!" Thomas, the Rock-of-Chickamauga, became the Rock-of-Nashville. He just sat.

Finally on the 9[th,] Grant issued an order replacing Thomas but then Grant received word from Thomas. Thomas had planned an attack for the 10th but heavy snow made that date impossible. Grant rescinded the order.

There were so many runaway slaves with Sherman's Army that they were slowing operations. Sherman believed in "White Supremacy." "All the Congresses on earth can't make the Negro anything else than what he is." One of the generals under Sherman had a name that brought forth Yankee laughter. His name was Jeff Davis. This Jeff Davis didn't care for the idea of freeing the Negro either. After crossing a river, Jeff Davis ordered the pontoon bridge cut. This caused many Negroes to drown and stranded hundreds so that they couldn't follow the Union Army.

On the 10[th,] Sherman's trail of smoke and inhuman atrocities came to a halt before the city of Savannah. Sherman blamed all of his war crimes on the other Jeff Davis. If the South wouldn't have left the Union, then Sherman wouldn't have had to make Georgia howl.

Southerners played the "blame game" also. The man Bragg had blamed for all his failures and had fired, William Hardee, was now entrusted with the defense of this beautiful city. Hardee's 18,000 had flooded the rice fields and built good defenses. It was hoped that they could keep Sherman's Army from re-supply from the Union fleet.

Not all the atrocities were committed by the Union. Wheeler's cavalry captured some Yankees and forced them to take a "loyalty oath" to the South. Now that they were good Southerners, the former Yankees were forced to join the Confederate Army. These were called "Galvanized Yankees."

Sherman took one look at those defenses and decided there would be no frontal attack at Savannah. He began to surround the city. Federal troops occupied homes in the area. Churches were desecrated by the ungodly barbarians. Horses and mules were penned within church walls so that the animals wondered through "Houses of God" and toppled the dead "Saints" gravestones.

As Sherman sat before Savannah, Gen. George Stoneman started his move from Knoxville against Southwest Virginia. Stoneman had 10,000 troops, mostly mounted, to raid against John Breckinridge. Breckinridge was now back in command of the department. On paper, the Shenandoah Valley Military District now ran from Harper's Ferry to Knoxville but with less than 6,000 men in the whole department, effective control was restricted to a thin strip of land along the railroads and major highways. For a couple of weeks, Breckinridge had been receiving conflicting intelligence reports. Everyday, Stoneman made movements as if getting ready to leave Knoxville, perhaps to reinforce Nashville. Breckinridge got those reports; he also got reports that Stoneman was getting ready to attack the Department. Breckinridge chose to believe that Stoneman was withdrawing. On the 13th, Breckinridge realized that he had guessed wrong!

The Union Army had left Bean Station, just east of Knoxville, on the night of the 12th and rode rapidly through the night. At dawn of the 13th, they attacked Kingsport. The town was lightly defended by 250 men from John Morgan's old command. Their new commander, Basil Duke, was not with them. He was sick in a hospital at nearby Bristol. There was no commander present; no one was expecting an attack; so as Stoneman's men rode, Duke's men drank! The men were rudely awakened from their drunken stupor; hangovers were intensified by rifle reports. When the smoke cleared, 18 Confederates were dead, 84 captured and the rest scattered.

As Kingsport fell so did Fort McAllister on the Ogeechee River below Savannah. When this fort went, Sherman could make contact with the waiting Union fleet. He could get supplies and the Union North would soon learn that Sherman was at the sea. This also sealed the fate of Savannah!

The Yankees, who invaded Southwest Virginia, had fought the "Devil himself" now they used one of Morgan's tricks against the South. Stoneman had a telegraph message sent to Bristol stating that Federals were defeated at Kingsport and were retreating.

General John Vaughn's Cavalry was at nearby Greeneville. He was responsible for the defense of Bristol. John Vaughn wasn't the South's most courageous, daring, gallant or smartest general. He knew that men got killed in battle. He didn't want that to happen to him or anyone under his command, so he sat at Greeneville. He only sent a reconnaissance force to Bristol to watch those Yanks.

It was unusual to invade in winter. It was unusual to attack at night but at 3 A. M. on the 14[th,] the Federals hit Bristol. It took only a little time for the gun fire to cease and for fires of destruction to begin!

As the Union plundered, they discovered a telegram sent by Breckinridge to the station master. Breckinridge wanted to know if the tracks were open to that city. Stoneman sent a reply that Bristol was safe. Upon receipt of Stoneman's message, Breckinridge informed the Confederate station master that he was sending two train loads of reinforcements forward.

"Station Master" Stoneman made preparations to receive Breckinridge's men. The tracks near the station were ripped up. As the two trains passed into town, the tracks behind the trains were ripped up. The trains were trapped; the men were trapped and 500 Confederates soldiers were now 500 Union prisoners.

Breckinridge had little to oppose Stoneman. He sent messages calling all forces including the home guard to defend Saltville. On the 15th, after a brief battle Abingdon fell into enemy hands and the burning began.

This day at Nashville, "The Rock" finally rolled. Thomas' massive army rolled over Hoods demoralized men. The South's left flank was mauled and fell back. The enemy believed that Hood would now withdraw but Hood found a good defensive position and remained in Thomas' front.

Thomas realized that Hood had not retreated so he attacked in a cold rain and snow storm on the 16th. He hit Steven Lee on Hood's right flank. Thomas threw all he could at Lee but Lee's line held. While attacking against the Southern right, Thomas sent his cavalry around the left hoping to cut the Southern retreat route.

It was late afternoon, when the Federals opened a massive artillery bombardment, which the Confederates couldn't answer. After being rocked with cannon fire, the Southerners were attacked along the entire front. The Confederate left broke first and then the center collapsed. Again Lee did great service. He moved to cover the retreat thus stopping a complete fiasco. Hood had less than 30,000 men in his whole army; now there were over 2,000 not in the retreat. Thomas had over 55,000 and 3,061 could not answer roll call this night.

It was also a cold rain in Southwest Virginia on the 16th. After trying Breckinridge's defenses at Saltville, Stoneman sealed the roads from that town and continued towards Marion.

The town of Marion was taken in a night time battle. There were many Confederates in Union uniforms or at least in parts of Union uniforms. Because the South could not supply its troops, its troops took from the Yankees. Many a Rebel back was covered in a Yankee jacket. In the dark, some Yankees mistook other Yankees for Rebels and shot their own men down. The town fell by midnight; looting and burning occurred.

At dawn of the 17[th,] the battle opened again on Fair Ground Hill at Marion. A few hundred Confederate cavalrymen held several thousand Union men at bay for several hours until more Union reinforcements arrived. Stoneman chased the Rebels toward Wytheville. At Mt. Airy (Virginia) Stoneman gave the little band of cavalrymen another licking and took their artillery. Now, all resistance at his front was gone, or so he thought.

There was a Confederate supply depot at Wytheville but no fighting men. Cannons that couldn't shoot were shipped to the depot for repair. J. Stoddard Johnson commanded five workers, "one (a) drunk private." Those cannon, that couldn't shoot, were moved to a hill west of town and rifle pits dug.

There were approximately 1,000 Union cavalrymen leading the advance on Wytheville when they saw the Southern line. Johnson and his men showed themselves at one cannon or rifle pit and then ducked down and ran to another. Here they would pop-up, show themselves and then run to another position. The Federal cavalry froze and observed the enemy line. A commander with "brass," a "drunk private," four workers, and cannons that couldn't shoot stopped the Union advance dead for over two hours. Federals, under a "flag of truce" demanded that the Confederates give up the town. Even now Johnson continued his bluff. He said he would give up the town but needed time to withdraw his command. The Yankees called his bluff and attacked those works. It was a fearsome attack that netted the invaders some holes in the ground and broken cannons. The cruel invaders burned much of the town.

Breckinridge realized that Saltville had been by passed "...it would not be creditable to remain there (Saltville) and surrender the whole department to the enemy...I supposed the lead mines to be quite as important as the salt works." Breckinridge decided to move on the enemy the next day.

What Breckinridge didn't know was that the Yankees had crossed New River and were destroying the milling facilities at the Austinville Lead Mines. The South's only source for bullets was being damaged.

In Savannah on the 17th, Hardee learned that General Lee would send him no troops. Sherman knew his force was overwhelming and sent Hardee a demand that he surrender the city.

In Tennessee, the general from Texas, Hood, retreated what little was left of the Army of Tennessee. It was more mob than army. Some men had no shoes and their feet bled as they retreated over frozen roads. Men recalled a better army with a great kill ratio under the command of Joseph Johnson, "Uncle Joe." As the army retreated south toward Franklin, verses from the "Yellow Rose of Texas" were reworded and sang openly at Hood.

> "and now I'm going southward,
>
> for my heart is full of woe.
>
> I'm going back to Georgia
>
> to find my 'Uncle Joe.'
>
> You may talk about your Beauregard,
>
> and sing of General Lee,
>
> but that gallant Hood of Texas,
>
> played Hell in Tennessee."

On the 18th, Breckinridge soundly defeated forces under General Stoneman at Marion. Stoneman used his colored troops to charge the Southern line and they took very heavy casualties. Despite the Southern victory, it was Breckinridge who had to retreat; his army was almost out of ammunition. Now, the defense of the South's food supply line rested on the shoulders of 400, mostly home guarders, at Saltville.

"No!" was Hardee's reply to Sherman; Savannah would not be surrendered. Even as he replied, Hardee was making plans to evacuate the city by the sea.

Farther north, a Union flotilla left Fort Monroe to attack Fort Fisher at Wilmington.

Former "Peace Candidate" Lincoln told the nation "The issue can only be decided by war." On the 19th at Washington, he called for 300,000 more men to replace the casualties his war had caused.

Hardee told Sherman that he would not give up the city but on the 20th Savannah was evacuated. The loss of another seaport seriously impacted the South.

Throughout this day, the 400 home guarders backed by artillery had kept 5,000 Yankees at bay. Each attack had been beaten back. Near dark, it began to rain. A Union cavalry unit circled the town and approached from the northeast. Southern defenders saw the Yankees coming but were not alarmed. There were many former Yankee uniforms in Southern service. The defenders thought that this column was the promised reinforcements arriving. The Federals were allowed to ride to the base of the forts before they were recognized as the enemy. It was too late and the South's last source of salt was now in enemy hands!

On the 21st, the saltworks were destroyed and the town fired. Major Union victories were won at little cost. Now, the South had almost no salt for food shipments and few bullets to kill Yankees with.

As the saltworks were being destroyed, Sherman entered Savannah.

Hood's Army continued to limp southward. The 21st was not a day of rejoicing in the South.

On the 22nd, Lincoln received one of the strangest presents every given a President. Sherman wrote, "I beg to present you, as a Christmas gift, the city of Savannah...."

By the night of the 23rd, the storm tossed Federal fleet was at Fort Fisher. The Beast Butler had watched land armies explode gun power under the enemy's line. Well, he tried the same thing at sea. A boat of Union gun powder sure scared the fish but did no damage at Fort Fisher.

On Christmas Eve, the Federal fleet of sixty ships pounded the fort. There were 6,500 soldiers ready to hit the beaches. The 500 Confederates returned fire but little damage was done to either side.

On Christmas Day, Federals hit the beach and had some success but at night fall Confederate troops closed in and the Yankees turned-tail and ran!

The fort was safe and the harbor of Wilmington was open but there was little else to celebrate in Dixie. This was the worst Christmas since white men had set foot in the southern part of this continent. The armies were decimated, the government in chaos, the economy in shambles, the enemy in the land, towns and cities blackened, farms and plantations in ruin, graveyards filled, hospitals full, prisoner-of-war camps overflowing, stomachs empty, disease rampant, famine widespread, loneliness and depression overwhelming.

Lincoln was well aware of the conditions in the Confederate States of America. He was pleased that he had caused a free people such suffering. It was now clear that the people of the South would not be freed during his Presidency. The "Protector of the Constitution" was wondering if the people of the South had had enough and were now ready to bow at his feet? To this end on the 30th, he authorized an "unofficial" mission to see if the Confederacy wished to talk about "Peace" (Surrender).

As the year 1864 was ending, the greatest religious revival in the history of this continent was reaching a crescendo! The revival was effected by the war and affected the war. Before the nations of the United States and the Confederate States were in war, the religious communities were already at war and it started well before 1861. The Ana-Baptists (churches like the Quakers) had adopted anti-slavery, anti-Southern stances years before the war. They wanted to define slavery as "evil" and slave holders as "sinners." There was a big problem with this doctrine; the Bible condones, not condemns slavery. To condone slavery, the Quakers decided to follow an "Inner Light;" that is "self-revelation." Soon the Inner Light was more important than the Bible. They soon ascribed to the "Higher Law" theory. This theory said it was okay to break the law to help a slave escape or murder the master and family.

Later, large denominations like the Baptist and Methodist joined the war. They were less militant but just as determined to define a God ordained institution as "evil." To do so they, too, had to disregard the Bible. Southern churches split because they believed that it was wrong to disregard the "Word of God" and follow what people decided. The churches split over adding to or changing the Bible. Because most Southerners believed the people of the north had left the Bible behind as the "True word of God" they were going to Hell. Thus, they became "Damned Yankees."

It was a war for political rights and freedoms but it was also a religious war. The Southern people viewed themselves as "Soldiers of the Cross" waging war against those who disregarded the Bible. Religion was always close to the great leaders, Davis, Lee, Jackson, etc. It was close to the common soldiers and those who tended the fires at home. Revival started in the Southern armies as soon as those armies were organized. After the reality of combat and death; after the reality that the South was losing, revival intensified and grew. The revival fires that helped start the war have never gone out! The southern part of this nation to this day is known as the "Bible Belt!" By 1864, the Southern people knew that they were losing the war and they believed themselves to be the "oppressed people of God." To please God so that He would aid the Cause it was important that every Southern heart be "right with God." It became almost mandatory, that to be a "good Southerner" one had to be a "good Christian."

It was during this time that the persona of General Robert E. Lee changed. The country was sinking to her knees both militarily and religiously. Everywhere but at Richmond there was loss. As long as there was a Richmond; there was a Confederacy. As long as Lee stood; there would be a Confederate Capital. Prayers by the millions ended with, "God keep and protect General Lee." It was during this period that Robert E. Lee moved from Christian, Southern, Gentleman, and General Extraordinary to a position only a little lower than the Holy Trinity. His memory still holds the same position in many a Southern heart to this day!

CHAPTER 20 JANUARY 1-MARCH 28, 1865

As the New Year dawned, the sun was setting for the Confederate States of America. People of the South prayed for victory; people of the North prayed for the South's defeat. Both sides knew that without a miracle, the Confederacy would die. Three mighty armies sat just waiting to crush the Confederacy. Grant was camped on Richmond's front door. Sherman was culled to strike South Carolina. Thomas had almost no Southern troops in front of his Tennessee army. In Washington, Lincoln and Congress were fussing over whose policy would apply when the free people of the Confederate States would not longer be free. Lincoln was still pushing to get Congress to approve the 13th Amendment. The Senate had passed the bill but the House wouldn't go along with destruction of the Constitution.

In the South, President Davis was reorganizing and recruiting for the showdown battles. There were few men to volunteer or be drafted into the army and desertion was rampant. There was much talk of arming the slaves. Few men wished to die for a lost Cause. The President wanted Lee to command all Confederate field forces and Congress said it would be open to any "Peace overtures."

On the 4[th,] the Federals decided to try it again. Those 60 ships and 8,000 troops set sail for Fort Fisher. There was one soldier who did not sail with the second attacking force; he was "Beast" Butler. He had completely messed up the first attempt. If there were women and children or civilians, Butler would have been successful but at the Fort, there were Confederate soldiers. Lincoln removed "The Beast" from command on the 7th.

On the 6th, the U. S. Congress failed to pass the 13th Amendment again. President Lincoln had had enough of this fair vote thing. He didn't believe in fair votes as he proved in the last election. The President went looking for Congressmen to bribe.

In a dieing South, the Yankee conquerors and citizens who cooperated with them (the Scalawags) started state conventions to apply to readmit their states to the Union. The Tennessee Convention adopted an anti-slavery amendment on the 9th.

Also on this date, Hood started moving what was left of his Army of the Tennessee toward Sherman in Georgia.

The slaves had heard the Union Army sing that they had "come to make you free." Many believed that and ran from their masters for "freedom" with Sherman's Army in Savannah. Many didn't know what freedom really was and didn't find out. These ex-slaves "...swarmed into the city and herded hundreds of ignorant victims into lock-ups, to be held until they agreed to enlist in the army—and then to be sold as substitutes for well-to-do draftees in the North." It was work in Southern slavery; to work in cruel Northern slavery, with the addition of probable injury and death.

About this time, the Union Chief of Staff learned about Sherman's Jeff Davis and fired a stinging letter off to Sherman. He wrote Sherman you have a "…almost criminal dislike of the Negro…you drove them from your ranks…." Sherman was grinning when he wrote back that he liked the Negro (and he had the dollars that prove it) and he was putting more of them in the Yankee Army every day.

Soon Secretary of War Stanton showed up and he too fussed with Sherman over Jeff Davis's treatment of the Negro. Stanton then told Sherman that the freeing of the Negro was now the purpose of the war. Without any authorization, Stanton took the property of slave owners and gave it to the former slaves. This violated every law on the books. Stanton thought that if Lincoln were to complain about his breaking any law, that he would ask, 'if Lincoln now was going to start upholding the United States Constitution?'

"Honest" Abe's "votes for dollars" campaign was paying off. The formerly "Honorable" Moses Odell of New York said that he would start supporting passage of the 13th Amendment. Now, other formerly "Honorable" Democrats also joined the gravy train. Lincoln gave Odell "an important" job. The Kentucky Representative took the floor and said that if Lincoln had told the truth about freeing the slaves, Kentucky would have fought for the Confederacy! Slave-holding Delaware's delegate also had bitter things to say about the Federal Government taking people's rights and property away from them. Another representative from New York wouldn't take Lincoln's bribe. He took the floor and said, "The Almighty has fixed the distinction of the races; the Almighty has made the black man inferior, and, sir, by no legislation, by no partisan success, by no revolution, by no military power, can you wipe out this distinction...."

The outrage of delegates was a reflection of the outrage of a large part of the population. Many people thought he shouldn't be President. He had suppressed the Freedom of Speech and the Freedom of the Press. He had jailed anyone thought to oppose him. He had lied about seeking "peace." The war and death went on with no end in sight. He had lied about protecting slavery in the Border States. The people of these states now knew they had been lied to and were fighting on the wrong side. For the good of the United States, for freedom and to help the Confederacy, he had to go. There were, almost certainly, many groups of brave patriots that pledged their lives to removing Lincoln's tyrannical government by killing those who were responsible for killing. John Wilkes Booth, an actor, was a member of one such group in Washington.

In Virginia on the 11th, 300 Confederates under Thomas Rosser captured 580 Federals at Beverly.

Oliver Howard

Frantz Sigel

In Richmond on the 12th, President Davis did not officially have a conference. Francis Blair, Sr. was not officially at the Southern White House. Blair did not officially give Davis a letter from Lincoln in which Lincoln stated that he was willing to talk "Peace." President Davis officially didn't say that he was open to discussing "Peace" with Lincoln; but they did.

On the 13th, John Bell Hood resigned as commander of the Army of the Tennessee. That army was a powerful force that had fought many battles and had a favorable kill ratio but that was before Hood. Many men who were there when he took command were not there to bid Hood "good-bye."

Also on the 13th, the most powerful armada the world had ever seen was before Fort Fisher at Wilmington. Almost 2,000 projectiles from 627 cannons on 60 ships, rained down on the fort. The incoming fire was so accurate and so overwhelming that Southern counter fire was almost ineffective. The Yankees landed on a peninsula above the fort and General Bragg's Army sat and did nothing.

On the 14th, Union forces moved closer to Fort Fisher. The fort's commander Col. William Lamb sent more messages to Bragg appealing for help. Bragg, with 6,000 men, did not move.

Starting this date and continuing until the end of the month, Union forces battled, beat and massacred the Indians in Colorado.

Everyone at Fort Fisher knew it was coming. On the 14th, the Federals launched a two prong attack. 2,000 Yankees moved from the peninsula and attacked from the east. Though out-manned, out-numbered and pummeled by two days of shelling, the Confederate defenders tore into the Union columns. Soon 2,000 Yankees were running for their lives.

The other attack of 3,300 men came from the west near Cape Fear River. Confederates made the Yankees pay for each foot of ground but the Union troops finally made their way through obstacles and breached the fort's wall. There were 500 Southern casualties, the fort's commander and 1,900 defenders were now Yankee prisoners. It had cost the North 1,341 men to close the South's last deep water port and Bragg sat.

On the 16th, Blair reported, in detail, about his meeting with President Davis. He told Lincoln that Davis was willing to "talk peace" and stop the blood shed. Lincoln said the plan did not call for "one common country" and he would not accept it. To Lincoln, "peace" meant the enslavement of the Southern people.

While Blair was with the President, Sen. Henry Lane of Indiana was introducing his House Resolution # 97. "Rebel prisoners in our hands are to be subjected to a treatment finding its parallels only in the conduct of savage tribes and resulting in the death of multitudes by the slow but designed process of starvation and by the mortal diseases occasioned by insufficient and unhealthy food and wanton exposure of their persons to the inclemency of the weather." In other words the Federal Congress signed the death certificate for Confederate soldiers captured in battle. Although, starvation and torture was already common place, this act made it official Union policy to kill captured, helpless men. Yankee history points to Andersonville as the example of Civil War cruelty. It is remembered that the Confederacy couldn't feed, clothe, or medicate either the civil population or its armies in the field. The Yankees had no such problems. The ill-treatment of Southerners was deliberate, not the result of want. Remember, the prison with the highest death rate during the war was at Elmira, New York.

What is rarely pointed out is that almost no Southerner had to remain in prison. If they would raise their hand and pledge to be a good a Yankee, they could go free. A small percentage did. Most of these enlisted in the Union Army and were sent to fight the Indians. These were called "galvanized Yankees." Most prisoners faced daily starvation, disease, and torture rather than to pledge to the "banner of tyrantity."

There was one group of prisoners that had no such option. These were the Yankee civilians Lincoln had arrested because they dared speak out against his oppressive regime; Lincoln's political prisoners.

Basil Duke

Stephen Ramseur

The last casualties at Fort Fisher occurred this day. Soldiers, sailors and marines, many of them drunk, looted the fort and stripped Southern corpses for souvenirs. Someone set the main powder magazine on fire. It exploded. 66 Yankees were wounded and 38 dead. The bodies of 13 were blown to bits and never recovered.

On the 18th, Lincoln again met with Francis Blair. He gave Blair a letter to President Davis. There were two phrases that Lincoln knew would stick-out in Davis's mind; "resisting the national authority" and "one common country."

Lincoln knew that hundreds of thousands of other men's sons had died in the war he started. He knew that more would die before the South was conquered; he wanted to make sure that one of those who didn't die would be his son. The President wrote Grant a letter on the 19th and asked if a place in "his military family" could be found for Robert. Soon it was Captain Robert Lincoln, a personal aide on Grant's staff.

In Richmond on the 23rd, Congress passed an act allowing General Lee to assume command of all field forces. On the 24th, the Confederate Congress again asked Grant to restart prisoner exchanges because so many were dieing. Grant did accept. Also on this date, Forrest assumed command of the Confederate District of Mississippi, East Louisiana, and West Tennessee. It was a large area but contained few troops.

John McClernand

Judson Kilpatrick

After Davis received Lincoln's letter, which was carried by Blair, he appointed three commissioners to talk "peace" with the North on the 28th. The commission was headed by Vice President, Alexander Stephens. On the 30th, Lincoln had safe conduct passes issued for the commissioners to go to Fort Monroe.

On the last day of the month, Lincoln's bribery officially paid off. The House of Representatives approved a bill allowing the proposed 13th Amendment to the U. S. Constitution to go to the states for approval. This amendment would outlaw slavery. Lincoln also appointed Secretary of State, William Seward as his representative to the "peace conference."

On the second day of the second month, Sherman started his movement on South Carolina.

He had appointed Seward to be his representative to the "Peace Conference" but on the 3rd, it was Lincoln who led his team. This shows his lack of confidence in Seward. President Lincoln lowered his status and met with the number two man of the Confederacy. The "Peace Conference" was held in the saloon of the ship, the *River Queen*. The ship was anchored off Fort Monroe. There was small talk and the President told a few stories which everyone pretended to enjoy. Maybe being in a bar made the President forget what he was there for. It was Vice President Stephens who suggested an "armistice" (stop the killing) until a formal agreement was made between the warring powers. Lincoln knew his military forces were squeezing the life out of the South and he wasn't going to stop. There would be no armistice. Lincoln went on to state that there could be "…no treaty with the Confederate States…for they were not a country in the eyes of the North." This, of course, begs the question, "If there were no Confederacy, what was President Lincoln doing setting on a ship at Hampton Roads?" It seems appropriate that the "Peace Conference" was held in a saloon.

Next, Lincoln countered Stephens saying that Confederate "troops must be disbanded…" and the Federal government allowed to take over his whole country. It was clear that the two countries had two different definitions of "peace." To the Confederacy, it meant no war; to the North it meant no Confederacy. Stephens then summed up Lincoln's "Peace Proposal" as "unconditional submission." Seward, who was only at the conference as "window dressing" spoke and said his President had not used those words. Lincoln just let his Secretary of State spin in the wind. Lincoln did not deny that was what he meant. The "Peace Conference" in a ship's barroom would not float or fly; it sank.

On the 5[th,] there was a minor battle at Hatcher's Run. Grant extended his lines south and west of Petersburg. This would force Lee to counter and further stretch the defensive line around Richmond.

Lincoln had done such a good job of corrupting the Northern election and legislature that he decided that he could do the same to the Confederacy. He presented a plan to his cabinet. He would ask Congress to give him $400,000,000 to bride the Confederate States. If a Confederate state would surrender before April 1st they would be given a portion of the money. When that state passed an amendment to abolish slavery, the state would get the other half of the money. His cabinet must have thought that Lincoln had not gotten over the effects of being in that bar; "...the Cabinet unanimously disapproved the measure...."

On the 6th, President Davis replaced James Seddon as Secretary of War with Maj. Gen. John Breckinridge. Davis then went to Congress to report on the "Peace Conference." His words echoed Stephens'; "...unconditional submission." He added that Lincoln would give no guaranties to the states or to the citizens except "...those which the conqueror may grant."

Fighting had been both great and small at Hatcher's Run. By the 7th, many a good man on both sides died but the Run remained in Confederate hands. The Yankee line was extended; so both sides won and both sides lost. Lee now had over thirty-seven miles to defend along the Richmond- Petersburg Line.

Congress had told Lincoln that they didn't like his attempt to steal the election by setting-up "make believe states" like the "Free State of Arkansas or Louisiana." On the 8th, they sent the President a bill saying that no Confederate State was "...entitled to representation in the electoral college." Lincoln already knew that he had cheated his way to re-election and didn't need his "Free States." He signed the bill and tried to pretend that it didn't apply to him personally.

Sherman's Union Army was in little rush to leave Savannah. It was the last of January or first of February before the last of the troops left the city. Everyone knew that Sherman was headed for South Carolina; many believed he would head for Charleston on the coast because that is where the war began and it was a military target. The greatest war criminal in the country's history wasn't worried about the military target; he went for a political target. In the war criminal's own words, "I could look forty miles in each direction and see smoke rolling up like one great bonfire...make little effort to restrain my army...when I go through South Carolina it will be one of the most horrible things in the history of the world." That great man who knew God's mind so well, President Lincoln, sent word that he was "praying for him." With very little Confederate opposition, Sherman had burned his way across the state and on the 15th the state capital, Columbia, was in sight.

On the 17th, the mayor of Columbia came to Sherman and said, "I have the honor of presenting you with the freedom of the city." Thus the mayor made it clear that there would be no fight to keep Sherman out. The mayor then asked Sherman for assurances that the city would not be burned. Sherman gave him assurances. What are a few more lies to a war criminal?

The last of Wade Hampton's cavalry took what they could carry and left town early in the morning. The grand Union Army entered town without a fight. They went straight to the capital building and raised the United States flag. A lady in residence saw the flag and said "Oh, what a horrid sight! What degradation! After four long bitter years of blood shed and hatred, now to float there at last. That hateful symbol of despotism!"

Throughout the day, the city filled with Yankees. The Union troops were in a holiday mood. Though February, the holiday was Halloween. Officers didn't restrain their troops but joined in the looting. The whole city, including the civilians, was there to trick and treat as they liked. An army of teenagers couldn't get enough alcoholic beverages to drink. Any store or saloon that might have the intoxicating spirit was broken into. Stores were looted whole sale by drunken Yankees. Homes were entered. Anything worth stealing or not worth stealing was taken. What wasn't stolen was damaged or destroyed. One resident shouted, "What are you, thieves or soldiers?" The thief-soldier's reply was, "Yes, Ma'am." On this devil's holiday, some soldiers entered the Catholic Church. They stole the "Sacred gold vessels off the altar...laughing soldiers taunted the nuns and blew cigar smoke in their faces. 'Oh, Holy! Yes, holy! We're just as holy as you are! Now, what do you think of God? Ain't Sherman greater?" Other Yankees were of the protestant faith so they stole the communion service at their church of choice.

Gang rape of any Negro female of any age was common. Some were raped and so brutalized that they were left "near death." Because Negroes were inferior beings, their rape was not considered a crime; white women were another story. Many white women had their dignity stolen but it wasn't condoned; "rape...unspeakable dishonor." After all, a white Southern woman looked a lot like a Yankee's mother or sister. They didn't want Confederate soldiers to deflower their women so it was considered a crime to rape a white woman. Col. Dayton of Sherman's staff said he shot a Union soldier dead. He was "out in the street...trying to rape a white woman." It was best to rape white women inside.

It had been a day of Halloween fun. "Hell was empty, and all its devils were in this devoted city, learning new deviltry from Yankee teachers. A perfect reign of terror existed." As dark approached the Grand Union Army which called itself, "the army that has come to set you free," decided to continue the fun with a big bonfire. "The city began to burn as dusk approached...hundreds of houses were on fire at once; men swore and women and children screamed and cried in terror; drunken soldiers ran about the streets with blazing torches..." At the fire houses, hoses were cut;

least, any citizen dare try and pour water on their fire. Drunken soldiers desecrated the Capital with a mock session of the state legislature. Later the Capital and went up in flames. The University of South Carolina Hospital, which was filled with Southern soldiers, went up in flames. Some homes had wounded Confederate soldiers in them; the Damn Yankees burnt them alive! Columbia was their bonfire! Union officers saw what their men were doing and raised the flask to the lips and shouted, "Damnation to the Confederacy!"

The members of the Union musical bands saw the flames, heard the cry of men being burned to death, they could hear women sobbing in the night as their homes burned and there was terror in the wail of the children. Band members were so moved that they put on a concert. Late into the night the Yankee National Anthem was heard. "Hail Columbia" was played and the strains of that grand spiritual, "Battle Hymn of the Republic" floated over the city of fire!

At least one Negro was glad that Sherman was there, "I have seen the great messiah and the Army of the Lord." Other Negroes were not happy the Union army was there because they stole and burned Negro property also. A woman who was born in the North but had cast her lot with the South, said Sherman's cruelties had not broken the Southern spirit but made it stronger. She declared I am a "much stronger Rebel..."

Sherman had lived in the South before the war and said the people of the South had treated him "with great kindness." Now Sherman had repaid their "great kindness." War Criminal, Sherman, at first blamed the people of South Carolina for the destruction because South Carolina was where the war started. Of course, this is like blaming the victim for being murdered. Then he said, "Jeff Davis is responsible for all this." Later, Sherman said he didn't know what his army was doing that he had not entered the city. Still later, he claimed that the fleeing Rebels set fire to some bales of cotton as they fled in the morning, winds at dusk fanned the flames and the city burned. It was God's fault, "God Almighty started the wind...." Sherman went on to say, "...I have never shed many tears over the event...(it helped) the end of the war."

Sherman didn't cry but others did. "Helpless women and children...some mournfully contemplated the piles of rubbish, the only remains of their late happy homesteads...children crying with fright and hunger...(men) sat bowed down with their heads buried between their hands."

On the other side of the state, Confederate forces were worried that they may be penned in at Charleston; so Fort Sumter, the symbol of Southern pride and independence, was evacuated.

The politicians in Washington wanted to be in on the rape of the South. Although, the Confederacy did not exist, the Senate this 17th day of February said it was okay to steal anything that the Confederate government owned but the Federals would not take any debt owed by that government.

On the 18^{th,} Sherman continued to destroy the city. The railroad depot, supply houses, public buildings and other homes were burned. Somewhere in the ashes was the home of Wade Hampton. Also on this date, Charleston fell into the tender hands of the enemy. Burning occurred there too.

The 19th saw more of the same at Columbia. There was an explosion at the railroad and about 20 Yankees died. Sherman said he was more worried about the death of one Yankee than he was about the whole city. A Southern lady did not feel that way, "…if only the whole army could have been roasted alive!" Southern residents of the city looked to their religion for comfort. Many looked forward to the time that Sherman would be confronted by God's wrath!

By the 20^{th,} "the trick-or-treat" was over and the Union Army left a smoldering pile of rubbish that once was Columbia. Some slaves left with the blue bellies. Sherman believed that he had crushed the Southern spirit but as his army left town, "many hissed and booed the blue coats, some spat on the soldiers, and not a few women undertook to lay violent hands upon them." These were not actions of a conquered people.

Also on this date, the Confederate House of Representatives authorized the use of slaves as soldiers. In a slave society, the slaves are inferior to the master. In a society at war, the hero is the soldier. By making slaves into soldiers, it is like turning inferiors into superiors. This was a hard pill for the South to swallow.

The destruction of Columbia, was more of a political victory for the Union but in the state to the north, the Yankees were making a great military victory. Wilmington was evacuated on the 21st!

In Richmond, General Lee was studying the map and making plans to cut loose from Richmond.

On the 22^{nd,} the port of Wilmington fell. The South's last deep water port was gone, Fort Fisher was gone, the great salt works were gone. The South was sinking fast. Lee called all his generals to assemble in the Carolinas; the balance of the Confederacy was to be left almost without defense. Generals, who had covered themselves with glory when the Confederacy was young, began to assemble but now they had no armies with which to fight!

General Lee reported to the President on the 23rd. The President was told that Joseph Johnston was back in command. Lee had told Johnston to consolidate all the troops in the Carolinas against Sherman. Most of Johnston's new force was also his old force so he used the old name, "The Army of Tennessee." Johnston was a realist, "In my opinion, these troops form an army far too weak to cope with Sherman...They're only calling me back so that I will be there to surrender..." This same day, Sherman crossed the Catawba River in South Carolina.

On the 24th, Lee expressed his concern to the War Department over the very high desertion rate. Many, a good man, decided he wasn't willing to die for a dieing Cause.

On the 26th Lt. Thomas Myers with Sherman's Army wrote: "My dear wife...We have had a glorious time in this State. Unrestricted license to burn and plunder...The people of the South have been stripped of most of their valuables. Gold watches, silver pitchers, cups, spoons, forks etc...I have about a quart (of rings, earrings, breast pins)...General Sherman has silver and gold enough to start a bank. His share of gold watches at Columbia alone was two hundred and seventy-five...The damned niggers, as a general rule, prefer to stay at home, particularly after they found out that we only wanted the able-bodied men. Sometimes we take whole families...But the useless part of them we soon manage to lose ...shoot at their bobbing heads as they swam rivers after the army units crossed over..."

Sheridan headed south out of Winchester on the 27th. His orders from Grant were to destroy the transportation systems Lee depended upon, the Virginia-Central Railroad and the James River- Kanawha Canal.

Sheridan had 10,000 men to advance; Early had very little to oppose.

March the first, found Sheridan on the march as he pushed Early out of Mount Crawford. Yankee state after Yankee state lined up to endorse the passage of the 13th Amendment. When it came New Jersey's turn; the state said, "No!"

On the 2nd, Sheridan sent George Armstrong Custer with 5,000 troopers to attack the left flank of Early's little army of about 1,500 men at Waynesboro. The side collapsed and the rout was on. Before the day was done, many Confederates were dead, 200 wagons, artillery and over 1,000 men were taken. Early and a few of his officers escaped. There was no force between Waynesboro and Richmond to oppose Sheridan's destruction.

Today Lee wrote Grant to see if there was any possibility of stopping this war. Grant informed Lincoln of Lee's letter on the 3rd and Lincoln said Grant could discuss no political issue but to press his military advantage over Lee. The advantage was very great. The Union had over 1,000,000 soldiers and plenty of supplies; the Confederacy had less than 100,000 and little supplies. On the 4th, Grant replied to Lee that all he could discuss was "capitulation." The generals couldn't do what the Presidents couldn't do.

While Lincoln was telling Grant, "no," he was also signing a bill to create the Freedmen's Bureau. The purpose of the bill was to steal Southerner's land and give it to the former slaves. It also was to help feed and clothe them. After the war, the Bureau was to also see that the ex-slaves were taught to vote Republican.

Sheridan took Charlottesville without a fight but did not burn the University. At the other end of the state, the Federals now held the Cumberland Gap.

Dirty politics had gotten President Lincoln a second term. On the 4th, he took the oath of office for the second time. Many in the audience hoped that maybe the second time he took the oath that the oath would take on him. Maybe this time, he will govern by the Constitution. Some who wanted to be there to hear him speak were in jail with no charges or trial. One of those that did hear him that day was John Wilkes Booth. It was a short address that is known as "Lincoln's Second Inaugural Address." When the speech is analyzed, it is almost a comedy routine.

His first knee-slapper came when he said, "All knew that (slavery) was, somehow, the cause of the war." He was really saying to his audience, "You are so stupid that you don't remember my First Inaugural speech; everything I said and did during the first two years of my term and how I wanted to ship every Negro, free or not out of this country." Also, he hadn't got around to telling Grant that the war was about slavery and that he, Grant, needed to get rid of those slaves.

The slaves "…were located in the Southern part of (the country)." This meant that Yankees didn't own slaves. He wanted all to forget that in his great Emancipation Proclamation that the slaves in Delaware, Maryland, Kentucky and Missouri were never to be free. Now, he lied again to the people of those states when Lincoln bribed the Congress to pass a bill to amend the Constitution. This bill would get rid of slavery where he had promised it would always remain forever.

He blamed the South for starting the war. Here he got a little truth into his speech, which could also be considered funny. How was it the South's fault; when they were "…seeking to destroy it (the country) without war…." That is to say, free people, in a free vote (something Lincoln didn't believe in), freely decided to form their own country. A free South, not at war with the Union, was still a threat to the Yankee nation.

Lincoln now showed that he held the Bible in just as much respect as he did the Constitution; that is to say, that he read both and believed in neither. Lincoln told those there that God was against slavery. Most of those there had read and studied the Bible. They knew that no where does the Bible say one bad word against slavery. Did anyone believe "Honest Abe?"

His concluding remarks have us rolling in the aisles to this day. "With malice toward none" Lincoln was saying "I don't even know Grant, Sherman, Hunter, Butler, etc." "With charity for all," was drowned out by the screams of Southern women his armies had raped and the cries of terror and hunger of their children. The crackling of the fires that burnt thousands of Southern homes, farms, plantations, towns, and cities were so loud that some didn't hear Lincoln say, "bind-up the nation's wounds."

Some said that the reason Vice-President Andrew Johnson's speech was so "rambling, incoherent" was because he had "taken too much whisky as a medicine." It may have been that he had to get drunk so that he wouldn't throw-up during his boss's speech. The tailor turned traitor, turned Vice President.

At Cheraw, South Carolina Sherman captured a Confederate cannon with a sign on it saying, "First gun fired on Fort Sumter." Sherman used it to fire a salute to Lincoln on his second inauguration. At least one Confederate soldier was executed and the town burned before Sherman left.

The Confederacy was disintegrating. The problems the country faced were enormous. The Congress of that country had been stuck in furious debate for sometime now but as Lincoln spoke and Johnson drank, they had reached a momentous decision. This date, they approved the design of the Confederacy's Third National Flag. No wonder, President Davis often accused them of not doing their share to help the country.

As Sherman marched, his atrocities continued. Seven Yankees raped and killed a teenager. Confederate cavalrymen caught the seven and slit their throats. Their bodies were placed near the home with a sign that read, "There are the seven." It was not enough of a comfort to the mother who later "lost her mind." After this event, other Yankees were caught; their throats slit and left laying along the road for the Federals to find. Sherman then gave orders to kill one prisoner for each Yankee so found.

At Winnsboro Sherman's men took the organ from the Christ Episcopal Church. They set the church on fire and played "the devil's tunes" (Battle Hymn of the Republic?) as the church burned. In their "unholy merriment" they stole a golden figure of Christ and unearthed a recently buried body. A brave Southern Belle stood on her porch and sang, "Oh, yes, I am a Southern girl, I glory in the name..."

Gen. Judson Kilpatrick shouted, "We'll soon see the proud women in Carolina, like those of Georgia, with tears in their eyes, begging crusts of bread from our men for their famishing children."

Some of the slaves took over the plantations and stole from the masters. Confederate soldiers tailing Sherman restored order, "Several have been shot and a great many severely whipped." The vast majority of the slaves remained loyal and protected the master and his property; "(this) was incomprehensible to the intruders."

On the 7th, Federals left Wilmington for New Berne with their sites set on Goldsborough.. Sherman entered North Carolina. This day, Lincoln spent issuing orders "permitting private persons" to control economic interest in "the insurrectionary states." Lincoln was paying off his political debts with Southern assets. The war was winding-down and the stealing was winding up.

Gen. Kirby Smith wrote the President on the 8th, he would step down as the commander of the Trans-Mississippi, if that was what the President wished. President Davis had little control east of the Mississippi and none to the west. He told Smith to stay where he was.

Joe Johnston had been sending Bragg every man he could in hopes of smashing the Yankees at New Berne. At the Battle of Kinston, which lasted through the 10th, Bragg's numbers weren't enough and the Yankees held the town.

On the 9th, what was left of the combined cavalry of Wade Hampton and Joe Wheeler attacked Judson Kilpatrick's cavalry at Monroe's Cross Roads, South Carolina. His men didn't think that Kilpatrick was much of a man or an officer; they had nicknamed him, "Kill Cavalry." He seemed more interested in burning, pillaging and banging on a Southern beauty he had picked up in Columbia, than fighting the Rebel Army. Wade and Wheeler woke him early and almost captured him. He escaped but his pants were taken prisoner. By pure numbers the Union came back and ran the Southern cavalry. The battle is also known as "the Battle of Kilpatrick's Pants."

Lee didn't know of the action at Monroe, SC when he wrote the new Secretary of War, Breckinridge, a letter. The Confederacy was in "full peril." Without supplies the Richmond-Petersburg Line must be abandoned. This didn't mean the end of the Confederacy. If Lee's force and Johnston's force could combine and defeat Sherman, there were still hopes for the Southern Cause.

On the 11th, Sherman brought his traveling band of murderers, thieves and rapists to Fayetteville, North Carolina. Sherman shouted at a Southerner before he burned his mill, "...Niggers and cotton caused this war, and I wish them both in Hell!" Sherman had three men and a woman hung and a wounded Confederate shot. Many men and women were "stripped naked and whipped" until they would tell where they hid their valuables. As the town burned on the 12th, Federal gunboats came up the Cape Fear River from Wilmington. The war criminal wanted the outside world to know just how brave he was. He sent a report bragging about pushing the Rebel Army. This is something like a man claiming to be a hero for swatting a gnat. He also loaded the boats with stolen goods.

On the 13th, the Confederate Congress finally completed debate and sent the President a bill so that the

South could use Negro troops. Davis signed the bill and then sent Congress a letter telling them that immediate action was required if the Confederacy was to survive and all Congress did was debate. This threw Congress into a tizzy. After only three days of debate, the Congress told the President that the charge was not true. It took another day of heated debate but on the 18th Congress ended its session; its last session.

Sherman thought that he was destroying Southern morale by his barbarous acts. When the army left Fayetteville a Southern lady said, "If I ever see a Yankee woman I intend to whip her and take the clothes off her very back…when our army invades the North, I want them to carry the torch in one hand and the sword in the other. I want desolation carried to the heart of their country! The widows and orphans left naked and starving; just as ours were left!"

Johnston knew he had no hope in an all out battle with Sherman. This old master of military discipline watched Sherman closely just hoping for a mistake. Sherman was headed for Goldsborough. He set one corps under Henry Slocum on the road toward Bentonville. Kilpatrick's cavalry was to provide advance intelligence for Slocum. Wade Hampton reported to Johnston of the separate column with less than 35,000 Yankees in it. Johnston knew he had far less that 10,000 men but that was the best odds he was likely to get. There was advanced skirmishing on the

18th and full battle started near dawn on the 19th. The Southern forces had been hastily assembled; although there were many outstanding commanders and many brave soldiers, they were not a fighting unit. Sometimes orders weren't followed and the army did not attack as a single unit. Despite the South's shortcomings, the Union left was smashed about noon and a rout seemed to be on its way. Much stolen loot was dropped as the Yankees took flight. Yankee unit, after Yankee unit, was mauled and sent scurrying off the field until the Southern attack encountered Jeff Davis. This was the Northern side of the family. The Confederate forces launched three main attacks against General Jeff Davis Union line. The line held. As dark approached both sides dug in. Johnston was determined to renew the fight at dawn. At dawn of the 20^{th,} Johnston received word that Union reinforcements were arriving. Before long Johnston got information that he was now facing Sherman's entire army. There was skirmishing but Johnston knew he had no chance of success and wouldn't sacrifice his men in a lost battle. Throughout the 21^{st,} Sherman moved more men toward Bentonville and started a flanking movement to trap Johnston. The two generals had played this game from Vicksburg to Atlanta and Sherman never won. Johnston withdrew from Bentonville that night, he wouldn't be flanked. However, when he retreated he had less than 75% of the army he attacked with.

The Union put massive pressure on North Carolina. Sherman up the middle, pressure from the coast and on the 20th, George Stoneman started a raid from Tennessee toward Western North Carolina.

The once mighty cavalry of Forrest was gone. He was no longer the mighty Forrest and James Wilson started a move toward a major manufacturing center of the Confederacy at Selma, Alabama on the 22nd. There were so many Yankees with so much that the South could only offer feeble resistance.

Sherman took Goldsborough on the 23rd. It was back to the old business of rape, loot and burn. One Yank raped a 65 year old woman and later a young girl. They were both white; he was shot by his own. Sherman was now looking toward Lee in Virginia. Johnston stood in his way but knew that what was left of the Army of the Tennessee wouldn't stop him. Sherman left his army of criminals and headed toward a conference with all the big brass at City Point. He, no doubt, took more of the riches of the South with him.

This day, Lincoln left Washington for a little "vacation." He took (Crazy Mary) his wife and son Tad. They went to City Point (today Hopewell). Their tour guide was to be Grant. They wished to visit burned-out homes, devastated towns and see the homeless women and children. Oh, and wouldn't it be lovely to see men die in battle on their "vacation?"

General Lee didn't know that he was to provide the entertainment for Lincoln's vacation. Lee was a gambler and everyday he saw the odds stacking higher against him. Maybe, just maybe, he could turn the odds around in one masterful stroke. Much planning went into the attack. Grant, never a great general, on the other side of the line never saw it coming. Confederate lines that were stretched thin were almost deserted as Lee consolidated his forces. Gen. John Gordon was given the honor and responsibility of leading the attack. The area chosen was just east of Petersburg; an earthen fort called Fort Stedman. At 4 A. M. Confederate artillery opened and thousands of "Marse' Robert's boys" poured into the Union line. The fort was overrun. About ¾ of a mile of what was Federal trenches were now Confederate trenches! Confederate troops headed toward the Union built, supply railroad. Other Confederates woke the sleeping Yankee President, at City Point.

Grant was taken by surprise! He rushed more troops toward the breakthrough than Lee had in his army. The Union trench line was designed so that one artillery position's fire, overlapped another. Thus, even though the South had taken one of the forts, artillery from other forts continued to pound the Rebel attackers. By 7:30 that evening, the hole in the Union line was sealed. Lee rode away from the battlefield in great depression. He now knew that the way he would leave the Richmond-Petersburg Line was by retreat not advance.

William Hardee

John Marmaduke

Late that evening Lincoln took the Union built railroad to an area close to Fort Stedman. He toured part of the battlefield; he saw some of the dead and heard the screams and moans of the wounded from both sides. This was a delightful "vacation!"

As Lee was attacking in Virginia, other Yankees were on the march in Alabama. The Union had stopped the South from using Mobile Bay. On this day, they started moving toward the city itself.

As lee was evaluating the failure at Fort Stedman, he received more bad news. Sheridan's cavalry, that had been destroying Confederate road bridges, canal and railroad transportation from the Shenandoah, were approaching Grant's line at Petersburg. Lee had nothing to even stop a cavalry unit! President Lincoln thought this was just a splendid vacation as he watched Sheridan's cavalry cross the James. Lee wrote the President that he couldn't prevent Sherman and Grant from linking up against him. Once they were together, Lee saw no way from keeping the combined force from taking Richmond. Lee told the President that if he maintained the Richmond-Petersburg Line that the army would be trapped and crushed. The only military option Lee saw was to abandon the line, combine with Johnston, and whip Sherman before Grant arrived.

Sherman came by boat to City Point on the 27th. There he, Grant and Admiral Porter met with President Lincoln on the *River Queen*. Sheridan's report was received. There was lots of drinking and planning. Sherman later remembered Lincoln telling the military brass that easy terms were to be given to any Confederate units that surrendered. The conference was continued the next day. The navy and army chiefs agreed; one more big push and the South was finished!

𝔚𝔞𝔡𝔢 𝔥𝔞𝔪𝔭𝔱𝔬𝔫

CHAPTER 21   MARCH 28, 1865- WAR'S END

The South never had as many assets as the North. The Northern population was larger plus they had immigrants from overseas from which to build an army. The Confederacy started from scratch to build a government, an army and navy. The South had little industry and was dependant on Europe for manufactured goods. As the war progressed, the South's ability to import decreased. Without the manpower to work the farms and plantations, production dropped. There wasn't enough food to feed or clothe the people. The cost of food went up; the cost of slaves went down. In some Southern cities, the starving people rioted. There wasn't enough food to feed the army in the field. Starved Southern warriors in rags looked like scarecrows. Without proper food, disease became rampant. Railroad rails and equipment were destroyed or wore out faster than they could be replaced. Burning of bridges slowed overland transportation. The telegraph wasn't reliable. Thousands were made homeless by Yankee burning. The whole economy was collapsing. Government services were breaking down. Confederate dollars were so worthless, that Yankees often lit cigars with the bills. There were many types of script money in circulation: there was Confederate money, United States money, state money; bank money, even stores issued their own money. Nobody knew what the value of money was. There weren't enough coins so un-cancelled postage stamps were used as change; until the post office ran out of stamps. The whole postal system, like almost everything else, was collapsing. The only things the South had in abundance were disease, death, pain, loneliness, heartache and depression!

By 1865, Chimborazo Hospital in Richmond was the largest hospital in the world. It had 3,000 beds but always had more patients than beds. An estimated 76,000 Confederate service men were treated here during the war.

On the 28th of March, Stoneman' force destroyed the home guard at Boone, North Carolina. On the 29th, he was at Wilkesborough.

Grant had over 125,000 men along the Richmond-Petersburg line; Lee, maybe 40,000. Grant kept shifting men to the west of Petersburg. He was trying to cut the South Side Railroad. Lee sent George Pickett and Fitzhugh Lee to Five Forks. Sheridan's cavalry passed to the west and around the Southern flank.

On the 30th, Grant kept the pressure up in the Five Forks area. Lee worried that Grant may strike else where on his paper thin line. Lincoln was making plans to return to his Capital while Davis was making plans to leave his Capital.

On the last day of March, Sheridan moved toward Dinwiddie Court House in force but stubborn, outnumbered Rebels pushed them back. There was skirmishing all along the line. Pickett realized that he was outnumbered at least five to one in the Five Forks area.

In Alabama, Wilson pushed Forrest out of Montevallo and destroyed the town. Elsewhere in Alabama, the Federals were tightening the noose around Mobile.

Lee sent every man he could spare to Pickett with the message, "Hold Five Forks at all hazards." With raw courage, the Southern boys dug in while singing *Dixie*. At this critical time, Pickett and some other generals were somewhat away from the front at a "shad bake" (fish fry). It was late afternoon when Sheridan's cavalry and Warren's Fifth Infantry Corps struck. Confederate defenders fought desperately and to the death but the Union attack had too much power. Pickett's Division disappeared that day. The line was broken!

At 4:30 on the morning of April $2^{nd,}$ Grant started a general assault toward the town of Petersburg. By 7 A. M. that Sunday morning, Lee's line was collapsing. The great general would hold a line until his army could retreat. A. P. Hill, one of Lee's most trusted commanders, fell to rise no more. Lee telegraphed President Davis at Richmond that he must leave the city. A messenger entered St. Paul's Episcopal Church as the minister was praying. He whispered in the President's ear and Davis quietly left the service. At 11 A. M., President Davis joined his wife and children and boarded a special train for Danville The Confederate treasury and important papers were on the train.

As the news of the President's departure spread; so, did panic and rioting. Government records, military supplies and cotton were set afire so that the enemy wouldn't get them. The fires spread beyond their buildings. Looters broke into stores. Inmates broke out of jail. Civil authority disintegrated. Robbery and fire spread throughout the city. It was pandemonium as citizens ran from Yankees, fire and rioters!

That evening as Richmond burned and the Petersburg Line collapsed, Lincoln sent Grant congratulations on a "magnificent success."

In Alabama, the news was no better. Wilson's cavalry overran Forrest's line and captured Selma The enemy captured 40 pieces of artillery, 2,700 prisoners and the important industrial center.

"Oh! It was too awful to remember, if it were possible to be erased, but that cannot be," a Southern Lady recalled April 3rd. Union troops in Richmond! The state capital building, which was also the capital of the Confederacy, now had a Yankee flag flying over it. Some slaves danced in the streets. The Federals stopped the civilian looters and then started the looting themselves. Some fires were putout; others burned themselves out. A great part of the capital was burned.

Petersburg was also occupied. There wasn't as much fire damage here. Lincoln and Grant entered the town after it was safe. Grant received reports that Lee's Army was moving toward Amelia Court House. He ordered Union units to move along a road parallel to Lee's line of march. Grant didn't want Lee to move south and make junction with Johnston.

Because the railroad was in such poor condition, it was noon of this day before the government train made it to Danville. The citizens were very pleased to have President Davis. Maj. W. T. Sutherlin's mansion was given for the "capital." The cabinet met and the

President issued a statement that the "most sacred cause" would continue.

On the 4th, Lincoln was back on the *Delta Queen.* No doubt he was back in the saloon too. The boat docked near Libby Prison. Admiral Porter and ten armed sailors escorted the Yankee President into the former Confederate capital city. Lincoln went to the White House of the Confederacy and sat in President Davis's chair. With his butt, he made a statement. The free nation of the Confederate States of America was conquered and its people were now enslaved by the conqueror. When the brass found-out that the boss was in town, more troops were sent to guard Lincoln. A quick tour was setup so Lincoln could see the damaged city. A few Negroes were found to cheer him but white people refused to welcome their nation's destroyer.

Sheridan's cavalry took Jetersville on the Danville Railroad. This would stop Lee from using the line and changed the direction of his army away from North Carolina.

On the 5th, Lee found no supplies at Amelia Court House. Time was lost. Lee sent orders to Lynchburg to send supplies to Farmville. Lee then started his army moving in that direction.

This day in Richmond, Lincoln came back ashore. He read a statement that the war would not end until the Federal government was again in charge and the government and armies of the Confederacy were disbanded. He said he wanted to call the Virginia State Legislature into session and force the state to vote to re-enter the Union.

The retreat continued on the 6th. Lee was moving toward Farmville and supplies. The army had to make it over the Appomattox River. Union forces were pressing hard. Some of John Gordon's men took a wrong turn and Dick Ewell and R. H. Anderson followed. When the army separated, the Yankees were there. In a bottom called Sayler's Creek the Federals attacked. Confederates counterattacked trying to break through the Union line but strong artillery fire beat back each attack. Cut off, surrounded and pressed, the only option was to surrender. For some Yankees, surrender wasn't enough. They continued to bayonet surrendering Confederates. Lee was watching from a hill some way off and saw 8,000 men become prisoners. "My God, has the army been dissolved?"

At Austinville, part of Stoneman's Blue Bellies hit the lead mines for a second time. The milling equipment was destroyed. There would be no more lead for the Confederacy from these mines. This action made no difference because there were no Confederate Armies left to shoot the lead.

On the 7^{th,} Lee got some supplies at Farmville. The master general was able to get his army over the Appomattox River. Lee gave orders that the railroad and road bridges were to be burned. The Confederate

Philip Sheridan

Jefferson Davis (U)

general in charge failed to completely burn either; Lee was angry that the Union pursuit wasn't stopped. That day, Lee also received a letter from Grant. After Saylor's Creek, there was no reason to continue the fight; Lee's Army of Northern Virginia was finished, said Grant. Lee wrote back that he didn't agree that his army was finished but did ask, what terms Grant would offer. Lee was keenly aware that he was headed toward Lynchburg and not toward a junction with Johnston.

This date, Lincoln sent Grant the following message: "Gen. Sheridan says if the thing is pressed, I think, that Lee will surrender...Let the thing be pressed."

On the 8th, Lee was moving toward Lynchburg; his next stop was to be Appomattox Station, where supplies would be waiting. The whole of the Union Army was pressing Lee but none had caught him. During the day, Sheridan's Cavalry and 6th Corps Infantry moved ahead of Lee's Army. Grant wrote Lee from Farmville, which was on fire, saying he desired "peace." There was only one requirement and that was for Lee's Army to lay down their weapons and not fight "against the U. S. Government until properly exchanged."

Early in the morning, General Lee was informed that a number of his officers believed that no link with Johnston could be made and that surrender was the best course. It was late in the day when Lee replied to Grant. Lee didn't feel that "the emergency has arisen to call for the surrender..." of his army.

That night the great general held his last council of war. The army lay near Appomattox Court House. The supplies lay at Appomattox Station. The county seat had been there for many years. When the railroad came, the station was built about a mile and one half away. Lee's scouts had brought him news that there was a Yankee cavalry unit between him and the supplies. Lee knew he could break through a line of cavalry but was there infantry behind them? It was decided to attack at dawn to find out. Again, there was discussion among his top commanders. Some favored surrender; others did not.

Now that all the fun was leaving the Richmond-Petersburg area, Lincoln decided to leave to and go to Washington the next day.

Near Mobile, the Federals attacked one of the main forts defending the city. The attack was repelled but Union forces were so strong that it was believed that the fort may be cutoff. So during the night, the important fort was abandoned.

Palm Sunday came on the 9th this year. As the sun rose, so did battle. Fitz Lee's Cavalry and Gordon's Infantry attacked. The Yankees fell back, it seemed that a saving victory was at hand but then the Confederates struck an infantry corps. The path forward and supplies were in firm Union hands. Part of Grant's Army attacked the rear guard of Lee's. The Army of Northern Virginia was pinned in and all hopes went out.

Grant knew his hordes had Lee boxed in so he sent another note saying, he had changed the terms since his last letter. Now, he couldn't talk "peace" only surrender.

James Wilson

Lee knew that further battle would only lead to further death; thus, he had no option but to negotiate with a man whose terms changed. "I ask a suspension of hostilities pending the adjustment of the terms of the surrender of this army..."

When the blowhard, Custer heard that Lee had decided to surrender, he wanted to be the big hero and he demanded the surrender of the whole army. Southern commanders ignored the windbag.

Wilmer McLean's home had been used by the Confederates at the Battle of First Manassas. The war was too close for Wilmer so he moved to Appomattox. The war followed him; now, his home had been selected as the place the two generals would meet. As Lee rode to the house, he told an aide, "I would rather face a thousand deaths..."

Those who pretend the war was all about slavery have a hard time at the McLean house. Lee, who owned no slaves, was surrendering to a Yankee who did. If the war were only about slavery, the generals were setting in the wrong seats.

Lee was in his finest dress uniform. Grant came in a mud spattered field uniform. Lee had more dignity in surrender than Grant had in victory.

In war, the victorious general is usually the greatest general but Grant knew who the greatest general really was. Grant wanted to know what Lee thought of him as a general. Grant kept asking Lee if he remembered him from before the war. Grant sure remembered Lee from the War with Mexico! Couldn't Lee recall him at all? "No." Grant was hurt. When Grant wrote his account of the surrender later, he said that Lee had remembered him well from the War in Mexico. Thus, saying that he was important in Lee's eyes.

It was Lee who called Grant's attention to the reason for the conference. Discussion of the surrender terms followed. During the discussion, Grant said that he didn't know Confederate cavalrymen had to furnish their own horses. Lee may have wondered just how intelligent Grant was. Some years later when Grant was President, everybody about him was stealing the government blind. When asked how all this thievery was going on while he was in the White House, Grant said he didn't know a thing about it. Maybe he was telling the truth. After the terms were agreed to, Lee left. Lee neither offered nor did Grant demand, Lee's sword.

Lee returned to his army with head erect but with no hat on. He no doubt was wondering how four years of death and destruction and the fall of the Confederacy could be God's will? His face did not portray the grief he felt inside. He rode looking to neither side. The word spread as to where the great general had been and why. Men removed their hats. Officers and men alike wept; many muttering, "No, no, no!" All who could, touched General Robert E. Lee or Traveler. Lee wasn't just their commander; he was so much more! The men called him "Marse (master) Robert." He was the "good master" and they his willing slaves. What ever he told them to do was the best thing to do; even if were to charge to their deaths! Lee issued his last order and the importance of that order to the post-war and even to this day can not be over emphasized! "Go to your homes and resume your occupations. Obey the laws and become as good citizens as you were soldiers." This is the reason that there was no massive guerrilla movement carried on against the conquerors after the war. Even when the Southern population suffered under the many unjust Union laws, there was no uprising. They would obey until their deaths, Lee's last order.

When word reached the cavalry, Fitz Lee ordered his boys to breakout and ride toward Lynchburg; which they did.

When Grant's Army got the news of Lee's surrender, there was wild cheering and the bands played. Then orders were given to stop the celebrating out of respect and honor for a fallen foe. When Lincoln arrived in Washington, the news of Lee's surrender was spreading.

On the 10[th,] Lincoln was serenaded and happy crowds came around the White House. Lincoln asked the military band to play an unusual request, "Play *Dixie*."

It was past noon, when the news reached the other President. Davis and party boarded the train heading for Greensboro, North Carolina.

Lee's General Order No. 9, which really wasn't an order but a farewell address, was issued this day. "After four years of arduous service, marked by unsurpassed courage and fortitude, the Army of Northern Virginia has been compelled to yield to overwhelming numbers and resources…you will take with you the satisfaction that proceeds from the consciousness of duty faithfully performed, and I earnestly pray that a Merciful God will extend to you His blessing and protection. With an increasing admiration of your constancy and devotion to your country, and a grateful remembrance of your kind and generous consideration for myself, I bid you an affectionate farewell."

Although, it was Grant that would be receiving Lee's surrender, Grant knew that he would always be inferior to Lee. This day, he told Lee that he would not be present for the formal surrender. Grant informed Lee that three "Commissioners" would be handling the surrender for the Union side. The three commissioners were three subordinate officers. Both Lee and Grant were Lieutenant Generals and Commanders of all field forces. General Lee appointed three of his subordinates as "Commissioners." Lee would not lead his army on its final march. The surrender of the infantry was scheduled for the 12th, almost four years to the day since the firing on Fort Sumter.

After the meeting, Lee spent much of the balance of the day in receiving Union generals. In the future, they all wanted to say, "I was there with General Lee." No one was known to have requested an audience with General Grant!

In North Carolina, Sherman was taking up the march on Raleigh.

On the 11th, the last defenses for the city of Mobile were abandoned. This day, the Confederate government train arrived in Greensboro.

In Washington, Lincoln addressed the people in a rambling talk, not speech, from a White House window.

He said he wanted "a righteous and speedy peace" but then said he had no idea how that kind of peace would come about because of his differences with Congress. He was still up-set because Congress had forced him to sign that bill saying that "his free states didn't count." He said he still believed it was a good idea. Then he dropped a bomb shell. In Louisiana, he wanted "the very intelligent" Negro and Negro soldiers to be able to vote. That is to say, Lincoln saw the Negro as a voting block for his party. Few people there thought that giving the vote to inferior Negroes was a good idea.

Mobile fell into Union hands on the 12th. This had been the last major city in the South under Southern control. The Southern defenders moved toward Meridian, Mississippi. Their plan was to move east and link-up with Johnston.

Wilson's Cavalry occupied Montgomery, Alabama, the first Capital of the Confederacy. Sherman moved on the Capital of North Carolina at Raleigh. Stoneman took Salisbury and captured 1,300 Confederates.

At Greensboro, the President and cabinet met with the highest ranking generals in the Confederacy, Beauregard and Johnston. The generals informed the President that they couldn't defeat Sherman and asked for permission to negotiate. Davis and his cabinet said that negotiations were a waste of time; the only thing the Yankees would negotiate was surrender. After heated debate, the generals were given permission to meet with Sherman.

The conqueror, Lincoln, had told the Virginia Legislature that he wanted (demanded) that they re-affirm their acceptance of the United States Constitution. The Legislature had declined and this made Lincoln angry. President Lincoln now said that this Legislature was not the "rightful legislature." He then denied that he had asked this un-rightful legislature, to vote themselves back in to the Union. This was Honest Abe at his best.

At Appomattox Court House, Gen. Joshua Chamberlain accepted the surrender. General John B. Gordon led Lee's Army. The long gray line of near starved, raggedie Confederates marched to the court house to stack arms and furl flags. They were beaten; not conquered. They who had fought with honor for the righteous cause of freedom paraded before those who had lost their honor and fought to suppress free men. The largest field force of the Confederacy was gone. Thus, one of the greatest armies in the history of the world, General Robert E. Lee's Army of Northern Virginia made its final review!

Lee had no home. Each year thousands of visitors watch the "Changing of the Guard" at the Tomb of the Unknown Soldier. There is no sign that reads, "You are entering Arlington National Cemetery, which was the ancestral home of General Robert E. Lee; stolen by the Yankee Nation!"

Joshua Chamberlain

These warriors were now at peace but their spirits weren't. Gen. Henry Wise told a Yank, "There is a rancor in our hearts you little dream of. We hate you, sir." A private wrote home, "Teach my children to hate them with that bitter hatred that will never permit them to meet without seeking to destroy each other." The Yankees made a poem of it. "Here's to the men of the Northland, our eagle a bird of prey! He soars high over Southern field- and shits on Southern clay!"

John Gordon

As the bad news spread across the South that Richmond had fallen and Lee had surrendered, many Southern units decided the war was over. They disbanded and left their post. Most of Lee's cavalry surrendered at Lynchburg. Some units broke-out and continued to ride. Later they just disbanded, also. In the Department of Southwest Virginia there were 600 soldiers and three brigadier generals. The men took a vote. Ten said the war was over and left for home. 590 men were still at war. Their bravery was "beyond praise." They marched south toward Greensboro where the President was reported to be.

On the 13th, Sherman took the capital of North Carolina, Raleigh, as he pushed Johnston. The Yankees knew it was all over. The hated draft was stopped and orders for more supplies were cut.

In the early morning of the 14[th,] General Robert Anderson raised the conqueror's banner over Fort Sumter. He was Maj. Robert Anderson when last he was at this place.

Sherman was moving toward Durham Station when he received a letter from Johnston asking if he were open to a conference to see if there could be "peace." Sherman replied that he was.

It had been four years since forces of the sovereign State of South Carolina fired on foreign troops occupying their soil. In the intervening four years, the biggest, most costly war ever fought in the western hemisphere had occurred. How high of a mountain would the bodies of over 600,000 Americans make? How deep of a river would the blood and tears shed make? What was the cost of the war material? How can you measure the amount of collective pain? How many homes were burned? How do you quantify loneliness? How do you account for fear, anxiety and not knowing where or how your loved one was? What was the cost of the heartache of never knowing? What value would you place on broken plans and lives? How do you value lost honor, dignity and rights? What was the sum total of suffering from 1861-65? Which one person was most responsible for the war and its suffering?

President Abraham Lincoln went to Ford's theater that evening. John Wilkes Booth was there but his part in this evening play had not been rehearsed by the other actors. The late President and his rude party stopped the action on stage until they could be seated. Then *Our American Cousin* continued for those who arrived on time. The play was interrupted again. This time it was the sound of pistol shot. Then the dramatic actor, John Wilkes Booth, boldly took center stage. He leaped from the President's box to the stage. The leap caused him to break his leg. He regained his composure and regained his feet. The last three words he spoke on stage were the most memorable words of his career. They were in Latin, "Sic semper tyrannis." These are the same words that were on the Virginia State Seal before and after the war. They mean, "Thus ever to tyrants!" Actor-patriot, Booth, had played his last scene and exited theater stage-left into the night. The audience was shocked by his performance and the President soon died because of it. The brave Booth knew he was risking his life to play his last part on the stage. He didn't know his three words, in a bit part, would change the world! He didn't know, couldn't know that he had changed history to this very day!

The day was Good Friday. It was the day that all of Christendom recalled, the Via Della Rosa (the way of sorrow), the cross, the pain, the death and resurrection of Jesus. All of this very painful day was necessary so the great act of eternal salvation could be opened to mankind.

𝕵𝖔𝖍𝖓 𝕭𝖔𝖔𝖙𝖍

That box at Ford's Theater could be considered a "Yankee Calvary" and the fire from Booth's pistol a very fast "purgatory." (Some religions believe that most men must pass through a fiery punishment to pay for their sins before they can go to Heaven.)

The real Lincoln was burned up in the flames from Booth's pistol shot. The Lincoln, who never joined a church or professed a personal belief in Jesus, was gone. The Lincoln, who lied to most of the people most of the time, was gone. The Lincoln, who detested Negroes and wished them all shipped from his country, was gone. The Lincoln, who did so many wrong things, caused a war that cost so much, was gone. What emerged was "Saint Lincoln "

Booth now became a type of "Pontius Pilate." He was a Southerner. The Yankees thought all Southerners wished Lincoln dead. Therefore, in the Yankee mind, all Southerners were like Booth, (who like Pilot, killed Jesus). All Southerners lost their honor in Yankee eyes. They were all guilty of Lincoln's death, all were to be hated and all were to be punished.

In the Yankee mind, the blood of Lincoln became similar to the blood of Jesus. It was atonement for all the evil things that had been done to the South and its people. It was the reason for and also atonement for, all the evil things they would do in the future. The entire South deserved and deserves ever punishment the North wished to dish out. Indeed, many, many attempts were made to officially connect Booth with the Confederate government; none succeeded.

What emerged from Yankee Cavalry is a completely different Lincoln than went to Ford's Theater. Now he was a kind, pure, Christian, saint, without earthly fault and the president that "saved the nation." To the Negro, he is "Father Abraham," who died to give them freedom.

The bullet from Booth's gun completely changed a man's entire life. The truth about who Lincoln really was, what he really did to both nations and what the people of his time really thought about him must never be recorded in Yankee history or taught in school!

Shortly after 7 A. M. on the 15th, President Lincoln died. Secretary of War, Edwin Stanton who had called Lincoln a "buffoon" now said his immortal words, "Now he belongs to the ages." At 11 A. M. Johnson became President. John Booth stopped at the home of Dr. Samuel Mudd and had his leg set, this day.

The living war President, Davis, left Greensboro moving south but there was little of the South left in which to move.

On the 16th, the President was in Lexington, North Carolina still heading south. On the 17th, he was at Salisbury. The dead President was laid in state in the East Room of the Northern White House while Sherman and Johnston were negotiating near Durham.

On the 18th, Sherman and Johnston signed the terms of surrender. Johnston got more out of Sherman than Lee did out of Grant. Basically full rights were restored to the Confederate soldiers. They were "guaranteed rights of person and property; the United States would not disturb the people of the South as long as they lived in peace..." One of the rights under the Constitution was the right to own slaves. Sherman allowed Southerners to keep their slaves!

Lincoln at Ford's Theatre

The Bullet that changed Lincoln

In the East Room on the 19^{th,} Lincoln had his funeral. His wife and son, Tad, did not attend. Capt. Robert Lincoln was the family representative. Grant got to stand alone during the brief service. The body was then moved to the Capitol rotunda so that the general public could pass by Lincoln's coffin.

The forces from Southwest Virginia linked up with President Davis at Charlotte. Wade Hampton suggested to the President that they cross the Mississippi and continue the war from that department. This day, in the Department of the Trans-Mississippi, Kirby Smith received a letter from John Pope suggesting that he surrender.

On the 21^{st,} John Mosby disbanded his men. This date, the train bearing Lincoln's body left Washington. It would take many stops and days to reach Springfield, Illinois.

On the 23rd at Charlotte the President approved of the terms of surrender between Sherman and Johnston. The President knew that Lincoln was dead but he probably didn't know that Stanton was practically running the Union government. Stanton had told Sherman the war was now "about slavery." When he saw the terms Sherman and Johnston had worked out, he was hopping mad! He got Johnson's approval to send Grant to Sherman to tell him the surrender terms were not acceptable! Grant arrived at Sherman's headquarters this day. Sherman was outraged that Stanton had rejected the terms. Grant ordered Sherman to go to Johnston and tell him that his word was not worth the paper they signed; he was just a "lying Yankee." If Sherman didn't do it, Grant said he would and that battle would begin in two days.

On the 25th, Johnston asked Sherman to renew the negotiations. Sherman said he would on the 26th.

On the morning of the 26th, Union cavalry surrounded a barn near the Rappahannock River. They were told that the man in the barn was John Wilkes Booth. The man would not surrender so the Yankees set the barn on fire. At about 7 A. M. a "religious fanatic and an unstable man," Sgt. Boston Corbett shot the man. Two men identified the body as that of Booth. The official autopsy shows that a man who was several inches taller than Booth was buried. It is likely the Yankees didn't shoot Booth!

Near Durham, Johnston accepted terms of surrender similar to those Lee had signed. The Army of the Tennessee passed into history.

This day, President Davis left Charlotte with the aim of crossing the Mississippi.

On the 27th near Vicksburg, an overloaded boat full of former Union prisoners-of-war was moving up the Mississippi. Some time before dawn the boiler exploded; the ship sank. Approximately 1,900 soldiers, who had survived fights with Rebels and prison camp, would not return home.

Joseph Shelby

On the 29th, President Johnson lifted the navel blockade of the former Confederate States, east of the Mississippi.

Stanton appointed a commission to try those accused of helping Booth kill President Lincoln. The officers were so anti-Southern they would convict anybody brought before them. Evidence was irrelevant.

Evidence was irrelevant to President Johnson also. On the 2nd of May, he issued a proclamation declaring that President Davis was behind the shooting of Lincoln. A $100,000 reward was placed on the Confederate

President's head. This day, the President arrived in Abbeville, South Carolina. A meeting was held. Most of the military officers wanted to surrender. Davis and what was left of his cabinet wanted to continue the war. Though they disagreed, he was still President and the war would go on. Abbeville was the site of one of the first rallies to take South Carolina out of the Union. It was the site of the last official government meeting. Davis and party left the town around midnight.

This day, word reached the Department of the Trans-Mississippi of Lincoln's demise. John Watkins of the 5th Texas penned a letter home, "Thou I dislike to see any one assassinated yet when I heard of Lincoln's death, I could but rejoice. When a man has injured a people who never harmed him and caused the death of hundred of thousands of his fellow beings for no good whatever, he deserves death, and every lover of peace should rejoice at it."

On the 3[rd,] more of Davis' cabinet resigned and started running for their lives. A number of Confederates were also running all across the southland.

On the 4[th,] Gen. Richard Taylor surrendered the forces of the Department of Alabama, Mississippi and East Louisiana. His forces had gone about 40 miles north of Mobile, toward Johnston. This day, Lincoln returned to Springfield.

On the 8[th,] Secretary of War John Breckinridge took it upon himself and dismissed what military forces that remained with the President. These were primarily the troops from the Department of Southwest Virginia, "…the long agony was over." They disbanded.

Without military escort, President Davis and party were captured by Union cavalry near Irwinville, Georgia on the 10th. Since Richmond, President Davis was the government and the government was President Davis. The "Cause" became the "Lost Cause."

Maj. Gen. Sam Jones surrendered his forces at Tallahassee. Blood-thirsty Northern bushwhackers caught William Quantrill and his men in Spencer County, Kentucky. Quantrill would die of wounds received on June 6th.

On the 11th, Brig. Gen. Jeff Thompson surrendered his force at Chalk Bluff, Arkansas.

The last land fight of the war occurred at Pelmito Ranch, Texas on the 12th and 13th. Yankees under Col. Theodore Barrett marched from Brownsville and attacked forces under Col. John "Rest in Peace" Ford. After two days of bloody fighting, the Yankees retreated. The last engagement was a Southern victory!

The governors of Arkansas, Missouri, Louisiana, and a representative of Texas met with Kirby Smith at Marshall, Texas on the 13th. Smith's subordinate, Jo Shelby, threatened to arrest Smith if he tried to surrender!

On the 22^{nd,} President Johnson opened more Southern ports to commerce. On this date, President Davis was chained and thrown into a damp dark cell in the lower recesses of Fort Monroe, Virginia.

On the 23^{rd,} the Grand Review of the Army of the Potomac was held in Washington. This time Grant was there to lead his army. "The Conquerors came…It was a march of victory and triumph…" There were many thousands of Yankees, who once were a part of this army, that weren't there for the march.

On the 24^{th,} the city saw the Grand Review of Sherman's Army. Their uniforms weren't very nice, their lines weren't very straight and there were Negroes and camp pets mixed in this parade. It could easily be seen that there was a lack of pride; these men marched without honor. The song to burn Dixie by, *The Battle Hymn of the Republic,* was played. Even the Union nation rejected their looting, burning and raping. The shopkeepers were glad to see them go. "Now and then the veteran looters glanced longingly at the windows of jewelry stores they passed." Their thievery hadn't stopped when the army crossed the Potomac. Sherman led his army of shame. At the White House, he dismounted and shook President Johnson's hand. When Stanton extended his hand toward Sherman, it was left hanging in the air.

The sound of war echoed through Mobile on the 25th. A warehouse with twenty tons of captured

Confederate gunpowder exploded. Buildings, warehouses, dock facilities, were laid waste; even boats in the harbor were sunk. Three hundred people were killed or wounded.

On the 26[th,] representatives of the Confederate Military Department of the Trans-Mississippi opened surrender talks with the Yankees in New Orleans. Gen. Jo Shelby wasn't about to surrender. He took his army to Mexico and disbanded.

On the 29[th,] President Johnson gave a general pardon to most Confederate prisoners of war. There were plenty of exceptions to the amnesty so that the Federals could keep anyone they wished in prison. In order, to receive a pardon, Confederate prisoners must take the oath of allegiance to the United States. The word "pardon" stuck in their crawls. Many prisoners protested because they weren't one bit sorry for fighting against Northern tyranny. Union prisoner of war camps began to empty the first part of June. To humiliate the Confederates one last time, the soldiers of the former Confederacy had to take the pledge while standing on a Confederate flag! Although most Confederates realized the war was over and staying in prison now made no difference, some prisoners refused to take the oath to the conqueror's flag or desecrate their own. Bewildered Union authorities simply released these "die hards" at the end of June.

On June 3rd, Confederate naval forces on the Red River surrendered.

"I here declare my unmitigated hatred of the Yankee rule..." Edmund Ruffin, who fired the first cannon at Fort Sumter, penned these words; wrapped himself in a Confederate flag and committed suicide on June 18th.

Confederate naval forces on the high seas captured two Yankee whalers in the Bering Sea on the 22nd.

On the 23rd, Confederate-Indiana, Brig. Gen. Stand Watie, surrendered the Confederate forces of the Cherokee, Creek, Seminole and Osage nations at Doaksville, Indian Territory.

Stand Watie

The C. S. S. Shenandoah captured six more whalers on the 26th and eleven on the 28th. The Shenandoah was never captured or surrendered. On November 6th the vessel was turned over to England at Liverpool.

William H. T. Walker

CHAPTER 22   IT NEVER ENDS

The war, Civil War; War Between the States; North against the South; War of the Rebellion; War of Northern Aggression; War for Southern Independence; Second American Revolution; War for Constitutional Government, didn't just start in 1861 nor did it stop in 1865. All history that came before affected the war; all history since has been affected by the war. On a personal basis, all preceding history both personal and group, affects what we do each day. What we do each day will affect what we do in the future. History can be viewed as a "River of Time." It started in the beginning and will flow until the "End of Time." We, individually, in groups, on a national basis and internationally, are a part of that flow.

The war was very large in scope. It is the second most important event in the history of this country. Its causes were myriad; its results are prolific. This nation has been involved in many, many military conflicts. It's hard to find a time when this nation wasn't involved in a military conflict. Out of all those conflicts, the one that has welded our national interest far more than any other, is the one from 1861-65. Its causes are still disputed, often to obtain individual or group power. The same could be said for its ramifications. Often its history is distorted for the same reasons. Hardly a week goes by that some national paper doesn't have a story about this one war. Why? Because it was such a defining period; it has defined all that came before it and all that has come since. Because the Yankees won, they have largely dominated the government, the media outlets and major publishing houses. It is they who have largely written the history. They wrote it the way they wanted it to be; not necessarily the way it was. For those who believe that truth is "relative;" it could be said that writing history is so important, that it shouldn't be left to historians. That "…the one war crime is losing. That is the reality, and the rest is sentimental nonsense." There are others who believe that "truth" is immutable; no matter how much cover-up, changing, rewriting or distortion that Truth can't be killed and can be found.

What follows is just a very light touch on some subjects in the post-war.

Big surprise! On June 30th all people charged as "Lincoln conspirators" or brave-patriots were found guilty. Four, including a woman, were hanged on July 7th. The four others were sent to a prison island off Key West, Florida. Dr. Samuel Mudd was sentenced to prison for life, because he was a doctor who treated a patient. He was released for the same reason. Because he treated patients during a yellow fever epidemic, he was pardoned in 1868.

The *Shenandoah* struck its colors when the captain learned the war was over on August 2nd. The ship was turned over to English, not United States, authorities on November 6th.

In September, eleven Indian Nations were forced to sign "a treaty of loyalty with the United States, and renounced all Confederate agreements." The Indians have fared no better than their Southern allies since the war.

Champ Ferguson was never charged with the massacre of Negroes at Saltville. He was hung on October 10th for killing those who defiled his wife and daughter. As a token gesture, members of the 5th U. S. Colored Cavalry watched him die. Many high ranking Confederate officials remained "shackled in some Federal dungeon." However, the conquerors had, by now, released some prisoners. Many Confederates went into exile in Mexico, Canada and England. Some former Confederates legally immigrated to other countries rather than live under a Union flag.

Capt. Henry Wirz commanded the Andersonville Prison during the war. He had written letters to the Yankee authorities asking that prisoner exchanges be restarted to relieve crowding at his prison. The Northern answer, "No." He wrote letters asking the Federal authorities to send Yankee prisoners food and medicine. The Northern answer, "No." He was well aware that Sherman had marched by and not freed the prisoners. At least part of the estimated 12,000, who died there; died by their own nation's hand. After a make believe trial, he was hung on November 10th for "cruelty to Federal prisoners..."

On December 1^{st,} President Johnson declared that the right of trial would be given; given to the Northern states only. The District of Columbia is not a state and there were many Northern political prisoners held there. So the District was included with the South and the territories, where no justice would be given.

On the 18^{th,} the Thirteenth Amendment to the U. S. Constitution was passed. This amendment outlawed slavery. The former Confederate States were allowed to vote on this amendment and most supported it.

The war with fields of battle had ceased months ago but the war of words was continuing and Washington was the big battle site. President Johnson and Congress were at odds over how to manage (take advantage of) the South; its people, its wealth and its politics.

The radical (Northern) Republican Party controlled Congress and they were men filled with hate and no morals. The delegates from the South had been "seated;" that is to say formally recognized as representatives of their given states. Now, Congress voted that their states were no longer in the Union; therefore, they must leave Congress. Their states had voted on the Thirteenth Amendment but they wouldn't be allowed to vote on the Fourteenth. According to the official Federal line, there was never a war between the

United States and the Confederacy. It was a "rebellion;" the states had never left the Union. After the gun fire had stopped, Congress declared that those states that were in the Confederacy were now "at war with the United States." If ten states rejected the amendment, it wouldn't become law; therefore the Southern states were "thrown out."

The Republican Party thought those delegates may object as what was left of the South was destroyed. It is called the Fourteenth Amendment. The politicians called the destruction of the South, "Reconstruction." These are but a few of the things the Fourteenth Amendment did. Those who fought for or helped the Confederacy were declared "criminals." Only males could vote; therefore, white Southerners could not vote. Former slaves were now declared to be citizens, thus, the only state voters left were former slaves and Yankee Carpetbaggers. There was no protection under the law for white Southerners. This gave rise to the KKK. Under previous law, when the government took a person's property, the government had to pay a fair value for the property taken. Slaves were property under the Constitution. Now, the Federal government said that they wouldn't pay for the property they had stolen. The government stole Southern property. The United States Government took all assets of the former Confederacy but refused to pay any debts it owed. These debts included the bonds the Southern citizens had bought. The government went even further. The states and many banks had issued (sold) war bonds. Now, it was against the law for them to pay the honest debt they owed. Thus, the remaining wealth of the South was stolen. The civilian governments were removed and military governors were appointed for each state. Southerners were not citizens of their own country; they had no rights. The South was a colony of the North. Union troops, enforced unjust Union laws "at the point of a bayonet." A Southerner could be jailed for whistling *Dixie*.

In this war of words over dividing the spoils of war, the South, The President fired a big shot on April 2, 1866. "Now, I, Andrew Johnson, President of the United States do hereby proclaim and declare that the insurrection…is at an end." What he was saying to Congress is that, 'President Lincoln started it; I finished it. It was a Presidential war. The President, not Congress, has the right to divide the South up as he wishes.' Congress, not the President, won this war. They impeached him.

The government of the United States of America had changed fundamentally. Before 1860, it was a voluntary "union" of states. When force was used on former members of the "Union," the founding principals of that union were destroyed. It was no longer a willing union, but from the Northern point of view, it could only be held together by force. So by 1865, the United States had become an "empire," enslaving several states and the people there of. The Federal Government had been created by the states, now it had turned on all of its creators. The passage of the Fourteenth Amendment officially changed the relationship between the states and the Federal Government; states were now subservient to the national government. Without powerful states to protect the citizen's rights, all the people, including those who wore Yankee Blue, lost rights. Thus, it could be said that in this war, even the winners were losers!

When the shooting stopped, there followed a stream of Northern Republican laws. Included was the "Black Code" whereby the un-free Southerners were regulated. At the point of gun, each southern state had to ratify the Fourteenth Amendment and all following laws before the state could re-enter the Union. States didn't re-ratify the Constitution. When the states left the Union, they withdrew their original ratification of the Constitution; therefore, these states have never ratified the Constitution. The southern states are not a part of the Union. Thus, technically, Southerners are citizens of their states but not citizens of the United States.

President Jefferson Davis languished in Fort Monroe until 1869. He spent much time in prayer and Bible reading as he awaited court decisions. He was charged with "treason." A court ruled that treason was a civil offense; that the U. S. authorities would have to try him in open civilian court not by military tribunal. It was known that the right of secession would come up and go to the Supreme Court. The Northern authorities knew the court would rule that the South had every right to leave the Union. Therefore, all charges were dropped and the former President was released.

There have been so many anti-Southern attacks by the government and the powers that be, that there isn't enough space to list them all. It can be said that, what was unacceptable law before 1861 is the law of the land, even to this day. The Yankee domination of the South by the government, politically and by economic means has never stopped. Some modern examples of this continued repression would include the illegal Voting Rights Act, the NAFTA Treaty and the attack on the Southern tobacco industry (while the Northern booze industry gets a free pass). The religious revival began during the war has resulted in a south that is more religious than the rest of the country; the Bible Belt. By its actions, the Federal government can now be seen as anti-Christian. It can be concluded that white Southern Christians are the most discriminated against minority in the country. Black raciest groups use the war to create racial dissension and finance their organizations. There seems to be no end to the attacks on the South, its culture, its heritage, its history, its politics and its economics.

Many of those who lived and fought during the war considered it a religious war. There are those who today say that "because the Yankees won the war that proves that God was on their side." That is to say that the Unionists were in God's will and the Confederates were not. If that were true, then no successful criminal should be in jail! If a strong man breaks into a weaker man's home, kills the man, rapes his wife, abuses the children, steals all and then burns the home, then God is on the side of the criminal, because he won. The victims were out of God's will. They were evil and only got what they deserved! Nowhere in the Bible does it say that, "Might makes right."

Although the war could be viewed almost completely as negative from the Southern point of view, there are provable positive attributes that have proceeded from the war. That is not to say that the price paid equals the benefits derived. Here are some positive things that have resulted from the war. There is great literature, inspiring poems, beautiful pictures, music, songs, statues, monuments, markers, and head stones. Starting during the war and continuing to this day, many a personal name is war related. Many names of places, building, parks and roads come from the war. A great deal of genealogy is war related. There are holidays to honor the war and those, who fought in it. There are a system of local, state and national parks because of the war. Military schools around the world, teach our war's history. The sound of musket and cannon are heard across this country as battles from the war are reenacted; some in areas that saw no action. Relic collecting is a national pastime and there are museums that preserve collections for the general public. There are gun and relic shows in all parts of this country. There are many organizations dedicated to the study of the war and preserving its history. Many people enjoy flying the Confederate flag and displaying bumper stickers about the war. Many people earn money selling and making items that are war related. These are just a few of the positive things from the war that impact our lives. Thus the war of our ancestors provides employment, income, pleasure and knowledge to this day!

The author believes he has lit one more candle in the dark that will illuminate the true history of the war era. It is his wish that it will be read, used and enjoyed. It is his prayer that the powers of darkness and ignorance will not extinguish that light.

C-2004

INDEX

C=Confederate U=Union

A

Abbeville, SC-452
Abingdon, VA-129, 337, 379
Adairsville, GA-289
Africa-2, 26, 65, 98, 102, 137, 205, 253
African Brigade (U)-177
Alabama-8, 22-3, 77, 101, 126, 146, 185, 199, 205, 209, 253, 310, 326, 339, 343, 366, 419, 422, 426, 427, 439,453
Alaska-2
Albemarle-79, 261, 287, 294, 356
Albuquerque, NM-78
Alexander, Porter (C)-124, 165-6
Allatoona, GA-346,-
Allatoona Pass-297
Amelia Court House, VA-428, 429
American Bible Society- 56
Ammen, Gen. Jacob (U)-344
Anderson, Bill "Bloody Bill" (C)-207, 343
Anderson, Maj. Gen. Richard (C)-162, 167, 185, 276, 277, 429
Anderson, (Col. to Gen.) Robert-26, 27, 29, 162, 442
Andersonville Prison, GA-249, 460
Andrews, James (U)-78
Andrew, Gov. John, (MA)-246
Appomattox Court House, VA-432, 440
Appomattox River-429, 431
Appomattox Station-432
Arapahoe Indians-369
Archer's Brigade-166
Arizona-45, 289
Arkansas-8, 30-31, 50, 65, 97, 101, 114, 137-138, 145, 147, 158, 179, 192, 206, 209, 217, 242-43, 296, 328, 349, 355, 401,454 "Free State of Arkansas"-401
Arlington National Cemetery-441
Armistead Gen. Lewis (C)-93, 189, 238
Army of Mississippi-65
Army of Northern Virginia-150, 264, 284, 286, 431, 433, 437,440
Army of Tennessee-319, 370, 371, 382, 408

Army of the Cumberland-206

Army of Kentucky-102

Army of Central Kentucky-56

Army of the Potomac-33, 47, 67, 181, 257, 361, 454

Army of the Shenandoah-295

Army of the Tennessee-219, 288, 333, 389, 393, 419, 451

Army of West Virginia-301

Ashby, Gen. Turner (C)- 67, 86-7, 103

Ashland, VA-89

Athens, AL-343

Atlanta, GA-57, 179, 218, 288, 292, 297, 308, 310, 315-19, 321-22, 324, 328, 332-38, 340, 343, 346, 354, 357-58, 360, 364-66, 418,-

Siege of Atlanta- 323

Atlantic Monthly Magazine-61

Attila the Hun-336

Augusta, GA-347

Austinville (lead mines), VA-200, 258, 269, 382, 431

Averell, Gen. William (U)-159-61, 205-6, 208, 221, 237, 258, 268-9, 273-5, 287, 295, 298, 301, 306

B

Ball Hill, GA-322

Ball's Bluff, VA-52, 62

Baker, Col. Edward (U)-52

Baltic-25

Baltimore, MD-24, 29, 59, 152, 158, 245, 302, 306, 317, 323, 340

Baltimore and Ohio Railroad-59, 158, 245, 323, 340, 351, 369

Banks, Maj. Gen. Nathaniel (U)-43, 65, 84, 130, 174-5, 217, 221, 226, 233, 243, 251-6, 258, 260-1, 292

Bannock Indians-148

Barksdale, Gen. William (Mississippian Brigade)-132-3, 185, 350

Barnum Museum-368

Batesville, AK-147

Baton Rouge, LA-101, 104,115

Battle of Brandy Station, Va-177, 181

Battle of Cedar Creek-328-9, 352

Battle of Cedar Run-102

Battle of Champion's Hill-173, 193, 244

Blair, Francis (C)-393-4, 397, 399

Blair, Gen Frank (U)-367

Blair, Postmaster General Montgomery (U)-343

Blunt, James (U)-137-8, 200, 354

Boatswain's Swamp, VA-90

Bonnie Blue Flag-22, 180

Boone County Courthouse, (W) VA-50

Boone County, IN-179

Boone, NC-425

Boonsboro, MD-116

Boonville, MO-34, 219, 349

Booth, John Wilkes (C)-222, 391, 411, 443, 450-2

Boston, MA-199, 295, 451

Boyd, Belle (C)-99

Bradford, Maj. William (U)-258

Bragg, Gen. Braxton (C)-73-6, 87, 127, 129, 177, 180, 209-5, 219-21, 225, 228, 230, 231, 234, 248, 317, 368, 376, 393-4, 415

Brashear City, LA-180

Brazil-348

Bread Riot-155-6, 209

Breckinridge, Gen. John (C)-74, 101, 142, 144, 211, 214, 249, 264, 280-2, 284, 295, 307, 345, 366, 376, 378-82,

401, 416, 453,-Secretary of War-416

Bridgeport, AL-209

Bright, Senator of Indiana-61

Bristoe Campaign-218, 221,-

Bristoe Station-106

Bristol, VA-TN-377-8

British and Foreign Anti-Slavery Society-175

Brooklyn *Eagle*-46

Brown, Joe (Governor GA)-366

Brown, John-6

Brunswick, MO-349

Brush Creek, MO-355

Buchanan, VA-304, 306-7

Buchanan, Admiral Franklin, (C)-327

Buchanan, President James-9-10, 22, 249

Buckner, Gen. Simon (C)-47, 63, 211

Buckland, Col. Ralph (U)-73

Buell, Gen. Don (U)-72, 75-7, 124, 127, 129, 226

Buford, Gen. John (U)- 181-2

Bull Pasture Mountain, VA-82

Bunker Hill, VA-34, 323

C

Crook, Gen. George (U)-
113, 258, 268-73, 342 , 275,
287, 293, 295, 298, 301,
308-9, 323, 332, 342
Cross Keys, VA-86
Couch, Maj. Gen. Darius
(U)-161, 166
Cub Run Bridge, VA-42
Cuba-55
Culp's Hill, PA-183, 186-7
Culpeper, Va-160
Cumberland, Gap, Va-60,
62, 66, 87, 102, 128, 146,
206, 209, 241, 248 ,411
Cumberland River-60, 146
Cummings, Capt. Authur
(C)-41
Curtis, Gen. Samuel (U)-65
Custer, Gen. George (U)-
190, 225, 249, 251, 347-8,
410, 434

D

Dahlgren, Col.Ulric (U)-
250-1
Daily News-46
Dakota Territory-128
Dalton, GA- 248-9, 289, 351
Damn Yankees-1, 6, 58, 81,
130, 142, 169, 179, 250, 252,
299, 339, 348, 367, 386, 405
Danville, VA-428

Danville Railroad-429
David-218
Davis, Coleman Smith (C)-
231, 233
Davis, Gen. Jeff (U)-418
Davis, President Jefferson
(C)-Numerous- Joe Davis
(Son)-262,-"Jeff Davis
Coffee"-240
Davis, Sam (C)-231, 468
Davis, Congressman Henry
(U)-154
Decatur, AL-319, 322, 365
Delaware-65, 338, 391, 412
Delta-242
Delta Queen-428
Democrats (U)-129, 170,
199, 314, 332, 353, 390
Department of Agriculture
(U)-84
Department of Alabama,
Mississippi and East
Louisiana-453
Department of the
Cumberland-51
Department of Ohio-147
Department of the South-67,
78, 146
Department of Southwest
Virginia-207, 249, 264, 276,
280, 295-6, 336, 345, 366,
373, 376, 378, 380, 442, 449,
453,-Southwest Virginia-

East Tennessee Department-
59, 128, 255, 313, 344, 366
Department of the Trans-
Mississippi-137,192, 235,
253, 256, 258, 262, 346, 354,
415, 449, 452, 455
Dewitt Jobe (C)-233
Diana-155
District of Ironton-45
Dixie-1, 24, 56, 62, 71, 192,
204, 210, 212, 309, 385, 426,
437, 455, 463
Doaksville, Indian Territory-
456
Doctor's Creek, KY-127
Dodd, David (C)-242
Dodge, General Grenville
(U)-232-3
Douglas, Stephen Douglas-
33, 200, 358
Draft Act-151, 197-8
Dred Scott Case-349
Dublin, VA-200, 269, 272-3,
275
Dublin-Pearisburg Pike
(Today, Rt. 100)-270
Duke, Gen. Basil (C)-154,
377, 396
Dunker Church-119
Durham,NC-442, 447, 451

E

Early, Gen. Jubal "Old Jub"
(C)-105, 110, 120, 142, 162,
167, 169-70, 276, 300, 306-
9, 311-6 -, - 318-9, 322-6,
328-9, 339-44, 347, 352,
364, 410, 432
Easton, PA-47
Echols, Gen. John (C)-221
Egypt-94
El Paso, TX-78
Elizabethtown, KY-141
Elkhorn Tavern, AK-65
Ellsworth, Col. Elmer (U)-31
Elmira, NY-204, 395
Emancipation Proclamation-
48-50, 54, 78, 98, 124, 137-
8, 143, 146, 156, 209, 211,
292 ,412
Emma-125
Emory and Henry College-
348
England-3, 11, 30-1, 51-2,
55-8, 67, 94, 97-8, 124, 142,
146, 149-50,156, 158, 174,
176, 180, 205, 209, 233, 253,
351, 457, 460
English, Robert (C)-233
Etowah River-291-2
Eugene-125
Evans, N. G. "Shank" (C)-
38-9, 43, 87, 95

Everett, Edward (U)-223
Ewell, Gen. Richard "Dick"-
40, 87, 108, 178, 181, 183-4,
186-7, 265, 277-8, 285, 429
Ewing, Gen. Thomas (U)-
208
Examiner-238
Ezra Church, GA-324

F

Fair Oaks, VA-91
Fairfax Court House,
Virginia-153
Falls Church, VA-34
Farmville, VA-429, 431, 432
Farragut, Adm. David (U)-
79-80, 84, 154, 326
Fayette, MO-343
Fayetteville, AK-138
Fayetteville, NC-416
Federal Hill, MD- 29
Ferguson, Champ (C)-348,
460
Fisher's Hill, VA- 341,
342,352
Fishing Creek, KY-60
Five Forks, VA-425-6
Florida-8, 22, 51-2, 54, 145,
153, 237, 245, 247, 317, 348,
372, 459
Floyd, Gen, John (C)- 46, 49,
51, 63, 95

Ford's Theater, DC-443,
445, 446
Forrest, Gen. Bedford (C)-
Numerous
Fort Berthold-128
Fort Bisland-157
Fort Delaware- 338
Fort Donelson-61-2, 71, 149,
349
Fort Fisher-345, 383, 388,
393-4, 397, 408
Fort Gaines-326, 328
Fort Harrison- 344
Fort Hatteras-48, 53, 141
Fort Henry-61, 71, 357
Fort Inge-52
Fort Jackson-79-80
Fort Jackson, LA-237
Fort Larned- 365
Fort McAllister-149, 152,
377
Fort Monroe-383, 399, 454,
464
Fort Morgan-326, 330
Fort Moultrie-156
Fort Pickens-51
Fort Pillow- 86, 258, 262,-
"Massacre at Fort
   Pillow"-259
Fort Powell-327
Fort Pulaski-77
Fort Randolph, TN- 356
Fort Smith, AK-209

9, 311-13, 316, 325, 332,
335, 412, 469
Huntington, IN-197
Huntsville, Alabama-101,
344

I

Illinois, 23, 30, 143, 182,
192, 241, 254, 329, 450
Imboden, Gen. John (C)- 280
"Immortal 600"-338
Independence, MO-102, 354
Indiana-61, 98, 175, 179,
197, 347, 349, 394, 456
Indianola-150-1
Indians-5, 23, 51-2, 56, 65,
103, 137, 148, 150, 206, 218,
245, 259, 262, 289, 339-40,
354-5, 365, 369, 393, 395,
460
Infamous Order Number 11-
208
Infamous Order No. 28-81
Ingles Ferry Bridge-272
"Inner Light"-386
Irwinville, GA-453
Isaac Smith -149
Island No. 10-67, 70-1, 77
Island Queen-341

J

Jackson, Gen. Thomas
"Stonewall" (C)-Numerous,-
Foot
   Cavalry,-38, 89,-"The
   Gospels"-69,-"The
   Stonewall" Brigade
   279,- Anna Jackson
   (Wife)-168
Jackson River Depot-84
Jackson, MS-199
Jackson, TN .....-86, 126, 139
Jacksonville, FL-153, 155,
245, 247
James Brothers (Frank and
Jessie) (C)-207, 343
James River-68, 84, 92, 196,
306-7, 313, 348, 368, 422,-
James River &
   Kanawha Canal-409
Japan-199
Jefferson City, MO- 34, 348
Jeffersonville (Tazewell),
VA-268, 269
Jenkins, Gen. Albert (C)-
115, 269, 271
Jennie's Creek, KY-59
Jessie Scouts (U)- 231, 301
Jesus-177, 444-6
Jews (Jewish)-56, 139

McGuire, Hunter (C)- 168

McIntosh, Gen. James (C)-65

McLaws, Gen. Lafayette (C)-118-9, 157, 167

McLean, Col. Nathaniel (U)-112

McLean, Wilmer (House) (C)- 434

McPherson, Maj. Gen. James-323

Meade, Maj. Gen. George (U)-123, 181, 183-4, 186-7, 189, 191, 202-3, 208, 218, 221, 230, 234, 253, 255, 257, 265, 276-8

Meadow Bluff, (W) VA- 295

Mechanicsville, VA-89

Memphis, TN-71, 77, 86, 150, 242, 244-5, 297, 303, 330

Mercedita-148

Meridian, MS-242, 244, 251, 439

Mescalero Apaches-46

Mesilla, NM-44

Mexico-53, 150, 158, 192, 435, 455, 460

Michigan-341

Midway Station, Nebraska Territory-355

Mill Springs, KY-60

Miller, Col. Madison (U)-73

Milroy, Maj. Gen. R. H.(U)-178

Mine Run Valley, VA-230

Minnesota-66, 103, 137, 186, 256

Missionary Ridge, TN-225, 228-30

Mississippi- Numerous

Mississippi River-52, 67, 71, 125, 154, 172, 242

Missouri-Numerous

Missouri Democrat-199

Missouri State Troopers-45

Mitchel, Brig. Gen. Ormsby (U)-77

Monitor.....-66, 78, 83-4, 141

Monocacy River-316

Monongahela-154

Monroe, John (C)-80

Montauk-151, 156

Montgomery, AL-23, 83, 86, 332, 343, 439

Montgomery, Capt. (C)-86

Montgomery and Atlanta Railroad-332

Morgan, Gen. John Hunt (C)-96-9, 102-3, 128, 138, 140-1, 145, 154-5, 197, 199, 201-2, 204, 230, 242, 264, 268-70, 272-5, 296, 300, 302, 305, 313, 336, 344-5, 378, -"The Devil Himself"-231, 273,

Q

Quaker "Quaker Cannon"-70,-"Quaker" gunboat-153
Quantrill, William (C)-206-8, 453
Queen of the West-149-51, 149, 158

R

Race Mixing-353
Raleigh, NC-274, 288, 438-9, 442
Raleigh-Grayson Pike (Cove Rd. Rt. 603 & Rt. 600)-274
Ramseur, Gen. Stephen (C)-352
Randolph, TN-125
Rapidan River-221, 230, 257, 263-4
Rappahannock River-103, 105- 6, 130-1, 136, 159, 161, 165, 167-8, 221, 450
Raymond, MS-173
Reading, PA-155
Ream's Station, VA- 332
Rebel Yell-184, 255
Red River-149, 251, 253-5, 258, 260-1, 287-8, 292, 456,-Red River
    Campaign-254

Reno, Gen. Jesse (U)-117
Republican Party-128-9, 302, 314, 340, 349, 361, 461-2,-Radical
    Republicans-247, 98, 247, 302, 343
Resaca, GA-289, 351
Reynolds, Maj. Gen. John (U)-112, 182
Richmond, VA-Numerous
Richmond *Enquire*-347
Richmond-Petersburg Railroad Line-401, 405, 421-2
Ricketts, Brig. Gen. James (U)-107, 119
Rio Grande-44
River Queen-399, 423
Roanoke Island, NC-62
Roanoke River-356-7
Rock Road (Rt. 11)-273
Rocky Point, FL-372
Rodney, MS-210
Rome, GA-349
Romney, (W) VA-53, 59, 62,-Romney Campaign 59
Rosecrans, Gen.William(U)-49-0, 124, 126, 129, 144, 180, 206, 209-12, 214-9
Rosser, Gen. Thomas (C)-347-8, 369, 391
Round Mountain, TN-56

Rousseau, Gen. Lovell (U)-76

Rude's Hill, VA-283

Ruffin, Edmund (C)-26, 4, 102,456

Rutland, VT-199

S

Sabine Pass, TX-146

Salem, AK-296

Salem (Church), VA-106

Salineville, OH-202

Salma, AL-84

Saltville,VA-200, 241, 258, 268-9, 273-4, 344-5, 347, 379-81, 383, 460,

    Massacre at Saltville 347, 348

San Domingo-244

Sanitation Commission-240

Santa Fe (Trail)-63-4, 68

Savage's (railroad) Station, VA-91

Savannah, GA-53, 57,77, 148, 151, 371, 375-7, 382-4, 389, 402

Savannah River-77

Saylor's Creek- 429, 431

Scalawags-389

Schenck, Robert (U) -82

Schofield, John (U)-369, 371

Secessionville, SC-87

Second Baptist Church of Richmond-69

Second Confiscation Act-98

Seddon, Secretary of War James (C)-136, 401

Sedgwick, Maj. Gen. John (U)-161-2, 167-8, 277

Selma, AL-419

Seminary Ridge-184

Seminole-30, 456

Seneca-51

Seward William, Secretary of State (U)-139, 348, 399,-Seward,

    Frederick (Son)-139

Shawnee-51

Shawneetown, IL-329

Shelby, Gen. Joseph "Jo" (C)-217, 354

Semmes, Capt. Raphael (C)-34

Shenandoah Valley Military District-34, 54, 67, 82, 86, 251, 257, 269, 280, 284, 295, 297-8, 316, 322-3, 326, 339, 341, 343, 351-2, 354, 364, 369, 376, 422, 457, 460

Shepherdstown, (W) VA-118,180

Sheridan, Gen. Phillip (U)-254, 279, 431-2

Sherman, Maj. Gen. William T.-Numerous,

White Supremacy-375
Wilkes, Admiral, Charles-150
Wilkesborough, NC- 425
Williamsport, MD-180, 191
Wills Hotel, DC-222
Wilmington ,NC-221, 327, 354, 357, 383, 385, 393, 408, 415-6
Wilson, Gen. James (U)-312, 427, 439
Winchester, VA-31, 34-5, 53, 59, 62, 65, 67, 84, 115, 178, 205, 280, 295, 314-5, 323, 328-9, 340-1, 352, 409
Wise, Gen. Henry (C)-33, 44, 46, 49, 51, 132, 441
Woman's Sanitary Fair- 308
Wood, Mayor NY Fernando (U)-176
Woodburn, TN-151
Wooster, OH-199
World War I (Great War)-257
World War II-196, 208
Wytheville, VA-200, 269, 273-5, 380-1

Y-Z

Yalobusha River-153
Yankeedom-231, 253
Yazoo City, MS-199, 244

Yazoo River-138
"Yellow Rose of Texas"-382
Yorktown, Va- 69, 82
Young, Lt. Bennett (C)-353
Young Men's Christian Association (YMCA or Y)-56
Zollicoffer, TN-50, 60
Zouaves-32, 40-1

1st Federal Corps-182
1st Massachusetts-37
1st Michigan-41
1st Minnesota-186
1st New York Cavalry-297
1st South Carolina Volunteers-79
2nd (West) Virginia Cavalry-275
2nd Massachusetts-41
2nd Michigan-37
5th New York Calvary-103
5th Texas-453
5th U. S. Colored Cavalry-460
6th Corps-352, 432
7th Kansas Cavalry-59
8th Illinois Cavalry-182
8th U. S. Colored Troops-247
8th Virginia Cavalry-241
13th Kentucky Cavalry-348
14th Brooklyn-41

14th Pennsylvania-271
15th Alabama-185
16th Illinois Cavalry-241
18th Corps-327
19th Corps-352
19th North Carolina-165
20th Maine-185
21st North Carolina-242
33rd Virginia-41

34th Ohio-275
50th New York Engineers-132
54th Massachusetts Colored Infantry-201
62nd Virginia Infantry-283
64th Virginia Infantry- 241
189th New York Volunteers-355

TEXT NOTES:

This book is not a research book designed to uncover new material or prove a new concept. The source work is easily available to any researcher. This book is designed as a textbook, although there are new ideas, new concepts and new perspectives presented; they are based on existing materials. Therefore, it was not necessary to footnote each quote used. Almost every quote in this book comes from one of the sources listed below.

The Civil War Day by Day by E. B. Long

The War of the Rebellion, the Official Records of the Union and Confederate Armies by the War Department

Sherman's March by Burke Davis

Voices of the Civil War (film) by the Editors of the Time-Life Books

Time Life Books (Battle Books) by the Editors of the Time-Life Books

A Southern Star for Maryland, "Maryland and the Secession Crisis, 1860-61" by Lawrence M. Denton

The Social History of Bourbon by Gerald Carson

North-South Trader Magazine

The Washington Times (Civil War Sections)

Sam (The Civil War experiences of Private Sam Davis) by Beverly A. Rude

The War in Southwest Virginia 1861-65 by Gary C. Walker

Hunter's Fiery Raid through Virginia Valleys by Gary C. Walker

The Truth about Slavery by Gary C. Walker

Gary C. Walker

- 506 -

ABOUT THE AUTHOR

Gary Chitwood Walker was born on May 24, 1946 in **Wytheville**, Virginia. He attended **Spiller Elementary School**. There, in the seventh grade the "war bug" bit him. The study of **Virginia History** exposed him to America's greatest war and started a fire in him that time has not extinguished. He was thrilled to learn of massive battles around **Richmond** and in the **Shenandoah Valley**. He asked the teacher, "What happened around here?" (meaning Wytheville). The teacher stuttered and stammered that something happened but she didn't know what it was. Twenty-five years later, Gary answered the question for himself and the rest of the world in *The War in Southwest Virginia 1861-65*.

In high school, Gary showed little aptitude for math but a great inclination toward history and geography. His fascination for **Civil War History** was heightened when he studied under **Miss Lelia Huddle**. He graduated from **George Wythe High** in '64.

Gary wanted to study history in college but explained, "It required three years of foreign language and I knew I could never get through three years, so I studied **Business Administration**." Nearly all of his elective hours were in the history-political science fields. The blending of the two academic fields, history and economics, gives Gary a unique ability to analyze **economic, historical** and **political events**. Coupled with his understanding of **psychology** and **sociology**, Gary gives a more comprehensive evaluation of historical events. Despite **Dyslexia**, he graduated with a Bachelor's Degree in Science from **Virginia Polytechnic Institute** in '68.

Shortly after graduation, Gary married his long-time sweetheart, **Sue Adams**. Together they produced sons, **Christopher Ewell** and **Kevin Forrest**. After graduation, Gary continued his education studying, among other things, creative **writing** and **photography**.

Gary's love of family history led him to write *Walker, Ben to Carl*. Later, he researched and wrote *Footprints*, a history of the Adams Family.

The *War in Southwest Virginia* propelled Gary from obscurity. Since 1985, one can often find him dressed in a Confederate uniform speaking to a variety of audiences. The **media** seeks him out for interviews. He enjoys signing books at **reenactments** and at **arts and crafts festivals**.

Encouraged by the public, Gary has become a **prolific** writer. He has authored *Hunter's Fiery Raid through Virginia Valleys, Civil War Tales Volumes I & II, The Truth about slavery, Son of the South* and a *Confederate Coloring and Learning book*.

The author is pleased that so many people have been **informed** and **entertained** by his books. He enjoys hearing from **students of history**, from **grade** school through the **doctoral** program, who have used his books as a resource. Gary is also pleased that non-academics have used his books to help in **genealogy** research or led them to uncover **relics**, buried since the war. Others have used his books to create **screen plays**, **paintings**, **carvings** and **sculptures**. Several **reenactments** have been fought based on his books. The **Virginia Defense Force** has used material from Gary's books in making a recruitment **film**. He served on the research and writing committee for the **Wythe County Bicentennial Pageant Committee**. A poem he wrote graced the back of the program. Dressed in a **Colonial** costume, to represent the "spirit" of the county's namesake, **George Wythe**, he opened the play. He also assisted in the mock **Civil War battle** scene. His books have been used by magazines and travel books as a guide to war sites and inspired many **Sunday morning sermons**. The author has been a **consultant** to many governmental and non-governmental institutions. His writing helped secure funding for **Hanging Rock Battlefield Park**, Salem, Virginia. His books have caused historical roadside markers to be erected and the **"Covered Spring House"** was built at Harrisonburg. His books have been placed as **memorials** in several libraries.

His books have propelled him into **leadership** roles with the **Sons of Confederate Veterans**, the **Civil War Round Table** and the **Point Lookout P. O. W. Organization**. Serving the **"Real Cause,"** he is the

Chaplain for several organizations. Gary served on the **Special Events Committee** for the **City of Roanoke**. He is also a member of many historic, reenactment and preservation groups.

Gary has received numerous **accolades** and citations for his work. Included are many **Certificates of Appreciation**, inclusion in *Who's Who in America*, the South and Southwest edition. On February 18, 1999, the **House of Representatives** of South Carolina, in assembly, gave the author a standing ovation for his writing on **Southern History**. On February 1, 2003, the **Town of Saltville** made Gary an **"Honorary Citizen."**

The author is pleased that so many from such a variety of **backgrounds** have found his books to be so **useful**, **entertaining** and **informative**. He still finds it amazing that a poor mountain boy with **Dyslexia** has come so far. Gary is mindful that without the support and patience of his **beautiful wife**, none of this would have been possible. Gary humbly gives credit to his **Lord** for the many blessings he has received.

Author's Other Books: To receive information on his other books, write; **A & W Enterprise 3747 New Spring Branch Rd. S. E. Roanoke, Va. 24014**.